I WILL

NOT

GROW

DOWN-

WARD

Also in the
DREAMS OF FREEDOM
series

## *RELENTLESS:*
## *AN IMMIGRANT STORY*

ONE WOMAN'S DECADE-LONG FIGHT TO HEAL A FAMILY
TORN APART BY WAR, LIES, AND TYRANNY

By Wudasie Nayzgi

AFTER RETURNING from exile to help rebuild her war-torn homeland, a young Eritrean mother receives devastating news, when her daughter is diagnosed with a dangerous heart condition. But her desperate attempts to secure the life-saving medical treatment available only outside of her newly-liberated country are thwarted, when fighting suddenly resumes. With the borders closing, limited options and time, and her husband taken away to serve an unending military conscription, she must make a terrible decision that could alter the course of their lives— do nothing and jeopardize the health of one child, or flee the worsening nightmare and leave her husband and second daughter behind, possibly forever.

*Relentless* is the powerful and inspiring story of an Eritrean woman who faced incredible obstacles, defied a ruthless regime, and never gave up fighting for the only thing that matters: family.

---

## DREAMS OF FREEDOM

ONE FAMILY, two powerful accounts of love, heartbreak, and determination from one of the world's most isolated and tyrannical governments in modern history.

It's 1991, and a bloody thirty-year conflict with Ethiopia has ended, earning Eritrea its first taste of freedom in over a century. But peace is a flower too easily crushed. Soon, the small Horn-of-African nation finds itself in the familiar grip of a new despot— their own beloved war hero and leader. Under his rule, families still healing are torn apart anew, and suspicion and desperation grow. In the midst of deepening oppression, one man and one woman, separated by circumstances beyond their control, will risk everything to save their children from this life of violence and give them the future they once imagined for themselves.

iii

# I WILL NOT GROW DOWNWARD

## MEMOIR OF AN ERITREAN REFUGEE

My Long and Perilous Flight
from Africa's Hermit Kingdom

Yikealo Neab

with Kenneth James Howe

BRINESTONE PRESS

BRINESTONE PRESS

Cover photo credits: Unsplash.com
Cover and interior design: Kenneth James Howe Copyright © 2018

Text formatted in Georgia 10pt.

NOTE: This is a work of memoir. All of the events in this book happened, although some dialog has been changed for purposes of clarity and brevity. Also, due to the sensitive nature of the story, the author has elected to publish under pseudonym. Therefore, selected names, dates, and identifying details have been altered to protect the privacy of the individuals involved. Otherwise, the experiences described herein have been rendered as faithfully as possible. The depictions of personal interactions are from the author's best recollection.

ISBN-13: 978-1-7292-2286-7 (pbk.)

# Dedication

My people fought for their freedom for decades. Hundreds of thousands of Eritreans — far more than the official accounts cite — gave their lives to bring that freedom to their children and grandchildren. They died never knowing the fruits of their sacrifice. But after independence, the peace and prosperity they fought long and hard to win remained out of reach. The exodus that began during the war continued for decades after it ended. Eritrea and Eritreans continue to bleed to this day.

I dedicate this book to all of my fellow countrymen and women, whether civilian or tegadelti, who perished in our long fight for freedom, as well as to all those who served afterward to safeguard that elusive prize, including, but not limited to, all National Service members, and all army servicemen and women.

Many of my fellow Eritreans left their fatherland to seek the freedom they were denied in their own country. I would also like to dedicate this book to those refugees who fled to every corner of the world, but especially to the thousands who lost their lives during their long and perilous journey to find that freedom, who perished while crossing borders, oceans, and deserts. This book is also for the many people who continue to languish in prisons inside Eritrea and in refugee camps and communities elsewhere.

One day, the face of true freedom will shine its light on all the people of Eritrea. I truly believe this. Praise be to the Almighty God!

Yikealo Neab
*October 10, 2018*

# CONTENTS

Dedication ············································································vii

Map of Eritrea ·····································································xi


*Khartoum, Sudan, 2010* - 1

## PART ONE
## THIS WAR WITHOUT END
## ETHIOPIA 1991

*Jimma* - 6

*Addis Ababa* - 24

*The Road Home* - 30


## PART TWO
## THE PRICE OF FREEDOM
## ERITREA 1991-2003

*Asmara* - 36

*Nefasit* - 57

*Ghindae* - 65

*Massawa* - 68

*Sawa Training Camp* - 72

*Red Sea to Assab* - 79

*Kiloma Training Camp* - 86

*Kebessa* - 109

*Tseserat Army Base, Asmara* - 115

CONTENTS (*cont'*)


## PART THREE
### FALLING APART
### ERITREA 2003-2007

*Asmara* - 148

## PART FOUR
### PUTTING IT ALL BACK TOGETHER AGAIN
### 2007-2010

*Asmara, Eritrea* - 190
*Tessenei, Eritrea* - 207
*Kassala, Sudan* - 212
*Shagarab Refugee Camp, Sudan* - 228
*Khartoum, Sudan* - 238
*Nairobi, Kenya* - 268


Editor's Note --------------------------------------------------------294
Acknowledgments -----------------------------------------------300
Glossary and Acronyms ---------------------------------------301

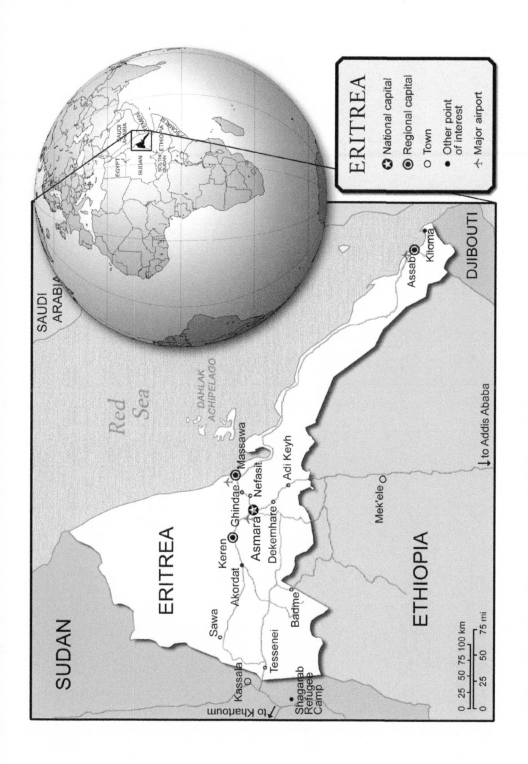

# Khartoum, Sudan

## 2010

THE MOBILE PHONE IN MY POCKET RINGS. From the number on the screen, I know it's Yohannes, and this brings a smile to my face. "Hello, my friend," I say. It has only been a day since we last spoke, but I am always happy to hear his voice in these troubling times.

As usual, the connection is weak and full of static. He says something, but the message is hard to understand. After another try, I realize he's telling me to stay home today.

"Is it because of the police?" I ask, worried. Could they be planning another raid in my neighborhood? Will they come to take us away for good this time? It happened to several of us not so long ago. They took me, but I was lucky enough to avoid prison. I'd rather not press my luck a second time.

He doesn't answer. He just tells me to wait where I am. "I will come over to speak with you in person."

The way my housemates act makes me realize they already know what Yohannes has to tell me. In our culture, bad news is always delivered in person, face to face if possible, in the comforting presence of friends and family. And in such times as these, there is an abundance of bad news and a scarcity of friends. Naturally, the first thing that comes to my mind is Yohannes's health. I worry his unmanaged medical issues have finally caught up with him. I have lost too many friends already over the past several years. It is a rough existence we live.

At last he arrives, and I can see from the look on his face that the news is both serious and personal. But it isn't about the police. Nor is it about the injuries he suffered while serving in the army. What he has to tell me concerns my father at home. "He has passed, Yikealo," he says. "I'm so sorry."

It shouldn't surprise me, and yet it does. Aboy — the term I use for my father — had been ill for a very long time, his body battered by a lifetime of hard labor. He suffered a stroke several years ago, which partially paralyzed him. But what wore him down most wasn't the physical toil, rather the emotional, the decades of bloody conflict his generation waged to win our freedom from Ethiopia. The enemy was especially brutal. But they were not unbeatable.

Then came my generation, and we squandered the freedom that came of our victory. I am ashamed by what we have done. We should all be.

So, by now, I should be numb to death in general, and even to my father's in particular. I left him in his sickbed knowing his time was drawing to an end. But it shocks me anyway. How can one ever prepare for such news?

It shames me that my first concern is for myself rather than him. I know I should return home to be with my mother in her time of grief. My fists clench with helpless rage because that is the one thing I can't do, return. I pace the room, which now feels like a cage. I thought I was free, but I am more trapped than ever.

I wonder what his final thoughts must have been. Had he wasted them on me, his runaway son? I am not his only child, nor even the only one to abandon him in this way. Others have left before me. Still, I was the last before he passed. Did he worry pointlessly for my safety instead of thinking about his own well-being? I hate that I was not with him at the end. I hate this feeling that I have betrayed him. It is as deep as the betrayal of my country.

My heart breaks because I will not see him returned to the earth from which he sprang, the earth he worked for so many years, held in his fingers, and buried his own parents in. It is the same earth that has been drenched in the sweat of our oppressed grandfathers, steeped with the blood of our heroic brothers. The earth that gave me my identity. And pushed me away.

So, who am I now?

I once thought I knew, but there is no certainty anymore. I have turned my back on all that I am. Now I am stuck in one land that does not want me, hoping to go to another that does not know me. Here among my fellow exiles, I am not home. And I cannot go home.

The tears come then, against my will. I grieve for my father, for his leaving this world without his son by his side, and for my mother, who must now bear this burden without us both. I weep for my parents' generation and for mine, that we knew only the most fleeting glimpse of liberty. I weep for my children, and for everything they have lost.

How could we have forgotten so quickly the sacrifices we made to be free?

# PART ONE

This War Without End

Ethiopia, 1991

# Jimma

THE EVENINGS HERE IN SOUTHWESTERN ETHIOPIA are generally pleasant, no matter the season. It's May, and we are heading into the heaviest rains of the year. Tonight, however, happens to be dry. A gentle breeze carries with it the aromas of fresh roasting coffee, wood smoke, seared meat and spices. The afternoon dust, kicked up by the tires of a passing minibus, pinches the nose. Beneath it all is the faint perfume from the jacaranda blooms outside the hotel where I am having supper.

I am an Eritrean man by descent, a Bihére-Tigrinya from Asmara, living in self-imposed exile in Ethiopia by circumstances outside my control. It's a complicated relationship my people have with this country. Ethiopia has governed Eritrea since Britain handed us over following the end of the Second World War. We have been fighting each other over independence for the past three decades.

With me are two Ethiopian colleagues from the local government office where we all work. Meseret and Abera are from the Amhara and Oromo ethnic groups, respectively. They know that I am Eritrean by birth, but they don't hold this, or our bloody conflict, against me personally. Nor do I feel any particular animosity toward them. Our people's histories are too deeply intertwined for such pettiness. Our anger is focused on our leaders. Besides, no one can say for absolute sure where one culture starts and the other ends. We are like stepbrothers to each other. Sometimes we disagree; more often, we do not.

Today, like most days, we share a common desire— to see the end of the bloodshed. Too many of our friends and family have died in this senseless, brutal war.

My residence here deep inside Ethiopia may seem contradictory, but it's not all that unusual. Ethiopia is actually home to many thousands of us. The war has been mostly waged far to the north, on soil claimed by my people, which has forced many of us to flee the violence, even if it means escaping into the land of our oppressors. But we don't just come to survive, we also come to improve our lives, to attend college, find work, and raise families. We come not because we agree with Ethiopia's rule over us, but because here we can enjoy some protection while staying close to our homes.

Ethiopia was ruled by the emperor Haile Selassie until his brutal reign ended in 1974, when Mengistu Haile Mariam's military *junta*, the infamous Derg, took power. The Derg ruled for ten years before Mengistu, bowing to international pressure, agreed to replace it with a civilian government. I arrived from Asmara shortly afterward, during a time of great optimism for both Eritreans and Ethiopians. But in the four years that have passed since then, Mengistu's authoritarian crimes have exceeded even the emperor's worst. The former Derg leadership, stripped only of their titles, still retain their positions of power and influence.

But recently, Mengistu's grip over his people has grown weak. Ethiopia's civil rebellion now aligns with, and energizes, Eritrea's resistance. Mengistu's armies have become spread thin by the country's many warfronts. In desperation, he and his loyalists lash out even harder, hoping to strangle us all. Their spies are everywhere, listening for seditious talk, making it increasingly dangerous to speak out to anyone anywhere in this country. Whether you are Ethiopian and dislike the current government, or Eritrean and wish for autonomy, you are always wary of publicly choosing a side. It's why I keep my political opinions to myself.

It isn't always so easy to do, however, especially when, as usual, the dinner conversation tends to gravitate toward the subject of the fighting. Tonight, it's the increasingly violent clashes between Mengistu's military and the Eritrean *tegadelti*, or freedom fighters, that fill the conversation. With help from the Ethiopian rebel group, the Tigray People's Liberation Front, the Eritrean People's Liberation Front has forced the national army to retreat southward from our shared border.

Like me, Abera and Meseret hope for a quick end to the conflict. Where we differ is on the subject of Eritrean independence. This is a hard pill for them to swallow. After all, they are patriots, just as I am. So much time and money has been invested in keeping Eritrea a part of their nation. So much Ethiopian blood has been shed.

And an equal amount of Eritrean blood.

I don't blame them for their inability to understand how important independence is to my people. For generations, their own government misled them, waging a decades-long misinformation campaign to discredit our fight. They have come to view our *tegadelti* fighters as *shifta*— a derogatory term meaning thugs or bandits. Naturally, contempt for independence-minded Eritreans is woven deeply into the Ethiopian psyche. Thankfully, it is not shared by all.

"There's an easy way to stop the war," Meseret gripes. He's in his early twenties, a recent graduate of Addis Ababa Commercial School with a degree in accounting, and the youngest of the three of us. Usually easygoing, always ready to give a smile and a compliment, today he is annoyed. It seems his impatience with the subject has reached an end. "This constant warfare has settled nothing and will create nothing worthwhile. Why not just allow Eritreans to vote in a referendum?"

"You wish for a vote?" I ask, surprised to hear him say it out loud.

"Why not? I am certain if given the chance, Eritreans will realize their foolishness and choose to unite with Ethiopia. Let us just get it over with once and for all."

I think this attitude is typical of his generation. They don't have as deep an appreciation of the relationship between our peoples as their elders, and they certainly don't understand how much Eritrea has suffered for so many decades. Meseret's personal investment in this war is relatively small, much smaller than those who came of age at the height of the Derg's violent reign known as the Ethiopian Red Terror. He expects peace and blames his parents' generation for preventing him from having it. He wants to believe that an easy political solution exists to the conflict, one that will favor Ethiopia, because, in his mind, *what is good for Ethiopia is good for Eritrea*.

Abera bursts out laughing at the question. The sound fills the small restaurant, causing others to glance over at us.

This only annoys Meseret all the more. He demands to know what is so funny. He easily forgets how deep and personal Abera's understanding of the strife is. More so, even, than my own. Unlike the two of us, Abera has actually fought for his country on the frontlines. In fact, he was originally a member of Mengistu's *junta* that overthrew the emperor. It was he and others like him who most felt the sting of betrayal when Mengistu replaced one authoritarian regime with another just like it, employing the same military *junta* to repress the very people who had once supported it. Years later, Abera fought unsuccessfully in the Ethiopian People's Revolutionary Party to unseat the man he'd helped put into power.

Today, he doesn't look much like a soldier. He's tall and lanky, more bony than muscular. And like his younger colleague, he's dressed in a casual suit. He's a businessman these days, not a killer, and instead of always presenting himself with soldierly stoicism, his demeanor now is relaxed. Only rarely does he allow us to see the toughened fighter he once was. He reaches over and clasps his countryman's shoulder. "I laugh because of how naive you are, young Meseret. It may be hard for you to believe, but most Eritreans would vote for secession rather than unity. Why else would they fight against us for so long?"

"A few stubborn and unruly resistance fighters? They are *shifta*."

"Do not dismiss them so easily, Meseret."

"You speak as if you actually believe their struggle is for the good of Ethiopia," Meseret accuses Abera.

"I am much older than you. I have seen and heard more than you. Better for us or not—"

"Or maybe you are stuck in the past with this old way of thinking."

"It's not old thinking," Abera counters. "It's a matter of accepting the truth." He turns his gaze in my direction. "But you don't have to take my word for it. Just ask our Eritrean friend, Yikealo. He can explain his people's feelings better than I ever could."


The war began the same year I was born: 1961. Nearly three decades have passed since then, and still we fight, despite the many tens of thousands of deaths on both sides. I have managed so far to avoid being swept up in the conflict, but it has always surrounded me. Sometimes, it seems very far away. Other times, it presses so close that I can almost smell the blood in the air, along with the gunpowder and burnt diesel of the armored vehicles. I have seen the victims, both civilians and soldiers, their bodies torn and bloody.

The news growing up, most of it crafted by the Ethiopian state-run media, was always heavily slanted in ways that belittled Eritrea's claims of autonomy. But those of us secretly supporting the resistance had our own means of spreading the truth. Unfortunately, it was only lies that the rest of the world heard. Lies were all they were ever interested in hearing. This way, they could go on believing that our war was just another tribal conflict on a continent where such conflicts rise and fall as frequently as the moon changes its face. For my people, however, the fight was always about one thing, getting back what is rightfully ours— our lands, our identity, our sovereignty. It's a fight we are never going to quit.

My country, situated in the Horn of Africa on the Red Sea, has a long history of occupation. In centuries past, we were ruled by foreigners from the region— Egyptians, Turks, Persians, Sudanese. The Italians were the first of the modern era, arriving in the nineteenth century during the European rush to colonize the continent. The opening of the Suez Canal in 1869 instantly transformed the Red Sea into a major commercial shipping route, and Eritrea's shoreline became a worthy prize with considerable military and economic value.

Our people tried to resist the European incursion, but any challenge was quickly put down. We were terribly outmatched, not in numbers or will, but in firepower. So, for fifty years, Italy was able to impose its will upon us. To be fair, they also introduced their art, culture, and technology. They built beautiful buildings, changing Asmara from quiet farmland to a bustling, picturesque city known as *Piccola Roma*— Little Rome. Most Eritreans, however, were barred from entering the Italian parts of Asmara during this period; only those serving Italian households were allowed there. Elsewhere throughout the country, far worse abuses than indentured servitude were being perpetrated.

After the region was seized by the British during the Second World War, we were handed over to the Ethiopian Federation like children in need of adult supervision. This was in 1952, and our new benefactor,

Emperor Haile Selassie, promised to guide us toward independence. But what he really wanted was our access to the Red Sea, since without us Ethiopia is landlocked. Over the years, the Ethiopian Federation summarily dismissed our pleas for self-governance or turned our voices against us.

By the time Haile Selassie unilaterally dissolved the UN-negotiated federation and annexed Eritrea in 1962, the secessionist movement had already built momentum. The Eritrean Liberation Front, a militant group of exiles led by Hamid Idris Awate, an Italian-trained *ascari* fighter and military strategist during the Second World War, had been operating in secret in Egypt since the early 1950s. In 1961, the ELF declared open resistance. Its military arm, Jebha, attacked an Ethiopian police post on Mount Adal, near the town of Akordat deep inside Eritrea, sparking our armed struggle for liberation known as *gedli*.

While the ELF grew quickly after that, it also became internally conflicted, eventually giving rise to the EPLF. Disagreements between these groups threatened to undermine the movement and end our struggle. But the promise of freedom is a powerful salve against such irritants, and the desire to defeat Ethiopia assured mutual cooperation between the factions.

The world's superpowers, who viewed their relationship with Ethiopia in strictly Cold War terms, willingly abetted the emperor's criminal activities. The American partnership with Ethiopia, for example, was a strategic maneuver, a direct challenge to the growing Soviet influence in the region. By leveraging these competing superpowers against each other, Haile Selassie was able to blackmail the West into providing him arms and money, which he then turned on us.

Eritrea had little such outside help, but lack of support did not stop us from building a strong militia. We resolved not to be denied our rightful destiny.

When Mengistu wrested power from the emperor in the Seventies, he tried but failed to convince Ethiopia's former allies to continue gifting the country money and arms, so he evicted them and invited the communists in. Now it was Russian weapons killing us.

Still we saw no outside help, and still we refused to give up.

As the Cold War thawed, the Soviets eventually grew weary of funding Ethiopia's expensive and seemingly never-ending war. When they withdrew, Mengistu turned to the Israelis for support.

And yet, in spite of everything, our movement persevered.

From the very beginning, Ethiopia portrayed our fight as illegal, our soldiers unsophisticated, and our efforts unorganized. Our freedom fighters were depicted as roving bands of guerilla soldiers who had little better to do than prowl the lowlands, harassing the police and threatening security. The *shifta*, they warned, did not reflect the greater will and wellbeing of the people. They offered nothing positive to the region.

All lies, of course. Nothing could be further from the truth, and Eritreans knew it.

Nevertheless, the rest of the world accepted these misrepresentations as fact. In reality, our movement was more well-organized, focused, and practical than anyone knew. We had no choice, being outgunned and outmanned at every turn.

Today, being known as *shifta* is a badge of honor, a title that tens of thousands of Eritrean freedom fighters have willingly taken with them to the grave in the hopes that their children might enjoy the freedom promised by their struggle.

I was born thirty years ago at the start of this war, so it is all I have ever known in my entire life. To be reborn into an era of peace, for my future children and the children of Eritrea to know only freedom and independence, that is my greatest and only hope. It is the hope of every Eritrean patriot.

But it is a hope I cannot openly proclaim, not while I'm still living in the heart of Ethiopia. Doing so wouldn't just be unwise, it could be fatal.


Meseret's eyes widen at Abera's declaration. My own eyes narrow as I turn my gaze toward him. It alarms me that he would so recklessly invite me to expose my thoughts in such a public place.

But I see no malice on his face. As a former EPRP member, his feelings about Mengistu and the Derg are well known among his friends. Mine are as strong as his, but far more private. I don't believe he is trying to bring me harm. He's just as impatient for change as the rest of us. Nevertheless, I think he underestimates the danger this puts me in.

There is a Tigrayan saying: *Haki tezaribka ab megedi babur dekis.* If you tell the truth, you may as well make your bed on the train tracks. If I speak openly now, will the train of consequences come and smash me to little bits? It's not in my nature to hedge the truth out of convenience, but sometimes even the truth must yield to prudence. On the other hand, how can I proudly assert my Eritrean heritage, if I deny who I am and what I stand for? I want to express my true feelings, but these are uncertain times, and I am in the company of uncertain friends.

I take in a deep breath and lean forward. My dinner companions mirror me so they can hear my whispered words. This is neither the time nor the place for making a loud public proclamation. The words I am about to speak are for their ears only. "Yes," I say, "Abera is right. If it came to a referendum, Eritrea would vote for independence. I am certain of this."

"Why?" Meseret asks.

I hesitate. My young friend is either willfully ignorant of how the Ethiopian government has mistreated Eritrea, both under Haile Selassie and then under Mengistu, or he is in denial of the truth. He has been brainwashed to believe otherwise since childhood. That the government has mistreated its own people in similar ways should be proof enough of their willingness to deceive. But I can't undo years of brainwashing over one single meal. It's worthless to try.

Abera gently encourages me to go on.

"Why would we vote for independence?" I ask. "Because we are tired of oppression, of being told what is good for us. We are tired of waiting for help from Addis Ababa that never comes. We must help ourselves. How can we be proud of our heritage, if we don't stand up for our right to self-rule?"

"If you feel so strongly about your heritage, then why are you here instead of fighting?" he counters. "Why do so many of you come to Ethiopia to live? For that matter, why do so many Eritreans leave their home at all?"

13

Ethiopians like to compare my people with the vehicle called Land Rover, because they think there isn't a place in the world we aren't willing to go, as if it means our ties to our homeland are weak. He doesn't understand that we leave because the terrible violence inflicted on us by those in power in Addis Ababa has given us no other choice.

I'm tempted to explain my own personal reasons for being so far from Asmara, my hometown, but I bite my tongue. That is a secret I must selfishly guard above all others, especially in such company as this. Instead, I allow myself to recall the terrible acts the Ethiopian military has inflicted upon my people since my childhood, of the secret police, the *Afagn Guad*, who terrorized Asmara during the Red Terror years of the 1970s. The horrible scenes fill my heart with anguish. Once more, I catch the scent of blood and fear of my people, even if only in my mind.

"How many of our villages has the government burned?" I whisper with a voice trembling with emotion. "How many of my people have been hunted down, captured, tortured, and murdered in Ethiopian prisons? How many more were taken without cause from their homes, never to be seen again?" I stop for a moment to compose myself. I can't allow myself to get so emotional. "Too many of my own friends and neighbors are gone, dead or forced to escape. Many are now exiles. Many died trying to find a better life. And many are stuck in refugee camps with no hope for the future."

Abera's face pinches, although I don't know if it's shame he feels at what his own government has done to us, disagreement with how I have portrayed it, or his own culpability in making it happen.

"They all *want* to return home," I say. "But how can they go back as long as Eritrea is not free? There is too much risk of persecution and imprisonment."

"But why fight? Why kill each other?" Meseret asks. "Why die? We can negotiate instead."

"We have tried, even from the very beginning."

"But Mengistu is not Haile Selassie. He knows he is losing the war. He will be willing to negotiate."

I try to remain diplomatic, even though I can feel my anger boiling up inside of me. "There is no chance of that anymore. Mengistu promised to correct King Haile Selassie's mistakes when he rose to power, but he only made them worse. He finally abolished the Derg after all these years, but the same people still rule the country. They control the security forces, the military, the police. And each day that passes, he and his followers grow more violent. He knows that if he is to remain in power, he can't lose Eritrea. But if Eritrea is to survive at all, we must be free. My people cannot suffer any longer."

Abera nods thoughtfully.

"Mengistu will not be in power forever," Meseret insists. "You must be patient. Our two countries are better together."

I sigh. "We can't wait. We can't trust that the next leader will be any better. We thought Mengistu would be, but he wasn't. It's long past time for us to choose our own path. For now, that path is revolution."

I look over at Abera, who is still nodding. But there is something new in his eyes this time, a darkness that alarms me. Perhaps it's because he is Ethiopian; he loves his country as much as I love mine, despite all the evil his leaders have wrought. Nothing will change that about him. And I'm then reminded of another Tigrinyan adage: *Anbessa indihir sinu ariukas zifeteweka keymesleka*. If a lion shows you his teeth, do not believe it's because he likes you.

Suddenly, the mood has chilled, and I have lost my appetite. I realize it's time for me to return home to Eritrea.

Two months have passed since I decided to return to my homeland, yet I have been unable to leave Jimma because of the fighting all along the border. As the balance of power slips further away from the sitting Ethiopian government, Mengistu loyalists ramp up their merciless campaigns against resistance fighters and civilians, even here, thirteen hundred kilometers from the front. His security forces make daily raids anywhere Ethiopian rebels or Eritreans live. His soldiers, weakened and demoralized, are either in active retreat or on the verge of defeat, and that makes them both dangerous and unpredictable.

Not all of his fighters remain blindly dedicated to him. Many simply walk away from their posts, which helps both the Ethiopian resistance and Eritrea's revolution. Some of those soldiers join the side they once fought. Here in the far southwestern part of the country, we have yet to see any fighting, but conditions still grow worse everywhere by the day. I fear I may have waited too long to leave.

The TPLF is advancing ever southward towards Addis, determined to strike at Ethiopia's heart to free the country from the clutch of its cruel despot. If successful, then Eritrea's war with Ethiopia should also end. The rebels gain ground every day, and victory seems inevitable. Yet Mengistu and his government stubbornly refuse to give up. We pray for his surrender, of course, but we are just as worried about the uncertainty that will surely fill the void if he does. Just as troubling, we have no guarantee the next Ethiopian leader will recognize our right to sovereignty.

Frustrated by the TPLF and EPLF surge, Mengistu has asked the United States to arrange meetings with their leaders. The talks are expected to be held in London, but he backs out at the last moment. Rumors spread that the man who vowed to fight "to the last bullet" has disappeared, and that Ethiopia's former Defense Minister, Lieutenant General Tesfaye Gebrekidan, is now in charge.

In Eritrea, the EPLF is marching toward Asmara, while the Ethiopian rebels of the TPLF, both alone and jointly with our mechanized units, are moving steadily southward, freeing Ethiopian cities and towns and overwhelming military strongholds as they go. Addis Ababa is caught in the middle, squeezed as if in a vise.

The military's commanders flee their camps, leaving armories unguarded. Police stations and other security posts are abandoned. Weapons caches are left unsecured. News arrives that the Southern Command's arsenal is being raided by civilians. Before long, towns are being overrun by gun-toting protestors, most of them youngsters. They speed up and down the streets in stolen pickup trucks and dusty cars, reveling in the imminent collapse of the government and military.

Fearing for my safety, I lock myself up inside the room I am renting. It was once part of a service quarters for a larger complex. The space consists only of a bed, table, and a pair of unmatched wooden chairs, so I have little to occupy myself through the long, tense hours as the chaos outside continues to grow. Some of my neighbors come by and ask me why I don't arm myself like everyone else. They are all Ethiopian, and although some of them know I am Eritrean, we are all on friendly terms, each concerned for the other's wellbeing. "Arm myself against whom?" I ask them. Despite my hatred of Ethiopia's military, I did not come here to fight them. "Mengistu's army is in retreat. I won't shoot them as they go." Others try to sell me their guns. They say I need them for my own protection, but I reject their offers. The thought of touching one makes me sick to my stomach. Firing one to kill, even in self-defense, is out of the question.

I am not a coward. It's just that I have seen too much senseless killing already. I have seen too many friends and relatives die. To kill now would accomplish nothing, change nothing.

Chaos spreads like wildfire throughout the city, feeding on fear and anger. Businesses and homes, mainly in and around the market area known as the Mercado, are looted. Gunfire echoes up and down the streets, sounding like exploding firecrackers. Rioters and shop owners shoot at each other. I hear about a man being killed while carrying away a stolen television set on his head, and I realize that what I am witnessing isn't the end of war, but the beginning of anarchy.

The offices of the Worker's Party of Ethiopia are broken into and everything inside is destroyed. Police stations, zonal command offices, security details are looted. I hear the vandalism is happening all across Ethiopia, in big towns and in small. While the anger is understandable, I wish they could see how they are only making things worse for us all. Loose papers blow through the streets like fallen leaves. I recognize the official government seal on some of them. With law and order now gone, what will happen next? Who will restore calm?

Outside the compound, smoke rises in columns from several locations throughout the city. Cars roar past on the street. People riding in the beds of pickup trucks yell and shoot off their rifles. I shy away from the glass to avoid being hit by a stray bullet or shot at simply by being visible.

After a while, I hear shouting outside, and when I cautiously peek out, I see a group of religious leaders, elders, and other citizens marching down the street urging calm. They beg us not to partake in any dangerous and illegal activities. After they leave, silence descends over us, broken only by the occasional gunfire and roar of a vehicle.

Later, there's a knock at my door. It's my landlord, Woizero Adanech, a frail woman in her sixties raising her two granddaughters alone. Their mother died in an accident and their father never returned from the fighting. She gives me the same advice as all the others, not to do anything to jeopardize my safety or invite danger here. Then she leaves, praying aloud for me and the other tenants.

Hours pass. I grow hungry, but I have no food. I don't store any here. I don't cook. Unlike so many other bachelors, I have shunned custom and never hired a helper to prepare meals for me. Instead, I have always taken my meals in restaurants.

When I left Asmara to come here years ago, my mother warned me against hiring local women to help with domestic chores, which is a common practice in Asmara. "Amharan girls like to seduce Tigrayan men to impregnate them and bear children out of wedlock," she claimed, referring to women of Ethiopian descent. She always considered Amharan and Ethiopian synonymous, even though they are not exactly the same. The Amharans, or Abyssinians, are just one of several Ethiopian ethnic groups. Tigrayans are another division, but we are found in both countries. "When that happens," she explained, "they have no choice but to marry each other." In her mind, it's just another way for Ethiopians to erase Eritrean identity.

Every Eritrean mother believes her son to be more desirable than any Ethiopian man. So it is the dream of Eritrean mothers for their sons to marry Eritrean wives and have Eritrean grandchildren. This is the emotional side of the issue, of course. On the logical side, marrying within one's culture simply makes life easier, as our language and traditions differ from those of the Amharan people. Suffice it to say, the choice of spouse is an important consideration for a mother. It's preferable that he or she comes from a known family with similar background.

As a reminder to heed her advice, my mother would always bring up my cousin, Kale Ab, who had two children with his Amharan maid. "I don't want you to be a failure like him, Yikealo." She never explained what she meant by failure. I suppose she thought it was self-explanatory.

Anyway, this is partly why I always took my meals in restaurants with my coworkers, rather than hiring someone to cook and clean for me. It's a decision that now forces me to make an even more difficult one— whether to leave the safety of my room for food, or stay put and go hungry.

Thankfully, some businesses are keeping their doors open during this chaotic time, offering up their goods and services to those willing to take the risk of venturing out onto the streets. They are determined to carry on as if this is all normal, or at least in hopes that normalcy will soon return. As my hunger grows and the chaos continues, I realize I have no other choice but to go to them. I carefully make my way to the market and back again with enough food to last a couple days. I'm unharmed by my little adventure, but the scenes I witness on the streets will stay with me forever.

Finally, word spreads that some of the town elders have arranged to meet with the TPLF leaders at their camp some distance outside of town. They beg the soldiers to help them suppress the lawlessness and chaos. There's a certain irony to their request, as the TPLF's success is what gave rise to this situation in the first place. But they recognize that nothing short of a military presence will restore order now.

After some discussion, the TPLF leaders agree to help. They dispatch a number of *weyane* — Ethiopian rebel fighters — who are joined by *hafash widib*, local civilians who had helped the resistance in secret. They arrive in pickup trucks and drive up and down the streets ordering everyone to turn in the weapons they stole. Instructions are given for drop-off sites on the main roads, where the guns will be collected. They warn that anyone caught with a stolen weapon afterwards will be arrested for theft.

The next morning, the drop-off locations are filled with guns, which are secured once again. Most of the weapons appear to be recovered, proof that the majority of people have already grown weary of the chaos and are fearful of arrest, but not all. Many guns remain missing.

More *weyane* are sent in to patrol the town and assume control of the former command post, as well as government offices and other sites. At last, order is restored. But it's fragile, and we don't know how long it will hold or what may follow.

Even with the TPLF reestablishing security in Jimma and the surrounding villages and towns, the situation grows more untenable for me. There is no work, leaving me increasingly frustrated. At the capital of Addis Ababa, the rebels are forcing the last of the army out of the city. Mengistu's regime has finally collapsed. Ethiopia sinks deeper into chaos, making it harder for me to return home to Asmara. I know it will only get worse in the coming weeks, so the first chance I have to get out, I take it.

With their advance into Ethiopia, rebel and Eritrean commanders have been releasing *tegadelti* and other political prisoners detained within the many dozens of prisons scattered across the country. Recently, POWs originally held in central Ethiopia were transferred to a prison nearby to keep them out of the hands of the TPLF as they pushed southward from Tigray.

I was aware of the prisoners being held here and always wondered what would happen to them once the Mengistu regime collapsed and Eritrea won independence. Now that both seem about to happen, I am relieved to learn our captured fighters will be bused back to their families. Several *tegadelti* from one of the EPLF's mechanized brigades are assigned to accompany their former comrades until everyone is safely back over the border into Eritrea. I and a number of other Eritreans petition the *tegadelti* and *hafash widib* to allow us to accompany them.

After a brief but tense discussion, we are given permission. I hurriedly pack my belongings. It doesn't take any time at all, as I have so little here to my name.

The TPLF rebel leaders arrange for three buses from the state-run service, Anbessa, to carry us all. From here we will head to Addis Ababa, which is now fully under rebel control. Then we will drive straight north for the long journey to our provincial capital of Asmara.

The former prisoners fill two of the buses and spill over into the third. Most appear to be in a state of disbelief over their newfound freedom. Despite how gaunt-looking they are, half-starved and beaten down, some manage to smile and laugh. A few of them sing. It doesn't take much encouragement to rally the rest of us into joining in.

I take my spot on the bus, as eager to return home as they are, yet wary of the risks. We could be ambushed by rogue loyalists bent on vengeance. The *tegadelti* are supposed to protect us, but they can only do so much. Still, I'm excited at the prospect of a new life in what we hope will soon be a free and independent Eritrea.

The road to Addis Ababa passes through overgrown forests and coffee plantations, and thanks to all the recent rains, everything is lush and green. The mood inside the buses grows ever more exuberant. The singing and clapping to celebrate our victory becomes loud. People tell stories about how the Ethiopian *weyane* and Eritrean *tegadelti* worked together to defeat their common enemy, which we still refer to as the Derg. Others talk about the friends and family members who lost their lives while imprisoned.

Along the way, we are stopped a few times by *weyane* soldiers, who now guard the roads and major crossings. They're clearly on edge, worried about attacks by those still loyal to Mengistu, so they demand our representatives produce proof of who we are and explain where we are going. Our *tegadelti* chaperones are equally as suspicious, so each time we approach another checkpoint, they disembark early and vanish from sight into the brush. Should a checkpoint prove to be held by loyalists, they will avoid capture and be better positioned to surround our attackers and retake the buses.

But at most of the stops, the paperwork is quickly verified and we are allowed to resume our journey without incident.

One stop, however, nearly ends in disaster. I'm in the middle of a loud discussion with Negash and Asfaha, two college educated men I have just met who were working for the Ministry of Agriculture before the fall, when it happens. We had been talking about how each of us intends to contribute toward rebuilding our country, when the bus suddenly stops in the middle of Asfaha's sentence, and someone pounds furiously on the door from the outside. Alarmed, I quickly look out my window and see that we have reached the Gibe River Crossing, a major security checkpoint a few kilometers south of the small town of Welkite. This close to Addis Ababa, the government's security forces are supposedly on the run, and the *weyane* are busy flushing out the rest.

The door flies open and an armed man rushes up the stairs. Dressed in khaki shorts and plastic sandals, he looks like a *weyane*. He also sports the typical large afro hairstyle of the rebel fighters, but in such times it's hard to tell who is who. He could be in disguise, a Derg soldier trying to pass himself off as a *weyane*. Or a *tegadalay*. Both anti-Mengistu fighters dress similarly, a fact that the president's loyalists have used to their advantage in the past to infiltrate and sabotage. They have no standard uniform; instead, they make do with whatever they can get their hands on.

The intruder starts shouting threateningly at our coordinator, demanding to know who we are and what we are doing. Out of nowhere from inside the bus, a *tegadalay* appears and shoves his handgun into the stranger's belly and tries to force him back down onto the road. There's a lot of yelling between them. Everyone stands up to see what's happening. Some of the passengers scramble onto their seats to see over the heads of the others in front. People in the back shout out in alarm. Tempers flare in the midday heat.

All at once, the rest of the *tegadelti* appear and circle the buses, rifles in hand. More shouts are exchanged. Finally, after some anxious moments, the *weyane* steps off the bus and waves us on.

Many of the passengers grumble that the standoff should have been handled better, that it could have easily cost lives. One soldier admits that he came close to killing the *weyane*. All he was waiting for was an order to do so. Others grumble that as long as we all have our papers, there should be no reason for anyone to question our passage. But the representative, an older *tegadalay*, tries to explain why it's necessary to have so many checkpoints. While he understands why everyone is on edge, he pleads with us to keep calm.

"Do not forget your responsibility," he chastises his fellow *tegadelti*. "You're here to protect the passengers, not fight. But," he adds, "if it should come to that, I will give the signal. You won't shoot anyone before that."

The directive sends a shiver down my spine. The scene had been so volatile that it is a wonder nobody got hurt. More troubling, at least for me, is the fact that soldiers who supposedly worked together to overthrow Mengistu's army, Ethiopia's rebel *weyanes* and Eritrea's *tegadelti*, are so quick to distrust each other again. If this is how they act, now that Mengistu is finally defeated, then what does it say about any future cooperation between our two countries?

# Addis Ababa

AT LAST WE ARRIVE IN THE CAPITAL, which is now occupied by the Ethiopian People's Revolutionary Democratic Front, formed by the merging of the TPLF and the Ethiopian People's Democratic Movement, a different anti-Derg resistance group that rose out of the Wollo Province in 1982. We are taken directly to a temporary shelter in the Gotera District of the city to await safe transit further north. There's a large depot nearby that is run by the Ethiopian Grain Trade Enterprise, and *gotera* refers to a specific type of storage container for grain. I have visited here a couple of times before, so I am familiar with the neighborhood.

Our accommodations are a set of dormitories most recently vacated by North Korean nationals. The official story is that they were students enrolled in various universities throughout the city, but it's an open secret that they were actually hired to serve in Mengistu's presidential guard. From the outside, the building appears intact, but all the furniture has been stolen from within, and the floor is littered with broken glass, wood, and paper. The empty spaces amplify our voices, creating eerie echoes and making it even more unnerving to be staying here so soon after it was vacated. I can almost sense the presence of its previous occupants. I dislike not knowing where they went, or if they plan to return. Our security detail tries to convince us they have fled the country and that we're safer here than closer to the general unrest that has taken over other parts of the city, but I'm not the only one with doubts.

In the late afternoon of our second day, the building is shaken by a series of large concussions. The TPLF soldiers, who are still in the process of clearing the city of dangers, inform our *tegadelti* escort what is happening. A warehouse nearby used to store army equipment, including large munitions, has been blown up by escaping loyalists to prevent the arms from being used against them. Our guards decide it's too risky to remain where we are, so we are advised to quickly evacuate. Many of us have little more than the clothes on our backs. Luckily, I had kept some of my items with me in a plastic bag. It isn't much, just a couple books, a pair of pants, underwear, and an extra pair of shoes, but it's more than many of the others have.

Having suffered debilitating injuries during their resistance fighting, some of the former prisoners require assistance. We try to help them, but our guards scream at us to hurry. "This place isn't safe anymore! Go now!" Nobody knows where we will end up, and neither the *tegadelti* nor their *weyane* counterparts say. The buses we took are gone, so we are forced to head to a safer part of the city on foot.

We walk for a couple hours until we have gone several kilometers. Finally, exhausted, we find an unfinished building for shelter. The three-story structure sticks up out of the barren ground like an old hollow bone split open. There is nothing to it other than bare concrete and rusting steel rods and cold cement stairs with old wooden boards and tattered plastic sheets spilling out. No water or electricity, and no protection from the wind blowing through the empty rooms. It makes a lonely sound in the gathering darkness. Nevertheless, it offers some protection and an elevated view of the surrounding area for the guards to keep watch.

As we approach, we are challenged by a man with a gun. He appears to be in his forties, and is dressed in old clothes. I can't tell if he's friendly or not. The *tegadelti* shout at him to put the gun down on the ground, and he yells angrily back in Amharic. Once more, we fear there will be bloodshed, but the stranger eventually complies. The gun is seized, and he's restrained to prevent him from bringing others. He is told that if he behaves, he'll be released after a while.

We are advised to sleep, yet we are all too anxious to do so. Without beds, mattresses, and blankets, we must lie directly on the cold, bare floor.

One man has a radio, and from it we learn that a well-known and re-spected international photojournalist, a Kenyan named Mohamed Amin, was critically injured during the attack in Addis. Many of us have heard of him, as he is famous for reporting about the various conflicts in Africa. Uncensored voices like his have been vital to informing the world about our struggles, although it often seems the world couldn't be bothered to hear them. We are all deeply saddened to hear that he lost an arm, and we pray he will soon recover.

The fire from the explosions in the city has spread to nearby buildings. In all of my years, I would never have imagined Addis Ababa burning at the hands of its own people. The image reminds me of the anarchy in Jimma. Is the scene repeating itself all over the country? And what of Eritrea? What of my beloved Asmara? We hear of loyalists hiding out in the city, causing problems. Are they willing to become martyrs to a lost cause? I can only pray that my family is safe. I dread the possibility of our *tegadelti* being forced to fight there, where there are so many civilians. What damage will the fleeing Ethiopian soldiers do to my home? How many innocent lives will they be willing to take as they go?

All at once, the need to be there overwhelms me.

The next morning, several Eritreans living in Addis show up with food, water, and other supplies. They had heard of our plight and decided to help. They give our *tegadelti* money for the long journey. Such generosity is ingrained in us, and we are especially grateful for it now, since we know it must be a terrible sacrifice for them, especially since their own futures are now uncertain. In such times as these, one might prefer to withdraw from the dangerous world, like a turtle burying one's head in a shell. But that is not our way.

The *tegadelti* are trying to figure out how we are going to continue our journey, since it's still too far to walk to get to Asmara, so it seems that this place will be our camp for a while. Given that there's little for me to do here, I ask if I can accompany the visitors back into the heart of Addis Ababa. I'm worried about some people I know who are still there. The ride back is much quicker than the walk was, and we encounter no trouble along the way.

By chance I happen to run into an old friend from Asmara, Belay, who surprises me with news that my younger brother Yebio is also here in the city. He's apparently with a group of Eritreans I knew from my days living here, so it's a relief to learn that they are all together and safe, but it doesn't stop me from worrying about him. Belay takes me to the Tigray Hotel in the city's northern economic center known as *Piassa*, where Eritreans are known to gather. Then they take me farther in to see if I can find my brother. I end the day unsuccessfully and vow to continue searching again tomorrow unless we are forced to move on. Yebio's friends promise to continue looking for him in my absence. They will tell him that I have returned home.

I begin my search the next morning where it ended the night before, then go to the Dehab Hotel, another welcoming gathering place for my people. Sure enough, I find a crowd squeezed into the tiny one-story building, many of them speaking a dialect of Tigrinya that tells me these are my fellow countrymen. They excitedly share news that the EPLF has finally wrested Asmara from the military's grip and are now sweeping through and flushing out the snipers. I'm stunned by how quickly everything is happening. Is it true? Could Eritrea finally be free after three very long decades of fighting? "Yes!" they exclaim, shaking me with unrestrained joy. "Yes, it's true! Mengistu is out! After thirty years— No! *After a hundred years or more serving others*, Eritrea has finally won its freedom!"

As excited as we are, our celebrations cannot go on unrestrained. We know there are Ethiopians nearby who won't be pleased to hear this news. They would use any excuse to lash out at us in resentment. Even now, it seems, the majority of them continue to believe the propaganda told to them by the very same government they despise. For them, the loss of Eritrea is the same as cutting a limb off of their own body. Like their fallen president, they would rather fight for the Federation until the last drop of blood has been spilled than concede defeat.

While there, I am pleasantly surprised to find two more old friends from Asmara. Weldu is my age, tall and skinny, with soft curly hair. Gebru is older and prematurely balding, but lighter skinned and more muscular than either of us. Handsome and charming, he has always had an easy way about him, and was especially popular with the young ladies back home. I expect them to say they are heading back as well, but I'm wrong. They tell me in confidence that they have been in Addis Ababa for a month making preparations to flee to Kenya. I admit I'm confused. I ask them if they have heard the news that Asmara is now free, and they nod and admit they had been expecting it. "Then why leave now? We should be returning home. Our country needs us."

27

They meet my question with wary silence. I can't imagine what might make them so afraid to speak.

"Listen to me," I tell them. "It's time for all the children of Eritrea to go back home. It's time to taste the freedom we have struggled to win for so long. We must now build our country."

But they don't hear me. They insist that I join them instead. Gebru seems especially determined to convince me to go with them to Kenya. My mind reels in confusion. What are they not telling me?

"If it's money you're worried about," Weldu adds, "we have enough for all three of us."

I thank them for the generous offer, but I have already made up my mind about going back. There's simply no other option for me. This is the time for homecoming, not running away anymore. What possible reason would I have to run even farther away, to another country where I would feel even more like a stranger than here? What reason would they, especially now when everyone will be needed to rebuild?

But then it comes to me, and I understand. Both of them had been active within the Revolutionary Ethiopia Youth Association in Eritrea. REYA had been created by the Mengistu regime with the professed aim of carrying out civic improvement projects, but its real purpose was to recruit our youth to spread his Marxist-Leninist propaganda. Now that Mengistu has been overthrown, my friends fear that their past association with the group, despite being coerced, will be viewed as a betrayal. They don't wish to be branded as traitors and sent to prison by whoever ends up becoming our leadership.

"You're still Eritrean," I tell them. "Surely our new leaders will forgive those who worked for groups sympathetic to Mengistu. I myself worked in a government office under his regime. Most of us did."

"Your situation is different," Gebru tells me. "Besides, it's too soon to know who will lead the country, and what they will do to people like us."

"Nothing," I argue. "They will do nothing."

"It's inevitable. The people who will take control are soldiers," Weldu theorizes. "They know only what it's like to rule using military tactics. Their language is military. Their thinking is military. It will be many years before they can learn how to rule any other way. Look at what happened here? Even after the Derg was abolished, Mengistu continued to rule as if the military was still in power. It's better that we leave now, maybe go to Europe, where we can wait and see what happens. Time will either prove us right or wrong, but I think it will prove us right." He takes hold of my arm and tries again to persuade me. "This is the safest thing to do. For *all* of us."

But I can't. It has been too long since I left my home, and I'm now feeling the time I have missed with my family and friends like a weight crushing me on my back, driving me forward. But there is another reason for my decision. I have long felt guilty for not taking a more active role in the fighting. All these years, I allowed others to spill blood while I stood aside and watched from afar. To flee now to some other country would only prove I am a coward. It would show how I have been lying to myself when I say I am Eritrean. I owe my newly freed nation, barely hours old, an incredible debt, and I intend to fulfill my obligation. It's time for me to repay it.

# The Road Home

EARLY THE THIRD MORNING IN CAMP I am shaken out of my sleep and told new arrangements have been made to take us to Eritrea. Soon after sunrise, three new buses arrive. I still haven't found Yebio, although I did learn from an aunt residing in the city that he's okay and plans on returning to Asmara soon. I wish I could have spoken with him, but I just have to accept that he knows what's best for himself. All I can do is follow my own plan and trust that we will be safely reunited one day soon.

The thousand kilometer trip north will take at least three days, as long as there are no more delays like this one. The regions we will travel through have experienced some of the heaviest fighting of the war and will be the riskiest for us yet. There are checkpoints everywhere, and our guards are constantly on the lookout. We are reminded over and over again to stay alert, as we might be ambushed along the way.

Our first notable stop is in the wool town of Debre Birhan, about a hundred and thirty kilometers northeast of Addis. Hundreds of former soldiers of the Tor Serawit, or Ethiopian army, now disarmed but still wearing their uniforms, line the main road. Very few of them look up at us as we pass. Of those that do, their eyes appear as empty as their spirits seem to be. Exhaustion and defeat cling to them like the dust kicked up by their shuffling feet. They know their president's final act was to betray them, for now it is widely known that Mengistu secretly fled to Zimbabwe with his family, even as his final order was for his soldiers to continue fighting for him. Now, they have nothing to show for their loyalty but the memories of their fallen comrades and an uncertain future for themselves.

We expect to reach Dessie, the administrative capital of Wollo Province, before stopping for the night, but we don't quite make it. Instead, we are overwhelmed by crowds of Eritrean people in Kombolcha, who put on a large feast for us. They have heard about the former prisoners in our company, some of whom endured years of torture inside Ethiopia's notorious prisons, like the one at Alem Bekagn. During the height of the Derg regime, thousands of inmates, both Eritrean and Ethiopian, were executed there. Its hideous reputation reaches much farther back in time, however, to the Italian occupation, when the fascist governor of Ethiopia, Rodolpho Graziani, imprisoned and executed hundreds of local people inside its walls. Prisoners taken to Alem Bekagn expected to never leave. Only those who escaped such a fate know how fortunate they are to be alive. The feast at Kombolcha is to show our heroes how much their sacrifices are appreciated.

It is a festive event, filled with food and dancing and films depicting the heroics of the EPLF fighters crushing Mengistu's army. In the midst of all the revelry, I find a familiar face, a childhood friend from the Asmara neighborhood where we both grew up. Tekle and I clasp arms in greeting. He has gained weight since I last saw him. And lost a lot of hair. We ask about each other's family, then he tells me he has been here a while, working for a company in the city. He doesn't yet know what he will do next, but he has no plans to leave anytime soon. We talk well into the night, and I end up staying with him and his roommate at their house. But as welcome as his hospitality is, I'm anxious to be moving on again the next morning. I long to see the familiar roads marking the ascent to Asmara and knowing my journey is finally coming to an end. I want to see my family and hold them in my arms. I need to know that they are all safe.

Tekle wishes me luck and safe travels, and he sincerely means it. We both know the road ahead is fraught with dangers. So far, we have been lucky. He credits the TPLF, which exerts enough control over the region to ensure peace and order. "But now," he warns, "you must watch yourself carefully. The closer you get to the border, the more likely you will run into retreating Ethiopian soldiers who won't hesitate to shoot you and *weyane* alike. And once you cross the border, the TPLF will no longer be able to help you."

That second day we drive another four hundred kilometers to Mek'ele, the capital of the Tigray Administrative region and birthplace of the TPLF. Once more, we are warmly received, but this time the crowds number in the thousands instead of the hundreds. Again, most who greet us are Eritrean, which makes the visit all the more welcome. I have many fond memories of this town, having traveled here from Asmara several times in the past for business. Each trip often lasted more than a month, so I have come to know many people and have lots of friends here.

The building where we will stay is one I have never been to before. It's well-appointed and beautifully decorated, and it bears the emblem of the EPLF, as well as the Eritrean flag from our time under the Ethiopian Federation. Inside, men and women and children dance in joyful celebration. When I see many of the younger ones dancing *tewedeb*-style, a trademark of the revolution, a smile comes to my face. *Tewedeb*, which applies to both the music and the manner of dancing, traces its roots back to the liberation front.

While the celebration continues, I convince two of my fellow travelers to accompany me to a local restaurant for a short break from the crowds. It was one of my favorite places to eat during my trips, and I am hoping it's still there. The former owner, whom I knew only as Mrs. Meselesh, used to call all of her customers "Doctor," since so many who dined there were physicians traveling through the area. This was especially true during the famine of the mid-1980s. After Mrs. Meselesh's death, her granddaughter, Tiberh, took over the diner. She was the main cook then, a friendly soul with a charming accent and a talent for switching effortlessly between Amharic and Tigrinya during her conversations. I'm eager to see how she and her family are doing.

The first person I recognize is Berhan. I remember I used to sit here and enjoy my coffee while watching her daughter, Tibletse, play off to the side. After Berhan recovers from the surprise of seeing me, she brings us glasses of the local drink, *suwa*, a fermented mixture of barley malt and a type of flour made by crushing dried buckthorn leaves. Each person has their own recipe, so there are no two *suwa* drinks exactly alike. Once we are settled in at a table, I ask about Tiberh, but Berhan tells me she isn't working that day, although she offers to fetch her. I tell her we can't stay long, as we are expected back at the celebration.

"That's too bad," Berhan says. "She will be sorry she missed you. But I know she will be happy to hear that you are still alive and well. We have lost so many friends over the years."

The time passes quickly, and soon we must leave. Berhan asks if I will be visiting others in the city. There are many old friends I wish I could see, but it won't be possible on this trip, as we expect to be departing very early the next morning. "Then we will see you again soon," she says, "when times are better."

My heart is warmed by the visit and the good memories it ushers forth. I bid goodbye to the family who always treated me so well, and wish them a prosperous and happy future. I promise to return, as she optimistically suggests, when times are better.

The final leg of the trip is the one I am most looking forward to, and the one I'm most concerned about. It feels like the closer I get to home, the more remote my chances become for making it there without incident. I have never actually traveled the long stretch between Mek'ele and Asmara before, so I don't know what to expect. I try to relax and take in the ever-changing scenery, rather than allowing my worries to ruin the trip. I'm not entirely successful, however, as every stop raises my anxiety.

A few hours after setting out, we reach the border and pass across it into Eritrea without much trouble. Now, we have only our *tegadelti* escort to protect us and can no longer rely on the TPLF. I still have an uneasy feeling that something is about to happen at any moment. Nevertheless, some of the tension inside me drains away, and I realize that part of it was from worrying about the Ethiopian fighters clashing with our own.

Our first stop inside Eritrea is the market town of Adi Keyh, whose name means "Red Village." It's a beautiful place, set atop a crescent of weathered hills. Nearby are some historical ruins I have always wanted to explore, but there is no time to see them now. While in town, I'm approached by a television reporter eager for an interview. Not surprisingly, he loses interest the moment I tell him I'm not one of the former prisoners or an EPLF fighter. It's just as well, as I have nothing to tell him that he hasn't already heard a thousand times before.

After a brief stop, we resume the journey.

My time on the bus comes to an abrupt end some forty kilometers shy of Asmara in the town of Dekemhare, which was developed by the Italians decades earlier as an industrial center. Much of it now lies in ruins. We are told we need to wait because of an incident in Asmara. It seems a lone Ethiopian soldier refused to surrender and is sniping *tegadelti* from his hiding place. They are still searching for him, and it's unsafe for us to proceed until he is captured. After waiting several hours, we are told that only the former prisoners will be taken any further. The rest of us must find our own way.

We are eventually able to hire another bus willing to take us to Asmara. Without the soldiers to protect us, we are all nervous again. But we arrive safe and sound. Within an hour, my family and friends converge on my location, and there is another big celebration. Excitement and hope fill us all. Every conversation focuses on a future of vast possibilities. In the midst of such optimism, I can't help but recall Weldu's and Gebru's pessimistic words, and a chill passes through me. For our sake, as well as theirs, I hope they are wrong. We must turn our eyes from the past once and for all.

# PART TWO

The Price of Freedom

~

**Eritrea, 1991 - 2003**

# Asmara

AFTER THIRTY YEARS OF FIGHTING, an immense weight is finally lifted away from us. Meles Zenawi Asres, former chairman of the TPLF and head of the EPRDF, takes over as President of the Transitional Government of Ethiopia. Isaias Afewerki, former secretary general of the EPLF, becomes Eritrea's Head of State until elections can be held to choose a president. Former military collaborators, the two men quickly establish friendly relations between our countries, turning our former foe into a new partner and forcing the international community to acknowledge Eritrea's *de facto* status as a free and independent nation.

In April of 1993, two years after throwing off the yoke of our oppressors, the Eritrean people will officially vote for independence in a free and open election. I can't help but wonder what my former Ethiopian colleague, Meseret, would say about that.

The following month, we will become the 182nd member of the United Nations. We will choose Isaias Afewerki to be our first president, and he will commit us to a program of moderate pragmatism and modernization. Within a year, the Constitutional Commission will draft the supreme laws of our new nation. This is how we honor the cause that saw so many lives lost. This is how we will march forward.


The celebrations last for weeks after Mengistu's defeat. During this time, we rejoice in seeing the faces of our family members as they return home, of friends and coworkers and former schoolmates we once feared dead. There are countless reunions, many happy, many more bittersweet.

Everywhere, women can be heard raising their voices in ululations of thanks. The sound beckons neighbors, who rush over and join in. Men laugh and shout and sing. Everyone dances. There is plenty of food and drink and music.

But there is also the serious business of reconciling those who remain missing.

The hardest part of ending a war is waiting to know if a loved one will ever return. Every day, I witness people standing out on the streets, anxiously hoping for that one familiar face to emerge from the steady stream of *tegadelti* and war refugees arriving from far away. They come on foot, in buses, and on trucks. Some are former Soviet-made military vehicles; others are Italian, their license plates printed in Arabic. Some of the returning fighters are able to walk; some cannot even stand. Most are physically changed, scarred, gaunt from illness and malnutrition, missing limbs; all of them are different inside. Every arriving *tegadalay* is pestered with the names of loved ones still absent. Every soldier, no matter how eager they are to see family, responds as patiently and attentively as they can manage. It has been a long journey, but at least they can say it's finally over for them.

Eager for news, we listen with rapt attention to their tales. Sometimes they are sprinkled with humor to dull the terrible edges, but usually not. We are horrified by the brutality they experienced, made proud by their acts of bravery and heroism, saddened by the accounts of those who sacrificed more than anyone should ever be asked.

As the weeks pass and the stream of fighters turns into a trickle, then a slow drip, many families lose hope of ever seeing their loved ones alive again. We are a nation hardened by hardship and sacrifice, yet it is still a terribly difficult thing to witness, harder still to endure, this gradual shift from hopeful expectation to mournful acceptance. We all know the costs of war— we were born with it engraved on our souls. We grew up experiencing it firsthand. We know the steep price to be paid for independence. And yet with peace now assured, how can we not hope and pray and expect to see our lost loved ones returning home safe and sound?

So begins our period of mourning, even in the midst of celebrations. This is a necessary part of the healing that will follow. We grieve in private and in public, individually and as a nation. Families unite, merging one's pride of survival with another's agony of loss. Mothers and wives of heroes join with the sisters and daughters of the fallen, tears of joy shed by some, tears of sadness by others. The young repeat tales of bravery and sacrifice they overheard their heroes tell. We are all strengthened by the blood that was spilled and the promise that no more will ever have to be spilled again, for freedom has been won at last, and no one will take it away from us ever again.

I cannot remember how many homes I visit during this time, alone or with my parents, my siblings, my friends. Countless are the numbers we have lost, the brothers and sisters, parents and children, and the mourning seems to be without end. Everyone has at least a cousin who died, an uncle, an aunt. A nation cannot fight for thirty years without this being true. Every family has sacrificed someone, whether on the battlefield or in another way. Others died for no reason whatsoever, innocent victims of a ruthless regime that often violated the conventions of war and civility.

Such was the case with my uncle. I was just a young man of eighteen, when I learned of his violent death. It was early one April morning in 1980, when we received an unexpected visit from three friends and neighbors of my father— Bokre, Andeberhan, and Zekarias. In our culture, such a visit is a sure sign that there is bad news to be delivered. No one is expected to bear such a heavy weight alone. In such times, neighbors become family.

As was customary, all were invited inside the house and asked to sit. Greetings were exchanged. There followed a moment of uncomfortable silence before my father turned to Bokre and asked the question we knew was coming. I can remember the exact words he spoke. I can still hear them in my head: "Are we okay?" He was always looking for the positive side of things, even in the face of certain tragedy. He wanted to know what we were facing so that we could work on moving past it.

Bokre sighed, and his shoulders slumped. I understood why my father chose him to speak for the group. As a teacher, Bokre was well regarded in the community, what one might call an Elder, even though he was only in his early fifties. But he was known for his ability to understand the troubles others endured and for choosing his words carefully. Speaking quietly, he told my father that his older brother had passed away.

Dad sat for a moment without speaking, clearly shocked. This was not what he had expected. His brother was a farmer. He was in his early sixties, so he wasn't young, but he was healthy and strong. Everyone expected him to live many more years. "How? When? Was it an accident? His heart?"

"They killed him," Andeberhan blurted out, furious. "Last week." He was shaking, his eyes flashing. A large man who rarely smiled, he was quick to anger. You never wanted to get on his bad side.

We looked to Zekarias, a man with an easy laugh and a reputation for working hard and drinking even harder, but he was uncharacteristically quiet. Bokre reached over and placed a hand on Anderberhan's arm to calm him down.

"They," my father growled. It was less a question than an affirmation. We all understood who *they* were: the Derg and its murderous agents.

"They accused him of being involved with the EPLF."

"Was he?" my father asked, for one was never sure of such things in those days. Eritreans often kept their loyalties to themselves for fear of betrayal, but also to protect loved ones from the consequences of their decisions should they be caught.

"What we know is that a man who spoke Tigrinya and dressed like a *tegadalay* tricked him into thinking he was a friend. As for admitting involvement . . . ." Andeberhan raised his fists and shook them in the air. "They took him from his farm. That is all we know."

"Then we don't know for sure if he is dead," my father decided. "There is a chance he might still be alive."

Of course, we hoped that this was the case, but we also knew that if he hadn't yet been murdered, then he was certainly in prison, where he was being tortured. The chances of him surviving such abuse at his age were small, and the longer he lived, the worse his suffering would become. It was often better to be a quick martyr than to endure the horrors of torture.

"This is all we know for now," Bokre said. "We will continue to check for details."

Confirmation of my uncle's death at the hands of the Ethiopian agents came a week later, although not from my father's friends. We heard it on the radio, from a broadcast made by the EPLF rebel station *Dimtsi Hafash*, the Radio of the Masses. *Dimtsi Hafash* had become our lifeline to the resistance, and from its reporting we learned of the countless people abducted from their homes or places of business, people like my uncle. All of those taken were informally accused of being involved in the rebel movement, imprisoned, beaten, and repeatedly tortured. Many were killed. And while it was true that some of them actually were involved in the resistance, not all were, or they were simply associated in some indirect way with someone who was. I didn't know if my uncle was *hafash widib*, a supporter of the resistance. All I remembered was a kindly gentleman who worked hard and was well loved by his family and friends.

My father mourned his brother's death; I mourned my uncle's. Neither brought an end to the war, but it did shape my opinion of it. It made me even more determined than I already was to join the fight, to do whatever I could to defeat the people bringing so much heartache to my family and my people.

Now, after the war has finally ended, I am deeply saddened to see how many of the martyrs are from my own generation, people who undoubtedly felt just as I had. I'm especially stricken when I hear from my old dear friend Yonathan that his younger sister is almost certainly among the casualties. We had all grown up together, played together. Yonathan is a couple years younger than I am, but we shared the same circle of friends. His sister would have been barely in her twenties.

He tells me that she joined the EPLF with a friend, both of them swept up in the wave of nationalism that rose after the Derg was supposedly disbanded. But the friend recently returned home alone. When Yonathan asked about his sister, she told him she was probably okay, but something in the tone of her voice said otherwise. He has since accepted her death and mourns her loss, just as we all mourn. We vow we will never forget their sacrifice.

The twentieth of June is officially designated as Martyrs' Day. Some sixty-five thousand *tegadelti* lost their lives, plus an unknowable but likely far greater number of civilians, both here and in Ethiopia. So many were taken on the field of battle; so many more taken in the streets or lost in cold, dark prison cells as they faced crimes they didn't commit or else waged in the name of *gedli* against an unjust, corrupt, inhuman regime.

As it always does, the ritual of celebration eventually ends as we prepare for the hard work of reconstruction. But mourning is an everlasting chore, a weight we carry with us for all time. With the arrival of each new day, our grief is reborn. So, each year, on this one special day we have set aside, we honor the fallen *shifta*, our heroic outlaw fighters. We march in the streets, renewing our promise to do our best to build the country they envisioned, the one for which they gave their lives.

We remind ourselves that their sacrifice was not made in vain.

Yonathan and I were once very close. This was before our paths went off in separate and unexpected directions several years ago, so I'm grateful for the opportunity to renew our friendship. We meet for coffee almost daily, often joined by two other old friends, Yemane and Aman, and we catch up on all the events we missed from each other's lives. Some stories are easier to tell, while others are shared only with considerable pain. There is so much to recall, but doing so helps us heal.

Yemane, for example, tells us about his years spent inside Asmara's Mariam Gibi Prison. Named after Holy Mary, the mother of Jesus, the jail was originally built as a maternity clinic run by nuns, but it was converted into a high security detention center and torture facility by the Derg for those suspected of being rebels. In the decade the prison operated, thousands of Eritreans were put to death within its walls. There is now talk of turning it into a museum, as much to show the world the atrocities subjected upon our people as to remind ourselves of the horrors we fought to rescue ourselves from. I haven't seen the inside myself, but I have heard from others what it was like.

Yemane's cell was barely four meters square and sometimes held dozens of men within its cramped confines. He says there are larger cells for upwards of one or two hundred prisoners. There was no privacy. Everything was shared, from clothing to blankets. Food wasn't provided; rather, it had to be brought in by the prisoners' friends and relatives. The interrogation rooms were located underground. He describes one

41

common method of torture called "helicopter," where a prisoner would be suspended with their hands and feet bound together behind their back. Then they would be dunked repeatedly into a well of water until they confessed to crimes, some real, some made up. A lot of people died while being tortured. There a rumors of mass graves on the grounds, which have yet to be confirmed, but given the numbers who went in and never left, it's a near certainty their bones will eventually be found.

In Mariam Gibi, the lucky ones were those who died quickly and suffered less. Of those who lived to see release, many now suffer some form of permanent disability. Yemane, who once had a generous, vibrant personality, is now solemn. He's deaf in his right ear from the abuse inflicted upon him, and pain, both physical and mental, plagues him night and day.

I feel humbled listening to the stories he tells. He has to position himself twisted to one side so he can hear us out of his good ear. His daily struggle is apparent by his gaunt body, his prematurely lined face, and the nervous twitch of his gaze. Terrible memories return to him at random moments, haunting him mercilessly. He confesses he can still hear the shrieks of the young Eritreans who shared his cell, even in the ear that is now deaf, shrieks of agony as they were being tortured. At night, he wakes up in a sweat hearing the voices of the Ethiopian guards as they call out the name of their next victim. "Gather your belongings, *shifta*," the ghost soldiers wail out at him, and he knows that it is a death sentence, for the order to collect one's possessions means there will be no returning to the cell. A prisoner quickly figured out that death was the only way one left the prison.

He had witnessed the guards give this very command many times: *"Gather your belongings!"* And as many times the poor victims, knowing their journey had reached its end, would turn to those remaining behind and utter the same brave words, their last: *Stay strong, brothers. Awet Nihafash. Victory for the Eritrean people. Justice will prevail.*

It's a terrible tragedy that so many never lived to see that it did.

Yemane had been a member of a secret cell of the ELF in Asmara, the same group that had called for Eritrean independence before the start of the war. In fact, it was he who tried to recruit me into the ELF weeks before he was caught and taken to prison. This was back when I was still an angry young man with a narrow view of the world and an even narrower role to play in it. I was eager to avenge the deaths of so many of my friends and family. Youth made me brave. Anger made me reckless. But it was naiveté that tricked me into believing I alone could make a difference in something as large as our fight for independence. It was folly that made me think I could, by sheer force of will, deliver us from our oppressors.

I was a teenager in 1978, when I learned firsthand how quickly and easily the balance of war can shift from one side to the other. At this time, the Derg held Asmara, the provincial capital of Eritrea, and they were beset by fighters from our own ELF and EPLF trying to free it. When at last they succeeded, expelling our Ethiopian tormentors, we believed with great confidence that independence would soon follow.

Despite our optimism, the siege had taken a heavy toll on those of us who had been trapped inside the city. Every basic necessity — food, water, firewood, oil — was either in short supply or impossible to get. People were starving to death. So my parents made the decision that we must go elsewhere and retrieve what we needed to survive. My father and older brother, Berhane, would remain behind to protect our small business, while my mother took me and the rest of my siblings to the family's ancestral village in the rural south. We were not the only family doing this. Hundreds of others were leaving every day.

We traveled by foot. For an entire day we trekked over rough track, up mountains and down valleys, through scrublands so thick with seraw, a type of acacia tree with long thorns, that we couldn't avoid it tearing at our skin and shredding our clothes. We made our way over scorching hot sand with little to protect our exposed skin. My younger brother and I took turns carrying our youngest sister on our shoulders. We did our best to avoid the fighting. I still remember how intense my relief was when we reached the old village and I saw my grandmother and knew we had finally made it.

The settlement was primitive by city standards. There was no electricity, no running water. There, in that remote location, hidden deep inside the forest, the Derg posed a much smaller risk than what we had witnessed in Asmara. But that didn't mean the occupants were any less involved in the war effort. In fact, it had become a sort of safe haven to members of the Eritrean resistance groups, particularly those actively fighting with the ELF, not just those who had fled the larger cities out of fear of being captured for being *hafash widib*. It offered me the perfect opportunity to learn more about the resistance efforts. Specifically, I wanted to know more about their experiences and motives for joining the movement.

The day after our arrival, I was surprised to learn that my cousin, Beyene, was an ELF supporter. He had left Asmara without explanation about a year before, although we all assumed he had come to help his uncle on his farm. The truth was, he had fled before he could fall into the hands of the ruthless security squads known as the *Dehninet*, a secret paramilitary arm of the Tor Serawit who operated to protect Mengistu's regime.

"So, you were recruited?" I asked, fascinated by the revelation. Not only was I curious how one went about becoming a member, but at the age of seventeen, I was seduced by the idea of *gedli* — not to become a martyr myself, although that possibility didn't scare me as much as it should have or would in later years — but to be a part of a movement that everyone was convinced was on the cusp of winning at long last.

"No, I was not recruited," was his blunt reply.

I had expected more out of him— if not in substance, then at least in spirit. Beyene had always been a good storyteller, animated and hyperbolic, often embellishing his tales with wildly expressive gestures and faces. He was a likeable boy, a sort of rebel himself, which many of us our age wished to emulate. He would sneak cigarettes, then smoke them anywhere he could find to avoid the scorn of relatives who disapproved of the habit. But he had terrible luck and always seemed to get caught.

Upon seeing my puzzlement, he sighed and shook his head. "I was thinking about it, about heading to the front to fight. I wanted to, but then . . . things changed." He shrugged. "I came here."

"I don't understand," I said, still confused. "What changed? Was it the way you feel about the war?"

"Feel?" He seemed offended that I would have to ask. "You know I help the ELF fighters nearby, supporting them, don't you?" he asked. I couldn't tell if he thought I had judged him a coward for coming here. Or a traitor for not wanting to stay in Asmara and fight. "Technically, that makes me *tegadalay*."

"I didn't say you were—"

"Do you know how many times I was nearly executed, how many times I barely escaped capture?"

This was all news to me. The only detail I knew about his departure was that his mom, my aunt, missed him terribly and talked often about bringing him back to Asmara to live with her. She had sacrificed so much to raise him and his older sister, fighting to keep them safe during the Derg's Red Terror, when children, especially boys, were vulnerable. She had had to do it alone because Beyene's father had been killed in an automobile accident when he was very young.

As to his question, I had no answer.

"At least three times," he told me defiantly. "Twice at Hiwet and once at Kokeb."

"The teashops?" I said, shocked to hear the names fall from his lips. Both places were well-known targets of the *Dehninet*, and we had all been warned to stay away from them.

Particularly brutal among the security squad were the strangulation team, or *Afagn Guad*, whose weapon of choice was the garrote, usually an old piano or guitar string. They all drove the same types of cars, typically Volkswagen or Fiat sedans, so they were usually easy to spot on the roads and avoid. Even their pathetic attempts to trick us by changing the registration plates didn't work. But they still got far too many victims. The *Afagn Guad* targeted the young, many of whom were innocent of any crime except for being born Eritrean. After torturing the poor victim to death, they would leave the mangled corpse on the outskirts of the city to be found by anyone passing by. So brazen were these agents that they would drive down a street in broad daylight and fire their Uzis into groups of people hanging around bars and teashops, like Hiwet and

Kokeb. They didn't fear retaliation or arrest, because there was no one to challenge them. Young men with large afro hairstyles, a trademark of the *tegadelti*, were particularly vulnerable, leading most parents to shave their sons' hair close to the scalp to protect them.

"This is why you left Asmara to live here in the village?" I asked incredulously. I had always viewed my younger cousin as my peer, but in that moment it seemed he had aged far beyond our years. Indeed, he didn't just look older, but he now spoke with a maturity I envied.

"I won't carry a gun, in case you are wondering," he said. "I have seen enough killing, and for the wrong reasons. Now, I only do what I am told to do for them, no more."

"No more? So, your feelings for the resistance have changed?"

"If you are asking if I would join now, the answer is no," he admitted. "I don't think it's worth it now to fight."

He continued to avoid answering my questions directly, and it was only after several more minutes of me pestering him that eventually brought out the truth.

"Why should I sweat and bleed for them?" he asked me. I could see he was getting upset. He was only half finished with his cigarette, when he threw it down and crushed it beneath his foot, before immediately lighting another. "Why should I give up my life, when they have forgotten what we are fighting for?"

"They?"

"The ELF and EPLF. From everything I have seen, it is now clear they can't agree on anything anymore. They are always fighting each other. How many of our deaths are from their own recklessness? What hope do we have that they will ever agree long enough to defeat the Derg? None."

Although I was surprised to hear him say these things, especially in light of our recent military victories, I had to acknowledge the opinion was one shared by others I knew. Disagreements between the groups was well known and a frustration for us all. Of course we expected there would be quarrels between factions. After all, the ELF holds much more conservative views than their left-wing brothers, who had split away from the movement a few years back. But that is always the nature of politics. Everyone always thinks they know best how to lead, so even the smallest

46

of disagreements can turn into divisive issues. I have seen this happen even within the same family, yet they always manage to set their differences aside for the greater good. It's what we hoped our fighters would see, no matter their personal politics. In this case, our very independence was at stake. Beyene's uncle, for example, had made just such a compromise. He provided assistance to the local ELF, even though his beliefs aligned more with the progressive policies of the EPLF, like mine. But because his nephew was assisting the ELF, he chose to help them, too.

Independence for the country must come above all else. That is what I thought. Surely, our petty differences wouldn't get in the way of achieving it.

But Beyene couldn't be persuaded to agree. "Their fighting between themselves is selfish and useless," he told me bitterly. "They are dying fighting each other, rather than for independence. Conflict is in our blood. We don't know how to live unless we are dying."

"But they are fighting together now to protect Asmara," I pointed out. "They have expelled the Derg."

"They are fighting to see who can become more powerful. To them, that is more important than freeing Eritrea. You just wait and see, Yikealo. This cooperation in the north won't last long. Today, they are working together, but I fear they will soon go back to fighting each other. And because of this, it will be harder than ever for us to win this war. The Tor Serawit knows this weakness and has gotten very good at exploiting it."

"Victory is too close now," I said. "And when we win, our fighters will work together to—"

"No!" he interrupted, shaking his head. "Believe me, cousin, they aren't thinking about how to win for Eritrea together, or how to build a new country together. They only think about how they alone can rule it once they get into power."

"Who cares who rules?" I naively replied. I was beginning to grow frustrated with him by this point. How had he lost his faith and his focus? "As long as Eritrea is ruled by Eritreans, we will survive."

He shook his head. "Just promise me, Yikealo, before you join the resistance and go to the front lines, take some time and observe how they really think. It would be a shame for you to die while we gain nothing toward our goal of independence. Or worse, die for a different kind of future that is free only in name."

I didn't press him after that. Privately, I believed he was dead wrong, despite the certainty of his doubts. Despite their philosophical differences, the ELF and EPLF had fought together to retake our capital. They had Mengistu's army in retreat, and that was proof enough that our leaders could work together when it was vital that they do so.

But I was the one who would be proven wrong.

Beyene's words coming true should have been enough of a warning to discourage me from trying to join the resistance, but they weren't. Later, I should have been discouraged by my uncle's capture and brutal murder. Yet even after Yemane's capture in Asmara, when ELF cells were being exposed one by one and their members rounded up and imprisoned, I remained committed to joining the cause. Even as the animosity between the ELF and EPLF grew, I was determined to do my part in the fight. Call it arrogance or youthful innocence, but I continued to hold out for an EPLF cell to join.

"You were lucky not to get caught," Yemane assures me. "Your connection to me could have been enough. But if you had joined, you definitely would have been captured. And then you would have spent years in prison, like me. Or worse, you might have died there."

"Better to die trying," I offer halfheartedly. Despite the wisdom of my years and the benefit of hindsight, I still feel guilty for escaping the warfront. "Besides, you don't know for sure what would have happened." I point to Yonathan, who was fortunate enough to avoid capture, despite being active in the same cell. "You never gave them any names. They tortured you, yet you never told them about us."

Yonathan stops Yemane before he can answer. "I am certain they already knew about me. That's why I left and went to Addis right after. Not because I feared Yemane would talk, but because the *Dehninet* must have already known I was involved. The moment I heard our friend had been taken, I ran. Does it matter if I was lucky or wise or cowardly in my decision? No. I'm alive now because of it, and Eritrea is still free. That is all that matters anymore. We will never forget those who sacrificed. But to honor them, we must now make our own sacrifices. It is our responsibility to build Eritrea, now that we are free."

I am grateful for the change in subject. Here at last is a conversation I am eager to have. And with my college education and experience, I know I should have no trouble finding a position, whether in the new government or in the private sector. In fact, I had expected there to be such an abundance of projects, whether related to infrastructure or commercial development, that I could have one of my choosing. But weeks after submitting a dozen applications for such work, I have yet to receive even a single acknowledgment they were received.

Aman tells me I cannot expect everything to change so quickly. "The government is starting from scratch. There is no money, and too much to do."

"Which is exactly why people like me are needed," I reply.

He shrugs, but it is Yemane's next words that strike a familiar and ominous chord in me, because they echo what Beyene told me all those years ago in my grandmother's village. "There is money, both from within and from foreign aid, but there is also too much arguing between our decision-makers. They must learn to set aside their pride and do what is best for the country. Otherwise, how can we be expected to move forward as a people?"

Without a common enemy to focus their efforts and enjoin them to cooperate, the old divisions between ELF and EPLF have risen anew. They now threaten to undermine any progress we have made, and swamp any plans for our future. Our country may have won its freedom, but we are still fighting.

The leader of the ELF cell in Asmara, a man named Berhe, disappeared around the same time Yemane was captured. Yemane has been trying to find him ever since his release from Mariam Gibi Prison, but he hasn't been successful. If Berhe is still alive, he has likely fled to Sudan, to join up with the surviving ELF leadership, who are now actively engaged in trying to disrupt the EPLF leaders in charge here in Asmara.

This time, I can't argue with Yemane's logic, as I once tried to do with Beyene all those years ago. I don't tell him not to worry about our choices in the past, as I argued with Gebru and Weldu in Addis Ababa. I have since learned that the past comes back to haunt us, as seems to be the case regarding the old feuds between the ELF and EPLF leaders. Experience has taught me that much. It has given me the perspective to see what I was so blind to then.

A few days after the conversation I had had with my cousin Beyene, just when it seemed the war was won, the balance suddenly shifted and with disastrous consequences for our struggle. Instead of retreating to Ethiopia, the Tor Serawit returned with heavy artillery, striking us while we were focused on our own petty squabbles. We watched as Soviet-made tanks passed through our village on a new offensive to take back Asmara. And they succeeded.

Our dreams disintegrated right before our eyes, and it was all because the ELF and EPLF could not formulate a single cohesive strategy to finish off the Derg. It took a civil war in Ethiopia to do that.

Now that it is all behind us, I worry we don't start our own civil war. Our leaders must be made to see the tremendous responsibility they have to honor the sacrifices of those who fought, both ELF and EPLF, and especially those who died. They must understand how we are still fighting for the same thing, the country we love.


It is now 1996, five years since the war ended, three years after our referendum for independence, and Eritrea is still struggling to settle into its new role of sovereign nation. But, after some misfires, we are at least making progress. The pace is slower than we expected, and the emphasis is still on military might rather than civil development, but President Isaias Afewerki promises more of the latter as he fills the ranks of his recently established National Service with young men and women. Our yet-to-be-adopted National Charter, the nation's Constitution, stipulates a mandatory eighteen-month term. It isn't an ideal situation for our country's youth, but there are far more civil projects than willing participants to staff them.

While the pace of progress remains slow, we try not to become frustrated by it. Our sense of optimism is irrepressible, our pride too strong. We have much to be thankful for and much more to look forward to. For starters, I am recently married. I met my wife Wudasie in 1992, when she applied for a job in the office where I worked. From initial introductions to friendship, our relationship quickly blossomed into mutual admiration and love. Like me, she is a college graduate who had been living and working in Ethiopia prior to the end of the war, although the difference is that she was born and grew up there, too. Her family fled to Addis Ababa, like so many others did to avoid the violence here; they returned after the war ended.

We took up residence in our new national capital of Asmara, renting a small house close to Wudasie's parents. We believe we will be able to contribute more meaningfully to our country's development from here, where the possibilities seem limitless. Just as our leaders are still trying to figure out, we simply need to learn how to get out of our own way to pursue them.

With her degree in social sciences from Addis Ababa University, Wudasie manages the staff at an international NGO that strives to meet the needs of a population still trying to recover from so much oppression. I obtain a position in an accounting department of one of the few international companies operating within our borders. While we both love our work, we set our sights higher. We have a burning desire to forge our own path, and we speak often and passionately about starting our own business, although we are still not sure what that might be. There remain considerable obstacles to any free enterprise, but none of them is so insurmountable as to discourage us, certainly nothing like the obstacles we would have had to overcome in the past. Independence has removed them. There is little to stop us from chasing our dreams.

After long consideration and careful preparation, we formulate a plan to open a small general store, a stepping stone to greater things. Our hope is to generate enough money from this enterprise to fund a more ambitious project in line with our professional skills and desires. The prospect is both exciting and daunting, yet we are confident in our strategy, and we know that one day we will attain even our most ambitious goals.

Ah, but peace is like a vibrant flower, bright and flashy, yet more delicate than it appears. Its petals are easily broken and quick to wilt if not constantly nurtured. In the years since the war ended, Eritrea has jealously guarded our peace, protecting it so it may blossom to its fullest potential. Some might say too jealously. But who could blame us, when outside influences still work to undermine our leadership? Additionally, we are surrounded on all sides by geopolitical unrest, which acts to remind us of what we have won, and what we can so easily lose.

Across the Red Sea to the east, tribal tensions are rising in Yemen. To the west and north, Sudan struggles with its own political and religious turmoil. And to the southeast, warlords have taken over Somalia after the government of Mohamed Siad Barre collapsed.

At home, despite cooling relations with Addis Ababa over lingering disagreements about the exact placement of the border between us, we are at least at peace. But then, on a hot morning in May of 1998, a band of disillusioned Ethiopians attack Eritrean security forces patrolling the border near Badme. They retaliate. People die. Armies are mobilized.

Eritreans everywhere hold their collective breath and wait. We cling to the hope that the flare-up will quickly extinguish itself, that it will find no ready fuel to reignite a war that has already burned through more tinder than either country can afford. We pray our respective governments will remember how much effort they invested in building our peace. Once, the presidents of both nations were like twin brothers to each other, both working hard toward a common goal. But now, they become like squabbling siblings. Neither one is willing to back down. Neither will make even the tiniest concession.

Weeks pass. The Organization of African Unity attempts to mediate the argument between the countries. A joint US-Rwandan plan is put forward, proposing that both militaries retreat to pre-June 1998 positions to prevent more incidents.

We watch nervously as our leaders perform the careful dance of diplomacy.

They say peace is a tricky path to walk, especially for a people so long accustomed to conflict. Even the strongest leaders can falter in the choppy wake of liberation, especially when it must navigate the turbulence of past animosities. Those who wield power become ever more susceptible to the constant pressures that seem to propel them toward conflagration. So it is for us. Our president, Isaias Afewerki, refuses the terms.

Within weeks, we are once more fully at war with our old enemy. Rather than being a reminder of what we might lose if we allow this to continue, memories of the previous conflict feed the discord. In engaging once more, we discard the sacrifices of our heroes. And any progress we have made in the years since the fighting ended evaporates like the fog that settles in the morning over our valleys.

Just as it seemed we would finally be able to realize our dreams, they are wrenched from our grasp.


Looking back, I guess we shouldn't be surprised at how poorly things have gone. Nation-building is such an incredibly difficult and complex thing to do that it seems inconceivable we didn't plan for failure. Perhaps it's because our people struggled for so long and fought so hard for what was essentially an unattainable ideal, that when peace was finally thrust into our hands, we didn't know what to do with it. It was a wholly unfamiliar notion to us, like a newborn baby given for the first time to a young and inexperienced father. Oppression may have been a yoke about our necks, but freedom carries a different kind of heft. It is so vast a thing, yet so unrestricting, that one can easily become overwhelmed by it, as we were.

Given such uncertain times, our friends and families advise me and Wudasie to wait before making any financial decisions about our future. So much about the nation's fate now depends on our leaders that it isn't a good time to be experimenting with our savings. Everyone is hopeful for a quick resolution to the conflict, but we all know it could just as likely drag on for many more years. What terrifies us more than anything else is the prospect of falling once again under another nation's power.

But even as the political strife threatens to upend our plans, a more personal reality takes precedent. Our young daughter Titi, now two years old, had recently been diagnosed with a heart murmur that could threaten her life if not treated. We won't know the full extent of the defect without more expensive testing, which can only be done outside of the country. Our only certainty is that the defect could easily get much worse as she ages. The news, when we found out about it, was crushing, but we had resolved to get her the best, most advanced medical care available, no matter the cost or sacrifice. Any parent would want that, of course. And since our current salaries barely even cover our modest expenses as they are, the only way we would ever be able to pay for a surgery unavailable inside Eritrea is by taking matters into our own hands. We had tried once before, but had been forced to postpone the plan when the government shut down the NGO where Wudasie worked. She has since found another job, but we lost a lot of ground because of it.

Are we being foolish to test fate once again, especially in such times as these?

A few days before Christmas, some seven months into the conflict, we take over the lease on a small market and begin selling general goods. We are terrified of failing and losing everything, so Wudasie stays on at her new place of employment, while I manage the store. We carefully reinvest everything we can save back into the business.

We have barely settled into our new role as shop-owners, when we learn Ethiopian soldiers have broken through our defensive lines to the south and advanced ten kilometers into the country. Memories of the previous war rush back with terrifying clarity. How can this be happening again? Have we not learned anything?

I bring a small radio into the shop to keep abreast of the news. Each hour brings more reports of death and devastation from the front. Our hopes seem fated to be dashed.

But then, days later, the conflict takes a positive turn. We receive encouraging reports that the OAU has forwarded a new peace plan for consideration by both nations. We wait, and when we hear that Eritrea has accepted the terms, we celebrate.

Except this time, it is Ethiopia who refuses them.

Fighting resumes.

Uncertainty grows. Each day dawns darker than the last, and just when it seems circumstances can't become any more dire than they already are, they do. The government recalls anyone with prior military training to duty, including any dismissed National Service members from the first three cycles. They have already served their eighteen-month obligations, but without a Constitution to protect them, the president himself becomes the law of the land. Now, no one can challenge his decisions.

Among the early conscripts are both of my younger brothers, including Yebio, for whom I had searched back in Addis Ababa more than seven years earlier, and my youngest sister, Ellen. She joined in one of the first cycles in 1995, right after she finished high school, and was dismissed a year before the new war started. Yebio was conscripted from his job and forced to train and serve. And Eyasu entered after he finished college. He has now been assigned to the training camp at Sawa.

Three of my wife's siblings also serve— two sisters, Arsema and Akberet, and one brother, Biniam. And both of us also have several cousins in the army. So far, Wudasie and I have both been spared— she because she is married, and I because of my age. I will soon turn forty, and will become ineligible.

The recall worries us all. Does it mean we are gearing up for another full-fledged conflict? The government takes no chances. It adopts a more aggressive position with regards to conscripting members into training, citing the defense of our country as our number one priority.

Wudasie and I refocus our efforts on our own priorities. What choice do we have? If we fail, we will be in serious financial trouble, and our daughter will never get the medical attention she needs.

As for the war, we pray it ends soon. Or, at the very least, that it doesn't reach us here in Asmara.

* * *

In these early tumultuous days of the business, I am always on the lookout for ways to generate more income. I get one such opportunity the following summer, after a relative with contacts in a large international construction company headquartered on the coast of the Red Sea tells me they need a provider for a variety of consumable goods. There are talks, requirements are described, proposals are made. The discussion is taken to higher ups in the company at Massawa.

Finally, in the first week of August, a meeting is arranged with the relevant decision-makers in their main offices. The drive to the coast is a hundred and fifteen kilometers over winding roads, but if all goes to plan, we will sign a contract the same day. It will require even more hard work for both me and Wudasie, and a lot more traveling, even the hiring of additional help, but the opportunity is too good to pass up.

On the morning of the meeting, I rise in the pre-dawn hours. The night's coolness seeps out of the bare floor and stings my skin. I put on my new suit and modest Italian-made shoes, expenses we can barely afford, yet felt obliged to make. If I am to convince my potential new business partners to take me seriously, I must look the part of a professional businessman. I even spent a few extra *nakfas* on a haircut I don't really need. I'm determined to convince them I deserve their consideration.

The chill in the air won't last long. The coast is far less temperate than the highlands of Asmara, and it will become very hot long before the day is over, so I relish it as long as I can. Hopefully, the deal will be done sooner rather than later, and I will be on my way back before the brutal temperatures of the lowland desert can sap my energy. As a native Asmarino, I'm unaccustomed to such extreme climates.

I carefully gather my effects before leaving the house— a brand new notebook and pen, as well as sample bottles of drinking water of various brands. God willing, I will be home before dark with good news for my family, and the promise of more money.

Shutting the door behind me, I make a silent prayer. I ask only for a little more certainty in our lives— for my family and for my business. But also, for my country.

# Nefasit

THE TAXI DROPS ME OFF DOWNTOWN. From there, it's a short walk of a few blocks to the bus terminal in the *Edaga Hamus* — Thursday Market — district of the city. The terminal occupies the bottom portion of a building facing the hospital. Just to the west is the city's slaughter house, already open and bustling with activity. A variety of older one-story buildings line the streets to the north and east. To the south is a Shell gas station, its familiar yellow and red sign faded by years in the sun and coated in fine dust.

It's a busy place filled with people coming and going and engaged in all sorts of transactions. Local buses pull in on a regular basis, delivering workers and picking more up to take away. Drivers honk and gesture impatiently at the crowds of people milling about. Many arriving travelers pause to browse at the nearby shops, snack bars, and street vendors hawking their wares. There is a noticeable scarcity of young men and women. Most of those present are dressed in uniform and carry packs as they make their way to and from their posts. Those eligible for service in the army, but not yet conscripted, have taken to avoiding crowded areas such as this one. Anyone eighteen to forty, male or female, is considered eligible. I am thirty-eight, but soon I will be too old to fight.

A handful of underage teenagers stand about calling out the names of various destinations, along with the number of available seats on each bus. After assessing my options, I hurry over to one shouting "Batsi! Batsi!" which is another name for Massawa. The boy, about fourteen, is standing in front of a light blue Mitsubishi minibus, and I can see that it's nearly full, so it will be departing soon. There are larger intercity transports available, but the smaller, more agile vehicles are the better option for me. They can more easily navigate the steep and winding roads that descend from Asmara, getting me to Massawa in a shorter amount of time. I want to do everything I can to guarantee I don't arrive late for the meeting.

Soon, we are off. On the outskirts of the city we pass the Asmara Zoo, its gates still locked prior to opening to the public for the day. Next, there is the Hindu crematorium. Then the War Cemetery commemorating those who died defeating the Italians during World War Two. It may be smaller than the British burial ground in Keren, some ninety kilometers to the northwest, but it's very well maintained and highly esteemed, as it contains the graves of Allied soldiers from over forty different countries who helped deliver us from Italian rule.

Just before we leave the Kebessa Plateau, we reach the Bar Durfo promontory, a convenient stopping point popular with locals and tourists for its sweeping views of the beautiful valley below. On this morning, like most other mornings, delicate fingers of mist weave through the forest canopy. The winding two-lane Arberebue-Embatkala road plunges down the side of the escarpment some six hundred meters before reaching the town of Nefasit. For the uninitiated, navigating the narrow roads can be an especially nerve-wracking experience. Driving it requires as much patience as skill for its steepness and for the variety of traffic it carries. Large trucks rumble up the pass belching smoke as they haul goods from the port at Massawa. Local residents, their carts stacked high with firewood or other materials, still move along it at a walking pace. And the twisting road is popular with local and international bicyclists seeking a challenge. Additionally, the surrounding forests are home to monkeys and baboons, troupes of which can suddenly appear out of nowhere and block the road or harass the unsuspecting.

Travel to and from Asmara was once augmented by a railway. Built in the early 1900s by the Italians at the cost of many Eritrean and Ethiopian lives, it ceased operations around the same time Emperor Haile Selassie was removed from power in the mid-seventies. The steam locomotives, or *lottorina*, were used by both tourists and commercial transportation companies. Parts of the track and tunnels can still be seen from the road.

There also used to be a seventy-kilometer long cableway locally known as *teleferica*. In its heyday, it carried as much as thirty tons of equipment and cargo each hour. Also built by Italians, the cableway ran for only a decade before the British, in a brazen act of post-war thievery, dismantled it and sold off the parts for profit.

If the trip were for any other reason, I might take the time to enjoy the scenery. The view is reputed to be one of the most beautiful drives in Eritrea, perhaps even in the whole continent of Africa. But today my thoughts are elsewhere. I'm engrossed in my papers, reviewing the details of the meeting that awaits me in Massawa.

The vehicle's abrupt stop a short while later, combined with the puzzled murmurings coming from the other passengers, jolt me away from my thoughts. I glance about and realize we have reached Nefasit, a town roughly twenty-five kilometers east of the capital. From my window, I can see the fog has cleared, offering a rare view of the ancient monastery atop Mount Bizen towering over us. The six-hundred-year-old structure, damaged by the Ottomans in the 16th century, is still in use. Many an Asmarino has made the difficult climb to the top, as the view is well worth the trek. But the monastery isn't what agitates my fellow travelers at this moment.

Before I can ask my seatmate what is the matter, a soldier appears on the road ahead of us and orders the driver to shut off the engine. The door slides open, and the bus rocks as another soldier enters. In a loud, commanding voice, he orders all male passengers to gather their belongings and get off.

My heart immediately sinks. I know what is about to happen, and so do the others with me. Such roundups were once frequently employed by the Ethiopian army during the War for Independence, both to press into service those willing to fight for the enemy, and to send to prison camps those who refused. The practice has recently been adopted by our own government to swell our own fighting ranks and to replace those who are dying in our new war.

The timing of the roundup, however, comes as a surprise. They typically occur in cycles, peaking as one round of military training nears an end and another group of trainees is needed to take their places. Anyone who might be eligible for service has made it a habit to keep track of these patterns, including myself. We know to avoid the usual hotspots and checkpoints at peak times and lay low. We are currently in the middle of the ninth cycle, not near the end, so this is when the risk of being detained should be at its lowest.

Is the army changing its pattern because we know it? Or are we losing the war that badly that it needs more soldiers faster?

The idea of us losing the war troubles me, but I am more angry with myself for not paying attention, not that I could have done anything differently to avoid this situation except remain home and hidden away until the war is over. That, of course, isn't reasonable. After all, I have a business to run, and a family to take care of.

The soldier is a young man, probably in his mid-twenties. His arms are well-muscled. A Kalashnikov dangles from his shoulder. He slaps a long, thin stick against his palm. It whistles with each swing and cracks when it hits his skin. He continues to bark at us, pointing to the side of the road and ordering us to stand in a line. He makes it clear we are now in the custody of the government. He refuses to answer any questions, and informs us that disobeying his orders will result in severe consequences. Running away is out of the question. Arguing invites a swift response, and it is delivered at the end of the stick.

One by one, we step out of the van and stand shoulder to shoulder, joining a dozen others who were already here before we stopped. There are roughly sixteen of us at this point, our ages ranging from the teens to well beyond the forty-year maximum. The soldier looks us all over and excuses two men, both elderly, who are allowed to return to the bus. They are permitted to leave. My heart sinks as I watch my ride trundle on down the road. I have little doubt as to what will become of those of us who are left behind.


The soldiers mill about, as if awaiting instructions from their superiors. Our group grows larger as more and more men are brought in. Some of the newcomers had been caught on buses en route to other places, just as we had. Some appear on foot from out of the surrounding hills and neighborhoods, or brought on the backs of pickup trucks. All are accompanied by stone-faced soldiers carrying rifles.

Having been caught unawares, we arrive dressed in all variety of attire, from street clothes to farming outfits. Some are so shabbily dressed that I doubt they'd expected to be seen in public at all, and I can't help imagining the chaotic scenes as they were taken from their homes and fields.

I wish I weren't as familiar with the routine as I am, but the stories we have all heard turn out to be far too accurate. Those of us deemed able-bodied will be shipped off to Sawa, a remote military training camp in the far western region of the country near Sudan. If we survive the brutal regimen, we will be assigned to a unit in support of the war effort. No opportunity is given to sort out personal and professional obligations. I try to convince myself that I still have a chance to be excused, in part because of my age, but also because my wife is midway through her second pregnancy, so I bide my time, preparing my argument for those with enough authority to make such decisions, rather than trying the patience of the soldiers here. I don't believe they have any power to excuse anyone unless they are clearly ineligible. Later, when I find the right person, someone who isn't worried about quotas or punishments, then I will plead my case.

The roundup throws this otherwise quiet town into a frenzy. Some of the new men are accompanied by members of their families. Wives and mothers cry out in anger, children in fright. The elderly and infirm beg for exemption. How will they be able to care for themselves if their sons are taken away? But the soldiers ignore them all. Occasionally, they lose their patience and shout them back into silence. They are rigid, although not entirely unsympathetic. I can see on some of their faces that they understand the hardship the conscriptions place on us. They are just as helpless as we are to stop it.

A miserable hush eventually settles over us, and in this uneasy quiet the soldiers go about their work, careful to reveal no emotion beneath their hard scowls.

At last they march us single file to an elementary school in town, where we are to be held. The doors are shut behind us and locked. We are in turmoil, our thoughts filled with regrets for the choices we made that brought us to this place, as well as with worries about our families and our future. Speculation spreads, prompting arguments, which spur even wilder rumors. An endless number of questions are raised, but too few answers are provided.

Rather than participate in what I feel is fruitless discussion yielding no solutions and only whetting our fears, I sit quietly away from everyone else. I need to focus on preparing an argument for my release. If I have any hope of being excused from this duty, it rests on my ability to find someone sympathetic to my plight. I hope my reasons are enough to convince them that my conscription will do more harm than good. First, there is the matter of our fledgling business, for which we have already gone into debt. It's a stretch to say that it serves the country, but I will make the point anyway. At this time, the market requires my complete attention, and my absence will disrupt it and threaten my family's security. It will also be a hardship for my potential commercial partners in Massawa. Next, there is my wife, who is carrying our second child. Her first pregnancy forced her into bed for the last four months, so she is in no shape to assume full responsibility of the family and the store *and* a fulltime job. And finally, what of my firstborn child and her heart problem? If I am taken away from my family, how will she ever have a chance to get better?

But as the hours pass without anyone coming to address our concerns, I realize I won't be able to use the business opportunity in Massawa as a reason to free me. By now, the deal will have already fallen through.

Soon, I am clinging desperately to anything positive. I concede that the lost business opportunity is a setback, but I can still come out of this okay. I pray to God, promising that I will work harder than ever, I just need the chance.


The guards return after a couple of hours with plain, dry bread for us to eat, but they don't stay to listen to our pleas. We have no appetite, but since we don't know when our next meal might be or what it might consist of, we eat anyway. I pass out the bottles of water I have with me to share. There is little more than a swallow for each of us, but it helps make the bread go down a little easier.

More men arrive, and I'm surprised when I see my brother-in-law among them, especially since he is a Swedish resident after having moved there years ago. He and my eldest sister, Saba, are newly married and were captured while traveling to the coast at Massawa for their honeymoon. As a foreign national, he is supposed to be exempt from conscription.

After getting over his shock at seeing me, he explains that only an official higher up in the chain may grant his release. "In the mean time, I must wait, just like you." This explains why he appears so relaxed about his detention. He is confident in his eventual release. I, too, try to show calmness, but underneath the surface I'm anxious.

Seeing him here turns out to be a lucky break for me, since he will be able to get word of my detention to Wudasie once he is released. At least when she hears, she will know what happened when I fail to return home tonight. I don't want her worrying about my whereabouts and whether I am safe.

It is a terrible thing to accept that one's life is no longer within one's control. So it is for me as of this day. As the hours pass and evening approaches, I'm forced to accept the very real possibility of a future separated from my family for an extended period of time. I continue to pray that I'm wrong, but I have to be realistic. I start writing out a list of instructions, which Wudasie will need to run the store. I pray she will somehow be able to manage, otherwise our investment will be lost forever.

After the briefest of bathroom breaks, we are locked back up inside the classroom, where we will spend the night. Some of the men lie down on the floor and use their jackets for cushions. Some sleep on top of the tables. Still others sit at the desks and rest their heads on their arms. I draw two chairs together to be my bed for the night, but although I am mentally exhausted, I can't stop the thoughts from rattling about inside my head like trees thrashing about in a strong wind. I check my watch a hundred times. It seems like each minute yields only grudgingly to the next. One hour feels like ten.

Morning comes at last, and the door opens. We rush toward it, eager to learn what will be our fate, yet dreading what it could be. The soldiers let us out without comment and allow us to gather on the school compound. Already the morning fog has cleared, and the sun beats down on us from a cloudless sky. We wait with empty stomachs to hear what their decision will be. But there is still no news.

The soldiers prowl along the campus perimeter, always on the lookout for anyone who might try to jump the fence and run away. No one is willing to challenge them. No one wants to risk getting shot, so we stay away from the edges of the property. It's hard to accept that we are now prisoners of our own government, our only crimes being that we are Eritrean, males of fighting age, and capable enough to carry a gun.

For all our waiting and praying and pleading throughout the day, they tell us nothing. And we have nothing to do to while away the hours, so the day stretches on forever. That evening, we are locked back up inside the building knowing no more than we did when we woke in the morning.

I spend this second night much as I did the first, in a state of agitation. My mind races, jumping constantly between possibilities I can't control and wish I couldn't imagine. I'm filled with self-despair and worry for my family. Their lives will change as much as mine is certain to do. How am I supposed to handle this? How are they? How long will this last? How will my daughter ever get better? And what of my unborn child?

Will I live long enough to see them all again?

# Ghindae

WE ARE ON THE MOVE AGAIN THE NEXT DAY. The activity brings relief from the monotony, but it also heightens the anguish we all feel. We're loaded like cattle onto trucks and transported under armed guard. Any soldier who allows someone to escape is considered negligent at best, traitorous at worst, and will undoubtedly be severely disciplined either way. In this manner, we have all been turned from free people into slaves, both us and the soldiers.

Entering a sprawling compound in Ghindae, a larger town some twenty five kilometers farther east, we see several large warehouse-type buildings and we realize we may be staying here for a while, perhaps even until the current training cycle is completed. I'm encouraged that it's still not too far from Asmara. I hope my wife gets word of my relocation and will be able to make the drive here, although I worry about her traveling in her condition. I don't want her to do anything to risk her life and the baby's.

We are ordered off the trucks with whatever possessions we have, then made to form a line. After some time, we are marched to a large storeroom with a tall, wide door. The air inside is stifling, but we're told to go in and not make a fuss. We have no choice but to obey. The door is slid shut, leaving us without ventilation.

Hours pass. On occasion, the door opens and we rush towards it, as much for fresh air as to beg the soldiers for updates and to pass along messages for our families. The guards here are a little more relaxed, now that we are off the road and the chances of escape are diminished. At least they seem more sympathetic to our predicament. We scribble notes on scraps of paper with details for where they may be delivered. The news, assuming it reaches our loved ones, won't stop them from worrying about us, but at least it will give their worries something specific to focus on.

There is no relief from the waiting, no reprieve from the uncertainty. Sometime before noon, we are given bread and water. It's the first food we have had since the crusty, tasteless bread of the previous morning. We aren't allowed to leave the heat of the storehouse, so we have no choice than to force the food down our parched throats. We need the nourishment. Then we sit and wait.

My thoughts torment me. Visions of the worst possible outcomes threaten to drive away the last of my remaining hope. I begin to fantasize that my contact who arranged the meeting in Massawa will learn of my predicament and come to request my release. This is how desperate I have become. After two days, the chance of this happening is next to none, yet I still cling to it.

At one point in the afternoon, I'm able to meet with Yordanos, the wife of my older brother Berhane. She tells me that as soon as she received news of my detention yesterday morning she has been on buses trying to find out where I am being held. "Wudasie isn't able to make the hard trip because of the risk to the baby," she says, confirming my fears and adding to my apprehension. She gives me a package of milk powder and *tihni*, a high-calorie roasted barley meal, which Wudasie put together after guessing what had happened to me. The *tihni* is typically given to people who are traveling to distant places or, in our current situation, for those who are conscripted to go to the military training camp in Sawa. It will help take the edge off my hunger and sustain me, if I'm not released. In the bundle are also a pair of plastic sandals, a fresh change of underclothes, pants and a jacket, as well as some small basic necessities. Seeing all of this, especially the sandals, the truth of my new situation finally hits me hard. I am no longer able to deny my fate. I am going to be a soldier for sure.

I give my sister-in-law some of the notes I have written. One includes instructions to Wudasie for negotiating my release. It's remote, but as long as I have any chance whatsoever, I have to take it. Another note includes details for running the market in my absence. When Yordanos is ready to leave, I thank her for her thoughtfulness. I don't want to let her go. I wish I could go with her.

After she leaves, I turn back to the dreariness of that unbearably long, hot, and monotonous day.

At five in the evening, the massive door opens again and we are ordered to stand in two lines, then we're marched into the nearby foothills. A large number of armed soldiers accompany us to ensure we don't escape. Once out of view of the compound, the man in charge tells us to stop where we are. Then, right where we stand, we are ordered to attend to our bodily needs. There is no effort to provide privacy. Some of us are lucky enough to hide our backsides against rocks or tree trunks. The guards mill about, clearly as uncomfortable as we are while we empty our bowels into the dirt. Like us, they are unwilling participants in this inhumane spectacle. The difference is that they have already been through what awaits us. Now they are part of the machinery and have a job to perform. They remain alert to anyone thinking about running away. None of them wants to be held accountable for an escape. More importantly, they don't want to be put in the position of having to shoot anyone, if we try.

We have only a few minutes before we're ordered back to our feet and marched to the compound again. Many men complain that they were unable to relieve themselves, having had so little to eat and even less to drink. But we're told that this is how we should expect things to be from now on. Such is life in the military. We will be expected to do whatever is demanded of us, when it is demanded, and exactly in the way we are told to do it. We must always be ready to comply immediately and without complaint. It seems the certainty I have been hoping to find has finally been delivered. It's just not the kind I had in mind.

As I close my eyes and try to nap, I'm aware of my fellow countrymen whispering or snoring around me. But the sound I hear loudest is the beating of my heart pounding in my ears. It's like the steady rhythm of war drums, ever restless, never ceasing, and I realize how foolish we were to think we had permanently silenced them.

# Massawa

LATER THAT SAME AFTERNOON, without warning, we are loaded onto a half dozen or so trucks. We expect to be taken west to the training grounds of the National Service camp at Sawa; instead, we are driven in the opposite direction. Some of us, myself included, foolishly take this as an encouraging sign. Perhaps it means we will soon be released.

But our hopes are quickly crushed.

As before, soldiers are assigned to keep close watch over us. They demand we sit on the hard bed of the truck and remain still. We do our best under the circumstances, but everyone is so tense, and the road is winding and rough. Yet every movement or sound we make elicits a sharp rebuke from the soldiers, as if they believe they can frighten us into staying silent and still.

The ride is long. We have no protection from the sun pounding down upon our backs or the dust that blows in our faces. Our bones ache from the bouncing. If we try to stretch, we are kicked or beaten over the head with a long wooden switch and yelled at to keep still.

At last, we arrive at a different compound. This one is called Emkulu and is already occupied with people like us, men who have been taken by force to be conscripted into the army. We later learn that the site had initially been established as a temporary accommodation for Eritrean refugees being repatriated from Sudan after the first war. The tents erected by the United Nations High Commissioner for Refugees still stand, although they are now worn and filthy. Additionally, four large Rubb-Hall shelters have been erected, but they are too flimsy to offer much in the way of comfort. The creaking of their aluminum frames in the breeze and the flapping of their plastic skins set my nerves on edge. The wind is constant, but not strong enough or consistent enough to carry away the stench of human waste from the pit-latrines.

In addition to housing repatriated Eritreans, the site also served as a transitional center for hundreds of Somali refugees being transferred from the Harsile refugee camp outside of Assab, far to the south, near our border with Djibouti. Somalia had already been deemed a failed state long before its leader, Mohamed Siad Barre, was ousted in 1991, but the man who deposed him, Ali Mahdi Muhammad, was never able to consolidate power from the various factions scattered about the country. Only recently, with the help of the United Nations, has Somalia seen any semblance of stability.

Our president must have learned from Somalia's example, which explains why he consolidated power as aggressively as he did and strongly resisted those who disagreed with him. But he ignored the mistakes of our other southern neighbor, Ethiopia. Like Mengistu did after overthrowing the emperor, Afewerki has become more autocratic. But it isn't too late for us. We just need to figure out how to regain the path that doesn't leave us worse off than before.

Once inside the former refugee camp, we disembark and are told again to stand in line. My muscles are stiff and sore. I'm weak with hunger, and parched with thirst. Thankfully, the soldiers treat us more humanely than before, perhaps because they know few of us will risk an escape attempt so far from home. They still have no information for us, however. We're simply directed to one of the occupied Rubb-Hall tents and told to wait.

The men already here invite us to join them inside. Some appear to be young enough to still be in high school. None of them is able to give us any idea how long we can expect to remain here, so we assume it will be more than just a few days. Near the opening at the other end of the tent, men sit in a circle on locally crafted mats and blankets playing *dama*, a board game similar to checkers. One of the players looks familiar, but it's only after I ask to join the group that I realize he's the younger brother of my friend Negash from Asmara University. We had only met once, but he remembers me as soon as I walk over. Right away, we begin to ask each other about people we know in common, which begins a lively discussion within the group about our predicament and the circumstances of our arrival here. All the stories share a common theme: We are the unwitting victims of the roundups. Most of these men, however, were taken in and around the nearby city of Massawa. As this had been my ultimate destination, I realize I would have been caught even if I had managed to avoid the detention in Nefasit.

In short order we learn what to expect regarding meals, water, toilets, and other basic needs. Much of what we're told is similar to what we have already experienced over the past few days. The conditions here are, in some ways, an improvement. At least the toilets are indoors now, and there is enough water to wash the sweat and dirt of the past few days off our bodies. But there is still nothing for us to do, at least initially, so we have little to occupy our time but sleep, chat, and play whatever games we can scrape together. We have no books or other reading materials. Nor do we wish to engage in any physically intensive activities, as the heat quickly saps our energy.

In contrast to our idleness, the rest of the camp is busy. People come and go in a variety of vehicles. More detainees are brought in, while others are taken away, never to return. I learn that the man I recognized earlier was able to produce medical papers showing a hearing problem and has since been released from military service. Another, a teenager from the same group, is excused because of a medical issue with his right hand. I can't help but be encouraged by their dismissals and hope that I will soon join them because of my own hardships. I may be in good health and free from physical impediments, but being so close to my fortieth birthday may be enough to warrant my release.

This is the sly curse of hope, how it forces one to ignore reality. Deep down, I know it will take nothing short of a miracle to win my release. Still, I can't lose faith. I must trust that I will soon be reunited with my family.

A local youth organization provides support for day-to-day chores at the camp. The kids are younger than eighteen, and whether they are forced to help or do so voluntarily, they are, for the most part, friendly and eager. In addition to distributing our food and water rations, they offer to run into Massawa to purchase any basic necessities we may be lacking. I am fortunate enough to have some money in my possession, and thanks to Wudasie's forethought I have her package, but not everyone is as well prepared as I am. Those who don't have must either share what others provide or go without.

We continue to ask for information regarding our fate, but still none is offered. We're given only orders: *Stand up. Make a line. Sit down on this side of the truck. Get off and go over there. Keep completely silent.* I am reminded of the saying that shepherds don't feel obliged to tell their herd where they are going. The sheep must simply comply. So it has become for us: we are their sheep. For the moment, there is little for us to do except obey. The rest of the time we spend sitting about wishing we were home with our families.

# Sawa Training Camp

A WEEK OR SO AFTER ARRIVING AT EMKULU, we are suddenly uprooted and taken away. This time, however, we're actually told of our destination before we set out. We are heading to Sawa at last, all the way over on the other side of the country. The news confirms our greatest fears.

Sawa holds over thirty thousand people and is Eritrea's largest and most active national military training camp. It also has a reputation for being one of the harshest. This time, when we are forced to sit on the floor of the truck beds for the long drive, we do so quickly and without complaint, because we're used to the routine by now, but also because our spirits have been crushed. We're again watched closely by the guards. I feel like a prisoner, not as an Eritrean citizen on his way to learn how to defend his motherland.

With a few exceptions, the trucks we have been transported on so far have been small, nondescript, and of no uniform make or color. Most are old, manufactured by the Italian automaker Fiat. None possessed any sort of visible military insignia. This time, however, I am on a large, modern Swedish-made Scania cargo truck. They pack in as many of us as they can fit.

The trip is as unremarkable as the previous ones were, with one notable exception. We make a brief stop in the city of Keren, where the local officials host a luncheon for us. I believe it's meant to cheer us up, and for certain the meal is a welcome change from our recent fare. But how can we enjoy it, when we are all held against our will, treated as somehow less than human, left to worry about how our families may be suffering? We have little to look forward to other than weeks of grueling military training under the harshest of conditions, all while knowing that many of us will be sent straight to the frontlines afterward, where some will inevitably perish. This, for a war we should not be fighting in the first place. We already won our freedom; the dispute now is about where exactly between the two countries the line should be drawn. This is a technical issue, not an ideological one. I can't believe after all these years we are still squabbling over such insignificant details.

While in Keren, I take the opportunity to ask about my wife's application for my release. All I am given is negative replies, which only deepens my despair.

We continue to Sawa after lunch, driving through more mountainous regions over twisting roads that make it impossible to judge how far we have gone. But shortly before evening, the landscape begins to open up, and the forest yields to desert. The scrubland stretches on as far as the eye can see. This tells me we are getting close.

Rather than entering the military camp directly, we're diverted to an area just beyond its perimeter. There, in a barren clearing occupied by nothing but rocks and brush, we remain for the next two days, waiting while the current conscripts finish their training and depart to their assigned units. We're given no pillows or mattress pads; we must make our bed on the bare, hard ground. Nor do we have any shelter above us. They force us to endure the nightly rains without any protection. During the day, the sun beats down on us without remorse. By night, we freeze. A daily ration of two gallons of water is provided to each of us for a shower. It's inadequate for our needs. Our meals are only slightly improved by the addition of canned meat to supplement the bread.

I know that one of my two younger brothers, Eyasu, is assigned here in Sawa, but it would be impossible to try and find him among the many thousands of staff and trainees, even if my own movements weren't restricted. I don't even know which of the six divisions he is in. Nor, for that matter, whether or not he has been reassigned since I last heard from him. The best I can do is silently wish him good luck and pray for his safety. If he knew I was here, he would do the same for me.

Then I think about my other two siblings in the Eritrean National Service, Yebio and Ellen. They are the babies of the family. Ellen is the youngest of us all, yet was one of the first to be taken into the ENS. She trained in the third cycle, whereas my brother, two years older, is from the eighth. From their occasional letters home, I know about the hardships they suffered during their rotations, and knowing what awaits me makes me even more worried. For them, the worst is mostly over. Also, they are younger and stronger. For me, now middle aged, it is only just beginning.

On the third day, we are relocated to a nearby farm whose cotton and millet fields stretch far to the horizon. We join another group already at work and get our first real taste of strict military regimen. The men in my group, most of them victims of the roundups like me, are formed into a single company. Another company is comprised entirely of inmates from the Sawa military prison known as Brigade Six, most of who tried to run away from the camp in previous training cycles. Many were captured as they tried to cross the border illegally into Sudan. The guards confide to us in ominous tones that they are lucky to still be alive, as they have been instructed to shoot escapees on sight. To my eyes, however, the prisoners don't look so lucky. They are gaunt, weak, covered in injuries, filth, and lice. Their eyes are either void of emotion or filled with fear. How can our country treat its own citizens so poorly? How can it punish them for wanting the very same thing we already won— freedom?

Service in the ENS can be extremely difficult, and many conscripted into it don't feel the same duty to fight as did those who volunteered during the War for Independence. It's not unusual to hear of someone deserting, whether intentionally or not. They go home on leave, often to care for a family member, and don't come back. When their absence is noticed, they are arrested out of their homes or taken in the streets. This is how bad it has gotten here since liberation. I have personally witnessed friends and neighbors being hauled away. And I have known others who didn't wait to be caught and instead tried escaping over the border. The journey to Sudan, the most expeditious option for us, is long and difficult, passing through hundreds of kilometers of unforgiving deserts and over inhospitable mountains. Most attempt the journey by foot. If they don't become sick or starve to death first, they risk being shot at the border. Others die after they are captured and before they get to prison. Still more die from the torture while incarcerated, or because of the labor they are forced to perform.

The physical conditions inside the jails are inhumane. Flea and lice infestations are common, and medical care is lacking. Prisoners often bake inside tin shelters by day, freeze at night. The psychological trauma is even worse.

There are many such places in the country like Sawa and the Brigade Six prison. Their locations are mostly kept secret by the government. Our leaders don't want the world to know that this is how we treat our own people.

Even those truly innocent of trying to escape, the well-intentioned who happen to run afoul of the military police, are given little consideration, if they're judged to be shirking their duty. Mehari, my mother-in-law's brother, for example, was arrested at the bus stop the day after spending a single night at home with his wife and children. He had been wounded in the knee while fighting and was recuperating in the hospital. Given that it was a holiday and he was close to home, he decided to pay them a visit. It was just for the one night, but he was supposed to be in the hospital recovering from the gunshot wound. He was caught the next day while returning and was given no chance to explain anything. They wouldn't have believed him anyway. The only thing they would have accepted was an immediate confession that he was trying to escape, which he wasn't. He was taken to prison without a chance to appeal.

While he was there, he managed to slip a note to a truck driver, which eventually made its way to Wudasie, his niece. It was a simple request for change of clothing. But when my wife tried to bring it to him, she wasn't allowed to pass through the gate. Instead, the guard demanded to know how she found out he was there. Terrified of being arrested herself, she fled. The fear she felt was just like the fear we all knew back during the time of the Ethiopian *Afagn Guad*, when everyone was suspected of being a *tegadalay* or *hafash widib*. Not even Mehari's older brother, an honored *tegadalay* still serving at the warfront with many connections to high officials, could do much about his situation. He was granted permission to visit, but that was all. Eventually, Mehari was released from jail, but not before many months had passed. And all because he hadn't been where he was supposed to be for one single night.

Roughly twenty of the prisoners at the farm are women. This shouldn't surprise me, and yet it does. They are treated just as cruelly as the men. Eritrea may be one of the few countries where both genders are obligated to serve in the military. Most have no choice but must enter the ENS soon after finishing junior high school, before marriage and parenthood disqualifies them. Growing up, however, girls and boys are treated differently. For example, my sisters weren't allowed to talk to boys, leave the house at will, or stay out past sunset. This is primarily for their protection. Boys are rarely given such restrictions. But once they are adults, women have equal opportunity for work and education. They own businesses and are expected to play an equal role in family decisions. And to fight. In fact, many women fought alongside men in the War for Independence, and they currently make up a large part of the army.

Still, to see them treated like this offends me. They are forced to sleep out in the open, unprotected, dealt with as harshly as their male counterparts. It's all part of the way our captors, at the behest of our military and political leaders, dehumanize us all.

For the task at hand, we are ordered to form a single line at the head of the field, each person separated from his neighbor by an arm's length. Then we are shown the other end of the field and are told to begin weeding. For a city boy like me and others not accustomed to this type of work, the task is more than just physically taxing. It's mind-numbing. Others take to it more capably, having worked in farming or similarly physical jobs with a lot of monotony. But after more than six hours of this backbreaking routine in the brutal sun, we are all equally exhausted and discouraged.

We do this for ten straight days.

This is how they try to break our spirit and make us forget about anything else. It works for some, but not all. Some people just get angrier than we already are. They retaliate by pulling up the crop plants instead of the weeds. It takes several of us to convince them to stop. Acting like this won't change a thing. It will only attract the guards' attention and bring hardship down on us all.

In addition to the field work, we're forced to chop down trees in the adjacent forest for firewood. In short order, our battalion clears another swath of land, adding to the acres already razed by previous conscripts. It saddens me to think about trees that once grew undisturbed for centuries now burned to ash so that we can cook our meals. It explains why so much of this land is now barren and blighted.

Each of us takes turns preparing meals for the group. We bake flat bread on scrap pieces of sheet metal heated directly over the open flames. We make our tea in pots blackened by the smoke from the still-green wood. We are provided reusable plastic plates, cups, and spoons, which we must keep safe. They are our first possessions as soldiers-in-training. If we lose them, we won't receive any more meals.

The hard labor is easier for those who are used to it. For the rest of us, we suffer from terrible aches and blisters that weep and bleed. The younger, stronger, and more physically fit among us take pity on those of us having difficulty. I'm lucky when a pair of men in my section take over cutting trees, leaving me with the easier task of collecting and loading the wood for transport to the camp.

After three nights attempting to sleep in the rain, an entrepreneurial seller arrives from the nearby village with large plastic sheets, which we purchase for a fair price. Again, some can't afford the expense, so those of us with money cover the cost. In short course, we have become brothers, each minimizing in his own way the collective discomfort of the entire group.

Even with the added protection, sleep continues to elude us, such that we rise each morning even more exhausted than the day before. Tempers flare. People grow careless, are prone to injury. One day, I am nearly bitten by a snake I don't see, even though it's in full view right in front of me. I'm lucky that the man working beside me happens to see it move and pulls my hand away before it can strike. He tells me that it is a very poisonous kind of desert snake called an Egyptian viper. Having grown up in the city, I don't know the different types of snakes, but I have always had a strong fear of them. For many days after that, the memory plagues my thoughts until I'm paralyzed with fear knowing I might not be so lucky the next time. So, when we are told there is finally room for us at the main training compound at Sawa, I'm actually relieved.

Our first afternoon and evening away from the fields is filled with the mind-numbing task of filling out documents, answering questions, and waiting. After we are done being registered, we're told to separate into two lines. Standing at the front are two officers, who will announce our assignments into the different training units. I end up in the larger group and learn we won't be staying in Sawa to train. "There isn't enough room here," we are told.

It's clear that Sawa is already stretched beyond its capacity. Four of the divisions occupy the permanent hangars. But two more divisions have been added, and they are housed in temporary huts constructed of palm branches, or *agefa*.

For the briefest of moments, I dare to hope that they will simply send the rest of us home until the next cycle. That hope is dashed, when we're told our training will be carried out at a recently opened camp far to the south of the country, near the town of Kiloma. My heart sinks. Kiloma sits on the coast of the Red Sea, in the lowlands of Denkalia, close to the border with Djibouti. It will be exceptionally hot, dry, and windy, and I will be as far from my family as I could possibly be while still remaining within Eritrea's borders.

We are given no uniforms and no equipment, only a single bed sheet, which we will take with us. Then we are advised to get some rest, since we will be leaving Sawa early in the morning for the thousand kilometer journey.

I have one last chance to bid those staying at Sawa good luck and goodbye. We tell each other we will meet again, hopefully under better circumstances, but we all know in our hearts how unlikely that is. Some of us probably won't live long enough to make it possible.

# Red Sea to Assab

WE SET OUT FOR THE LONG JOURNEY hours before dawn the next morning, while much of the country is still cloaked in darkness. I know from the stories my siblings and friends have told me that Sawa is a big place, not just the training camp, but also the town nearby. Of course, I have seen very little of it, and now I will leave it without having had the chance. My greatest disappointment, however, is missing my brother, Eyasu. Even a brief moment to exchange hugs would have lifted my spirits greatly. Instead, we are forced to leave the place exactly as we arrived two weeks before, whisked off in the back of a truck like prisoners.

This time we are accompanied only by our future trainers and a handful of other administrative staff. There are no armed soldiers guarding us. Either there are none to spare, or the army believes we are convinced there's nothing to gain by escaping. After all, we already gave them our personal information, and they have made sure we know what happens to those who are caught. We would not like to be taken to prison and forced to toil in the fields for months on end.

Nevertheless, some still run. They plot their escape in secret, letting no one else know of their plans. They sit patiently, quietly pretending to be just as resigned to their fate as the rest of us. Then, as soon as the driver slows down at a tricky turn — and there are many on the steep, twisting Asmara-Nefasit Road — they jump up without warning and leap over the side before anyone can react. We hear them crashing through the brush as they run away, disappearing within seconds.

Nobody tries to stop them. Some of us shake our heads and roll our eyes. We secretly pray for their success, but we also know their chances are slim. Those who fail to show up in Kiloma will be noted and possibly hunted down. Their families and neighbors will be interrogated. Maybe the ones who run don't have such worries or connections. They might be loners. Or maybe they lied about who they are and where they are from.

Or they don't believe they will be caught. Maybe their personal circumstances are so dire — a sick family member, starving children, a business to run — that they would rather take their chances. They don't consider the possibility of laboring for years on a prison farm. Or they believe it's still a better fate than going off to fight on the front. As far as I am concerned, ten days of backbreaking toil is enough to cure me of such desperate thoughts.

The truck continues on, stopping for no more than a few minutes at a time. On this journey, there's no luncheon in Keren, no welcoming party to help us forget our misfortune. We drive directly to the coast, but because of the winding roads, we don't arrive in Massawa until after dusk. One by one, we pick ourselves up, stiff and sore from the bumpiness of the ride and the hardness of our seats. Thirsty, hungry, and emotionally drained, we climb down off the truck.

Considering how many of us there are, the place is unnaturally quiet. Nobody feels like talking. We're told we will be boarding an old military freight ship for the oversea leg of our trip to Assab, Eritrea's second major port city. The journey far to the south will take a full two days over the Red Sea.

Even though the sun has gone down, the air remains stiflingly hot. The wind blowing off the water offers no relief. Our view is limited by darkness, and the spotlights illuminate only the shipping containers stacked all around us, leaving much of the rest of the world hidden from view. Not that there is much else to see. I have been here before, and I know what little there is. Not much lives in this barren and dry environment. To the west, pressed right up against the water, as if they succumbed to gravity and slid down the hills, are the port buildings and other structures. To the east is the endless roiling ocean. Both land and sea seem eager to crush us like bugs between two hands.

Rising up over the metal containers, like giant fingers, are the massive cranes that move them. Trash and other debris litter the ground. The air smells of oil, fish, and diesel. I have a terrible feeling this might be the last time I will see this dreary scene.

The trainer assigned to our platoon, Mulueberhan, orders those of us in charge of each unit to make sure our members are standing properly in line. He is a short man with a wrestler's build, squat, muscular, and intense. We are all afraid of him, so we do as he says without question. We fold our bed sheets in half, then drape them about our shoulders and try to stand as quiet and still as we can, which is nearly impossible given our state of exhaustion. The men standing before me sway like weakened trees in a heavy windstorm, ready to topple over at any moment. I, too, find it difficult to stay upright. While we await further instructions, bread and cans of food are distributed. Everyone is starving, yet we have little enthusiasm for the meal. We're tired and want nothing more than to lie down and shut off our minds, even if it means being on a boat that will take us to an even worse place than we have already been.

For a moment, I'm struck by how hopeless we all look. To someone else unfamiliar with our situation, we might easily be confused for prisoners of war or victims of human trafficking. In fact, there are a few inmates from the Sawa prison among us, men who have been given a second chance. How they have come to have it, I don't know. It doesn't surprise me that they are here, instead of attempting to escape a second time along the way. The will to run has been beaten out of them. The knowledge of the consequences is still fresh in their minds.

One of them, a Muslim in his mid-thirties named Mahmood, tells me he ran away from Sawa a month before finishing his training, only to be recaptured in a *giffa* in Keren and sent back. He can't say why he wasn't imprisoned longer, but he suspects his assignment to Kiloma will be punishment enough. I ask what he means by this, and he says he heard this new training camp is much worse than Sawa. "I don't know exactly how," he says, "only that the food is terrible, the trainers are as brutal as the insects, and the heat is unbearable. Also, there is no electricity in the camp."

He offers no other specifics, although I sense he knows more. And it frightens me. In my mind, Sawa was bad enough already that I have a hard time imagining anything worse.

"Why did you run away?" I ask. "You were almost finished with your training."

"I have a family. I have two children to feed. I would have stayed, if I had faith the government would honor their promise to limit our service to only eighteen months. But we know they won't. They have already broken this promise many times. I could have been patient and done my time, but how can anyone be patient, if there is no end to be patient for? If I have no idea when I am free, how can I help my family? I can't just sit and watch them starve to death. So I escaped. I knew I had to do it to save them. But I wasn't lucky, and they caught me, and now I am back to the beginning again. Whenever I think about my family, I'm sickened by how helpless I am."

At last, the commander of the company shouts for our attention. He gestures to Mahmood, who stands in the front of the line. *"Arkib!"* he orders. "Line up! Move!" And we fall in behind the other men already shuffling toward the boat. The vessel rises up before us like the gate to hell has just been opened and we have no choice but to march right in. If what Mahmood has said is correct, what awaits us will surely be as bad, if not worse, than hell.

The ship is meant to carry large equipment, armored tanks, ammunition, and other military cargo. The rails are high and solid, so once we are on board, we can't see the water, even when we stand as tall as we can. Not surprisingly, the senior members and trainers take to the upper deck, where the ship's crew accommodations are located. There's more room up there, a view of the sea, fresh air, and they have more freedom to move about. For us, forced to share the limited space on the main deck with so much equipment and so many crates, not even the open sky and stars above offer any solace. There isn't even enough room for everyone to lie down anywhere. We number so many that we must sleep sitting up, leaning against the hard metal or wooden crates, or else laying on top of one another.

At last, we are underway. The engines rumble and the air fills with the choking stench of exhaust. I try to relax. My last worry before I yield to exhaustion seeds my nightmares: What if the ship is overloaded for its capacity?

* * *

Morning arrives an eternity later, but daylight promises only more torment. By our calendar, it's the *Ge'ez* New Year, or *Kudus Yohannes*. This is a major Christian holiday in our country, although the day is significant for us all, as it marks the end of the rainy season. We typically celebrate with parties and feasts and entreaties to Saint John for a bountiful harvest in the coming days. But none of us on the boat is in any condition to celebrate, whether mentally or physically. Our spirits are broken, and our bodies weakened by the unbearable heat, and the lack of fresh air and food. All we are given to slake our hunger and thirst is a solution of dissolved sugar in water, stale bread, and cans of thin sauce to flavor it. We use our bed sheets to shade us from the merciless sun, but it makes the air underneath even more rank with the stench of too many bodies packed into too little space.

Many of my fellow conscripts are sick. Some can't stomach the motion of the boat on the water. Others are vomiting because of disease. Some men pretend to be sick so they can get a reprieve to the upper deck. But not all requests for medical attention are granted, nor are many of the requests to visit the bathroom.

Imagine five hundred men packed tightly onto the sun-baked deck of a boat, no room to lie down, much less move about. No shade or breeze. No escape. Any exposed metal burns the skin on contact. Five hundred men, many carrying only a small bundle of personal possessions and the single bed sheet given to us in Sawa. We occupy every inch of space not already taken up by the supplies the army transports with us.

Having lost our will and our dignity, it isn't long before we begin to lose our civility. Some of the men grow selfish. They act like boors, taking up far more space than their share. They stretch themselves out, and intentionally drop their limbs on top of other people without permission or apology, hoping the offended party will move away rather than argue. Others grow quick to anger. They yell if someone snores or talks too loudly. They shout or curse if someone touches them.

With little to do, no place to go, and no interest in adding to our collective misery, I sit as still as I can in one spot and stay there. The air is stifling, rancid, hard to suck into my lungs. To occupy my mind, I observe the men around me and make up stories about them. Eritrea is made up of at least nine distinct ethnic groups, whose people arrived from all over the Horn of Africa and the Arabian Peninsula, so there is also a wide range of looks and skin coloring among us. But their appearances don't always help tell me about their origins, as even the Habesha people can have light, brown, or dark skin, which we call *red*, *kederay*, and *tselim*, respectively. I can't be certain where they are from until I hear them speak. I listen and hear Tigrinya, Amharic, Arabic. It makes me wonder how we'll ever be able to communicate with each other as soldiers.

There is one group of a half dozen or so who are unmistakably Rashaida, a tribe originally from Saudi Arabia. The Rashaida are nomadic and Sunni Muslim. If they are here, it's because they were probably taken from the coastal areas north of Massawa and the islands of the Dahlak Archipelago. They are a close-knit society and rarely intermingle with other ethnic groups. If the army is conscripting them, then we must truly be desperate for fighters.

The differences between us are striking now, but soon I think we will all be the same, even the Rashaida— Eritrean National Servicemembers, soldiers. Christian or Muslim, city-born or farmer, *kederay* or *tselim*, educated or not, we will all be expected to fight side-by-side. Any differences between us will be stripped away, leaving us in our most elemental forms, not as men, but as interchangeable pieces in the government's war machine.

By midday, the heat presses down on us with such intensity that we become little more than baking mounds of flesh. The stagnant air wrings the sweat from our bodies. I rest my head on my arms and try to sleep, but all I get is short, fitful naps— a dozen, a hundred, brief respites that leave me more tired than before. I am jolted awake each time, not by the occasional shout of some angry man or slap of a wave against the side of the ship, but because some new worry for my family rises in my mind. I try to push the thoughts from my head, to convince myself that Wudasie is taking care of herself and our daughter, that she is managing the shop, her health, and her pregnancy. But I know that even in the best of circumstances my hopes are unlikely to be true. No single person could carry all that alone, not even my strong wife, and it makes me angry that it is all left to her to do so. I wish I could help, but there is nothing I can do for her now. Worrying solves nothing, only makes me feel my helplessness all the more. I keep reminding myself of this, but I can't stop myself. After a while, the resentment takes hold inside of me, spreads, turns optimism into bitterness. How can this be happening?

As children, my siblings and I used to sneak extra sugar into our tea than our mother permitted. The sweetness complemented the somewhat bland *kitcha* we ate, a traditional unleavened flat bread made of wheat. Recently, I had committed to consuming less sugar in my diet, to eating healthier. My body has slowed down as I approach middle age. It's a cruel irony that I am now relying on sugar water to stay alive.

Any reasonable person would be able to see that such treatment is inhumane, an outright violation of basic human rights. But there are no reasonable people overseeing us now, and no courts to judge our keepers.

Nightfall finally comes, bringing respite from the intolerable sun. Despite the eternity of insomnia, it proves far too fleeting. All too soon, the next day's torments recommence.

By any measure, it's the worst experience I have endured in my entire life. I am sure many of my fellow conscripts feel the same way. Do they, as I have started to think, feel that any release from such torment would be welcome? I chastise myself for considering the coward's way out, even if only in a fleeting moment of weakness. All I can do is pray the experience will prove to be the worst of all that is yet to come. I tell myself that if I survive this, I can survive anything.

At last, we're told we have reached our destination. Somehow, we have all survived. By the grace of God, we have survived.

But what fresh hell awaits us next?

# Kiloma Training Camp

THE SHIP DOCKS AT THE PORT CITY OF ASSAB, which is known for its large market, beaches, and nightlife. Nearby are an international airport and a defunct oil refinery that once supplied much of Ethiopia's energy needs. The refinery was shuttered in 1997. Some thirty-five thousand people live here, mainly in the central part of town called Assab Kebir, but the number of inhabitants is shrinking as a result of Eritrea's growing isolation and its choking effect on trade.

South of the city stretches thirty kilometers of empty road. At the other end is Kiloma, the closest settlement to the training camp. The road is like a seam stitching together two starkly different landscapes— the sun-scorched sands, rough azure gray of the Red Sea, and red and yellow salt pans on the left; and the rusty amber, black, and gray of the broken and worn Dankalia Desert to the right. I have traveled around Assab many times before, both for business and leisure, and have always considered it to be one of the most beautiful places I have ever seen, from the simple, clean architecture, to the picturesque Afar *sambukh* fishing boats left stranded in the shallows. There is an honesty to this place, a pure, unforgiving, unremitting solitude that forces a man to shed all his deceits. The sky can be the purest of blues, the salt air untainted by the scent of civilization. The inhospitable landscape tolerates no weakness, yet fortifies the strong.

Today, however, I take no pleasure at all in revisiting the region or facing the new reality it forces me to confront. Today, I don't see the beauty, only the harsh truth of what my life has become, because today I am not a free man.

We are taken by truck to Kiloma, a town in the Debubawī K'eyih Bahrī or Southern Red Sea Administration. It sits at an average elevation of only eleven meters above sea level. For comparison, my home in Asmara rises to well over two thousand meters. The seaside town is flat.

The ground is covered in crushed volcanic gravel in every burnt hue of brown, red, and black. A low ridge of worn mountains occupies the inland horizon. Beyond them, invisible to us at the moment, the land sinks to more than one hundred meters below sea level. The volcanically active region known as the Danakil Depression is considered the most inhospitable environment on the planet. Only the hardiest of creatures manage to survive there.

We arrive at the camp in the middle of the day, when the heat reaches its peak, blasting like a furnace and leaving the ground sterile. A brown haze hovers everywhere, not moisture but dust kicked up by the ever-present wind. Almost nothing grows here without assistance, just a few stunted acacia and doum palms. It's so hot that we are grateful for the tepid water our trainers provide us upon arrival. First we slake our thirst with it. Then we try to wash the grime and stink of the past several days off our skin. We bathe using plastic buckets, and dry ourselves in the open air. A lucky few have bits of soap to dissolve the grease; the rest scrape away the caked dirt with handfuls of gravel.

The camp was once an Ethiopian military base. Now, the frames of dozens of twisted and burnt-out war vehicles sit rusting in the desert, some half buried in drifts of sand. The abandoned metal pieces poke up out of the ground like fossil skeletons, voicelessly telling stories of the deadly fighting that occurred here between the EPLF and Mengistu's army in the months leading up to May 1991. There are only a handful of buildings, mostly quarters for the staff. As Mahmood said, there is no electricity. Two of the three battalions will be stationed and trained here at the former base. The third, we are told, will be located a couple kilometers away at an even more remote site. The new conscripts altogether number well over one thousand. In our entire battalion of four hundred, there is a single female, a young member of the ENS who works in the kitchen. I can't help but wonder what she did to deserve such punishment.

As for walls or fences to pen us in, there are none. We are free to leave, if we choose, but there is nowhere for us to go and almost certain death for anyone who tries to escape.

The nearest settlement is little more than a village of a few structures offering no safe haven. There are other settlements farther away, but it would be extremely foolish for any of us to try and walk to them. Other than fishing, I can't say what the permanent residents do to survive or make a living. Maybe their entire existence depends on supporting the camp's operations.

The indigenous people are called the Afar. They are mostly nomadic, with a range extending from southern Eritrea through Djibouti and into eastern Ethiopia. After many generations, they have learned to cope with the extreme conditions.

While the camp staff occupy themselves with preparing for the training cycle, we are given the rest of that day and the next to recover from our ordeal on the boat. The break is sorely needed, and far too brief to erase the abuse our bodies have endured so far.

On our first official day of military training, we are roused out of our sleep at four-thirty in the morning by the trainers' shrill whistles. Several men grumble their usual complaints, but our superiors quickly shout them into silence. They make it clear that this is to be our new routine, and there is little we can do about it other than get used to it. Already dressed in the uniforms we were given the day before, we jump up off the bare ground where we made our beds and quickly fold our bed sheets and blankets into bundles to be stored away. We are told to wash and toilet, but not how much time we have to do it, so we rush through these activities for fear of not having enough time.

Then we wait.

The next time the whistle blows, we rush to line up. Those who don't run, or who run too slowly, are forced to lie facedown on the ground, then ordered to crawl over the coarse, hot sand. I am called out along with some others. The razor-sharp stones lacerate the skin on my knees, palms, and elbows. The pain is terrible, and within minutes the wounds are caked in blood and mud. Biting flies add to the torment. After that, I try to make sure I don't give them any reason to reprimand me. But no matter what I do — no matter how hard any of us tries — we all get punished more than we deserve. Even the quickest and most attentive among us is subjected to this cruelty. We are all at the mercy of our trainers and their moods.

After roll call, we are forced to run as a unit into the desert. Leading us is an ENS member, whose main job is to translate our instructions into Arabic, Tigrinya and two other regional dialects. When we reach our destination, he orders us to empty our bowels. Then we run back to camp, where we are handed over to our trainers. Even after such a short distance, my legs feel like dead wood. I have no energy and am on the verge of collapsing from exhaustion, yet I somehow keep going. I tell myself it will be worse if I quit. So I persist, finding strength where I never knew I had it.

We run everywhere, no matter how severe the heat or our thirst. Even when we aren't training, we run. We don't stop running until an hour before noon. In this way, they break us down, both physically and mentally, until we have become little more than empty shells. After weeks of this, they work to build us back up again, filling us with new ideas and determination, turning us into something better suited to their purpose.

We train to handle weapons. For many of us, it's our first hands on experience with firearms, and despite the seriousness of the subject, even those of us revolted by such things are caught up in a sort of competition to see who can properly dismantle and reassemble their rifle the fastest. Not surprisingly, our instructors encourage this sort of behavior in us.

Then comes several days of shooting practice at stationary targets with live rounds. Our proficiency scores are recorded. Some of the men believe if they perform poorly at this task, they will avoid being assigned to the ground forces engaged in active fighting. But this will prove to be inaccurate. One man, who I know made it a habit to intentionally miss the majority of his targets, will end up on the front after his training is finished.

We also receive instruction on combat techniques and survival. We learn to crawl, climb, jump, hide, and evade. We spend many hours over many weeks moving around with stealth and speed over the hard, rocky ground, like a leopard stalking a gazelle. All of this is carried out beneath the blazing desert sun.

After lunch, we are given time to rest in one of the buildings. Each platoon of roughly fifty men is assigned its own room. Inside each room are *medeb*, mud block platforms raised roughly five or six inches off the floor. To me, they look like coffins half-buried in the packed earth. Some of us have *meshemae*, plastic sacks used for grain, which we spread out on top of the *medeb* to act as a barrier of sorts. Over this, we lay our blankets. Finally, our bed sheets. This is where we rest, waiting for the next whistle to blow. When it does, we rush out into the heat for our next round of training. No one wants to be last into formation.

How we learn to hate that whistle and the merciless shouts of our trainers. We learn to fear the sun. And even the open air. The insect problem is especially bad here. Besides the biting flies, there are mosquitoes and ants and scorpions. Everywhere we go, we are being yelled at, hit, bitten, or stung. But the worst are the rats and snakes. I fear the snakes the most.

We train until the shadows grow long, then we retrieve our blankets and bed sheets, get back into our lines, and march toward our sleeping area, an open field next to the buildings. We march until the order is given to stop. Then, right where we stand, we make our bed for the night. We smooth away the loose rocks, and lie down on our thin, makeshift mattresses. We sleep in formation wearing our uniforms so that we can be ready at a moment's notice.

If we have need of the toilet in the middle of the night, we must notify whoever is on patrol. There is no leaving our bed without permission. As for where we go, the entire desert is at our disposal.

Once the sun sets, the heat leaks away from the ground, and the air grows cold. When the chill becomes too unbearable, usually an hour or two before the morning whistle, we pull the blanket out from beneath us and wrap it around our bodies.

Our uniform consists of thin brown trousers, short sleeved shirt, and plastic sandals called *shidda*. While suitable to the climate, the clothes do a poor job of protecting us from the physical abuses inflicted by the environment and the rigors of our training. Soon, everyone's arms and feet are covered in weeping, bleeding sores. Our bodies are given no time to heal, so the wounds are constantly reopened. Many become infected. If they heal, they leave scars.

The trainers show us no sympathy. In fact, the sight of blood seems to enrage them. For some people, the injuries get so bad that they fall ill. If they become so severe that they prevent someone from participating, the unit leader will report it to the trainer, who beats the trainee without mercy. If after repeated beatings, they still don't participate, then the trainer, having no other option, leaves that person alone. The beating is resumed the next day, then the next, until the man is "persuaded" to rejoin the group.

Whenever one of us is unable to line up, we move them into the shade and cover them up with their bed sheet to protect them as much as possible against the wind, dust, sun, and pests.

One member of our battalion, Yacob, takes it upon himself to ensure the sick receive their daily food ration. He does this out of the kindness of his heart without waiting to be asked. In fact, I have seen him walk all the way across camp to buy *injera*, a spongy flatbread sold by the local vendors. Often, the quality of the bread is so poor as to be ridiculed, yet we still eat it. Yacob is so selfless that I have seen him spend his own money to buy food and medicine for those who are very sick and can't afford it themselves. He is young, strong, and very smart. Being from Keren, he speaks Bilen, a Cushidic language also spoken by those in Kassala in eastern Sudan, although he is also fluent in Tigrinya and Arabic, so he's able to communicate with most of the trainees. It's him we seek out first whenever we are in need.

As part of our fitness training, we must march over very long distances carrying our rifles and supplies— plastic jugs of water, picks and trowels, medical stretchers, and other equipment. One day, our endurance is tested to the limit when we are roused out of bed an hour earlier than usual. The march begins at four o'clock. We head south through the pre-dawn darkness toward the border with Djibouti. After the sun rises over the sea, it bakes our left side. On our return, the same side is exposed once more to the setting afternoon sun. Not once are we allowed to eat or drink anything. Our breaks last mere minutes.

It is pure torment, being forced to carry water we cannot drink. Our trainers check the containers constantly to make sure they remain full. I am charged with leading my squad, and so I have the responsibility of ensuring we all keep up with the rest of the unit. I lose count of how many times I have to encourage my fellow team members to quicken their pace. Of how often I must relieve those who fall behind by shifting their burden to myself or another. By rule, I can't take their weapons, but we are allowed to redistribute the rest of the supplies. I make sure the heaviest objects get passed around every few minutes so that no one tires too quickly.

I can't say what distance we walk, but I do know that it is almost twelve hours before we see the camp again. Twelve hours of near constant marching. Never have I been so happy to see a bare patch of hard ground. But our trainers don't release us right away. Instead, they force us to stand in formation until we are on the verge of collapsing. Then they give the order, and we fall to the ground in exhaustion, hunger, and pain. The bottoms of our feet are ruined. Not even cool, fresh water can ease the torment or replace what we have sweat away.

This is only one of many tests of our endurance, but thankfully it turns out to be one of the worst. We all know what our instructors are doing. They're training our minds and bodies to tolerate the worst conditions imaginable, to be ready for any challenge we might encounter on the battlefield, yet still have enough strength held back to be capable of fighting. They're pushing us past what we think are our limits. They're making sure we won't break when the time comes.

Although, some of us do. Somehow, I'm not one of them.

We are given the day after our forced march to recover. It takes until nightfall before our bodies begin to feel almost normal again. Still, it takes another week before the strain on our arms from carrying the supplies fades away, and the blisters on our feet stop tormenting us. The scars left behind are our trainers' gifts to us, meant to remind us forever after, not of our pain, but of our resilience.

In a park in the middle of Asmara, on a road called Martyr's Avenue, stands a rusty metal statue commemorating our War for Independence. It doesn't depict the figure of any *tegadalay* hero, although every Eritrean who sees it immediately understands its connection to the freedom fighters and its significance to our nation's sovereignty. The sculpture consists of sheets of metal bent into the shape of a giant pair of *shidda*, much like the ones worn by my country's freedom fighters during their thirty-year struggle. They are very much like the sandals worn by myself and my fellow conscripts now. Light, airy, easily crafted from old tires and just as easily repaired, they are supremely functional. They represent the strength, persistence, and pragmatism of our people.

They are a symbol of our strength of will.

But also a daily reminder of how little has changed for us since we won our freedom.

Our conditioning isn't just for our bodies, but also our minds. We receive classes on Eritrean history and politics. Thankfully, these are delivered in the same shaded structure we use for weapons handling and eating. The walls are constructed of stacked rocks without mortar, blocking some of the wind and dust, while tree branches laid over the top shade us from the Dankalia sun.

The history classes are meant to indoctrinate us with the proper mindset regarding the current conflict, as well as instill a strong sense of national pride, both of which will fortify our resolve in combat. The lessons are taught in both Tigrinya and Arabic, Eritrea's two other official languages, besides English. Being a college graduate, I am already familiar with much of the material, as are some of my fellow soldiers-in-training. But not everyone has had the benefit of a formal education. Some of the men here never finished high school. Others are entirely illiterate.

None of these details matters to our instructors. We are all treated identically. They assume we know nothing, or that what we do know is either incomplete or incorrect. They consistently depict Eritrea in the most favorable light, whether it is deserved or not. Our nation's failings and those of our leaders are either ignored or denied outright. How can we ever progress as a nation, if we don't recognize our failures and correct them?

We are also never tested on the material. Our trainers don't care if we learn it or not, only that we do not challenge these views. They measure their effectiveness by how we carry ourselves as Eritrean soldiers; we pass their test by showing how willing we are to defend the fatherland.

While the lessons provide respite from our physical ordeals, they are an assault on reason and objectivity, so I privately resent them, and I am grateful we aren't forced to suffer listening to them every day. I see it as a form of brainwashing. With each lecture, I can almost feel pieces of my identity and independence slipping away, the holes left behind to be filled in with half-truths and outright lies. It's too reminiscent of the propaganda Ethiopia fed to us every day for decades.

While I am able to resist the psychological assault, I fare far less well with the physical. For whatever reason, I can't seem to tolerate the food they provide to us, which is mostly a type of lentil soup called *ades*. I try to eat it, but my stomach rejects it. And I'm not the only one. Most of the men can't bear eating this soup and instead subsist mainly on sweetened tea and *kitcha* flatbread. Sometimes, even the bread is almost inedible. By the time we get it, it has become so hard and dry that we joke it could stop bullets.

I know I am losing weight, even though there are no mirrors or scales to confirm it. The bodies of the other men are my mirrors. A few in the group, however, seem to thrive, despite the wretched diet. They don't have any trouble eating the lentil soup. Not only do they finish their own rations, but they ask for more *ades*. It is hard not to resent them. They don't know the agony of constant hunger like the rest of us do.

The trainers aren't fed the same diet. Their lentils are properly washed and cooked with good quality oil. Onion and tomato paste is added for flavoring, while we get none. They get yogurt and *bagayit*, a preparation of cooked spiced meat, to supplement their meals. They can also purchase their own groceries in Assab, so they eat much better than we do.

When we complain to them about the food, they tell us a story about the time President Isaias Afewerki was a *tegadalay* leader in the resistance. "It's a known fact," they say, "that they ate lentils for every meal every day for years. Just lentils and bread. And they defeated

Mengistu's armies. Only on special occasions did the farmers from the local communities bring fresh meat and vegetables so that they might celebrate whatever holiday it was or recent victory they had achieved. Whenever Isaias heard a soldier complain about it, he would tell them they were welcome to go to bed with an empty stomach instead."

I would eat the lentil soup, if I could. I would rather do that than go to bed hungry every night, but the more I try, the more violently my body rejects it. Now, after several weeks of such abuse, my stomach doesn't seem to be able to hold much of anything at all, not even the canned vegetables or meat we sometimes get in our occasional field rations. Each meal is a battle between the misery of throwing it up and the agony of keeping it down.

To maintain my energy, I rely primarily on our daily rations of tea and bread, as well as the milk powder and *tihni* my sister-in-law delivered to me at the detention center. I share whatever I can, but I have to be careful doling out these supplies. Without them, I would surely suffer worse than I already am. Fortunately, my brother-in-law learns of my situation. He works in an office at the nearby port, so he's able to procure more of the *tihni* for me on occasion.

There is no mess hall in the camp, no kitchen. All of the cooking and heating are done on open fire pits using wood we gather as part of our daily responsibilities. Other supplies are transported in from the Zone Military Division in Assab each day, including our bread, which is prepared there ahead of time. The meals are served to us in shifts within the shaded structure. The leaders of each unit designate who will serve for that day. This sometimes causes problems, as we come from many different areas of the country and have many different backgrounds and customs. Some men feel they shouldn't have to serve, or be served by, certain others from different ethnic groups. Or they believe they should always be served first. I try to be sensitive to this, but I have to remind them that the army is a secular institution in such cases and blind to religion. Everyone must share every burden equally.

As to the gathering of firewood, the only trees around us have thin, hard branches full of thorns. Because the wood is so dry, it burns hot and fast. And since we are not cutting down live trees, I do not feel as bad as I did when we were in Sawa. Not that there are forests here, but at least we are not killing what is alive. The sun and winds do a good enough job of killing things first.

One day, I step on a piece of wood, and a thorn pierces the bottom of my sandal and enters deep into my foot. When I try to take it out, a piece breaks off, forcing me to limp back to camp, where Mahmood uses a needle to dig the thorn out. It's agonizing, so while he works on me, he distracts me with a story about a fellow trainee's recent misfortune. This soldier was bitten by a poisonous snake and had to be rushed to the hospital in Assab. He doesn't know if the man survived, as the venomous snakes here are deadly. This is how limited our availability is to even the most basic of medical care. A shiver goes through me, as I remember the snake I saw in Sawa.

"In Sawa," he tells me, "if someone is too sick or injured, the trainer can send them directly to the hospital, where a medic might decide if they need a break from training."

Here, there is no medic to make such a determination.

I mention the man in Nefasit who was excused for his hand, and Mahmood explains that only a medical review board can excuse a conscript from training. "There is no such board here," he adds. "So there are only three ways to leave training in Kiloma— finish the course, sneak away, or die."

One day in late October, nearly four months into my training, I'm called into the office of the brigade commander. I have no clue why I'm being summoned, so I'm nervous and fear the worst. But instead of a hostile reception, I receive a cordial welcome. My puzzlement grows when a female member of the National Service assigned to the region's Central Command introduces herself to me and asks me to sit. The appearance of a female is startling enough, but then she offers me coffee and once again urges me to have a seat, and all I can think is that something terrible has happened at home.

Finally, when I'm settled, she hands me a package from my wife and tells me that it arrived by way of my brother-in-law, with whom she shares a common friend. Still perplexed, I open it up to find more of the lifesaving supplies of powdered milk and *tihni*. On top is a letter from my wife. I dread opening it up, fearing the kind of news that might necessitate such personal treatment from someone like this. Despite my status as a lowly conscript, I am still an Eritrean. We all are. Some cultural norms, such as the delivery of important news, are blind to rank.

In her delicate handwriting, Wudasie tells me how she and the family are getting along. Titi, our daughter with the heart defect, is still as healthy as we could hope for her. The murmur is still there, but at least it doesn't appear to be getting any worse. Wudasie is still actively re-searching treatment options, including seeking assistance through international aid programs, but it's so hard because the options are extremely limited. Tears well up in my eyes, for I know how fiercely protective she can be of our little girl, and I hate that my conscription has forced her to carry so much of the burden all alone on her shoulders.

I expect next to hear about our market. Instead, the news is about the arrival of our second child, another girl. For a long time, I can do nothing but stare at the words on the paper as a mix of emotions overwhelms me. I feel so happy and relieved, but also so helpless.

At last, I compose myself. I make a promise — to myself and my growing family — that I will survive this test, no matter how extreme the hardships. Wudasie's strength buoys me. I will do whatever it takes to return to her and my two daughters.


None of us wants to be disciplined, but even when we do our best to avoid it, punishments are doled out almost daily. Sometimes it's for the smallest bit of negligence or stupidity, sometimes for an entirely made-up infraction. Most of us aren't foolish enough to intentionally invite the trainers' anger, because deserved or not, the punishment is always far worse than the offense requires.

The trainers make sure we witness this cruelty firsthand, as if we need to be constantly reminded that we're no longer in charge of our own lives. The punishments are delivered most frequently at lunchtime, when the sun is at its peak and we have little choice but to watch. The offender is forced to stand like a statue in the blazing heat, a heavy load on his back and no water to drink. Or he is forced to crawl over long distances on the hard, sharp ground while being whipped with a stick.

We are told that the other battalion in the camp is punished more than ours. I don't know if this is true, or whether, if it is, it's because their trainers are more cruel or the conscripts more negligent, but it makes me glad I wasn't assigned there. As for the third battalion, I can only guess how its men are faring.

The trainers try their hardest to break us. And most of us try just as hard not to be broken. Some inevitably fail. We try to be flexible, to bend so we don't break. Then there are those who refuse to bend at all, who remain defiant. They are slow to learn that it's useless to act this way. They only make their lives harder.

I have come close to breaking several times, yet each time I somehow manage not to.

In between training sessions, we're given time to attend to our personal matters. Yet even in such moments, we are always expected to act with strict discipline and follow every rule. There is no excuse for laziness or misbehavior. We must always be vigilant.

Laundry takes up most of this free time. We have more generous quantities of clean, fresh water here than we did in Sawa. A truck appears on a regular basis, probably from the Harsile Reservoir in Assab, to fill the large storage tanks nearby. The tanks are under constant guard to prevent abuse and sabotage.

We also have a supply of plastic buckets for transferring the water into several large tubs located behind our building, which is where we wash our clothing, bed sheets, and blankets. There are no machines. It must all be done by hand— or rather, by foot. We step into the tubs and mash our clothes about as if we are making wine. Then we hang the washed laundry up to air dry.

To bathe, we stand inside a screen of rocks that protects us from the wind and dust. The water isn't heated, not that it needs to be. In the middle of the day, the air is so hot that our skin dries within minutes.

If we have no additional chores, then we are allowed to catch up on our sleep. It does not come easily, nor is it as restful as it could be, since we are always worried about catching the roaming eye of an angry trainer. We have little access to books, just the few that people had with them when they were rounded up. There is no television or radio. Our trainers and other staff don't often volunteer news, so we have to rely on the letters we receive instead to inform us of happenings outside of the camp.

It's frustrating not knowing more. Information about the war comes to us piecemeal. We learn the fighting at the frontlines is raging, but what exactly does this mean? Are we winning? Are there a lot of casualties? Are other countries coming to help, as Somalia did toward the end of the last war? What about the United Nations? How are the peace talks progressing between our two governments? Speculation runs rampant, spreading through the camp like a deadly disease. Without knowing what is true and what isn't, arguments sometimes result. A few of the men have managed to become friendly with our trainers and occasionally convince them to share whatever information they are willing to impart. Teame, for example, a bright and charismatic city boy with an easy manner, engages well with almost everyone in the camp, including the trainers, whom he will often join uninvited during meals. Sometimes they kick him out, but once in a while they will tolerate his presence. Afterward, he is usually full of the latest news, which he willingly relays to the rest of us. I'm always wary of the accuracy of such information. Some of it is surely outdated by the time it reaches us. I also suspect our trainers tell him things to suit their needs, which includes keeping us misinformed.

One member of our unit has been lending me his Bible. I find that reading it helps restore my spirit, when I am at my lowest. On one such occasion, a trainer from a platoon in our unit, an ENS member from one of the early training cycles, enters our building specifically in search of me. I know right away what he wants, which is for someone to carry water for him to bathe. As trainees, this is one of our regular chores and, as a unit leader, it is up to me to choose who will do it. I keep a notebook to make sure no one is unfairly burdened more than others.

But he stops me when he notices what I am reading.

"Don't you know that religious books are banned in camp?" he snaps. "No Bibles. No Qurans. We are not Christians or Muslims here. We are soldiers, *Eritrean* soldiers. We can't be fighting each other over such things as religion."

This all comes as a surprise to me.

Eritrea, like our former guardian, Ethiopia, has long supported religious freedom. The two main religions, Christianity and Islam, have coexisted mostly peacefully for many generations. Animosities between the two exist, but they are either uncommon or rarely acted upon. It's the practitioners of less common religions who are persecuted more often, whether by citizens or by the government. But this has never been an issue here in camp.

"That is the rule," the trainer warns me. "Do you wish to be disciplined?"

Thankfully, he doesn't wait for my answer. Nor does he confiscate the book or order me outside for punishment. He tells me what he wants, and when he's gone, I put the book away for good. It's yet another reminder that the military considers itself the only source of inspiration for its soldiers.

The routine is becoming mind-numbing. With nothing to challenge me intellectually, my brain feels as if it is shrinking. I lose focus. My attention drifts. As I grow more used to the strict routine and less concerned about surviving it, my thoughts turn increasingly to my family and our uncertain financial situation. I worry how my wife and daughters must be faring without me. I worry about how Titi's heart is holding out. And how Wudasie is managing everything all by herself.

These distractions nearly get me into trouble one day. I am walking through the camp, my mind far away, when a shout brings me to a stop. The commander of our battalion calls me over. I had passed him without seeing or acknowledging his presence.

"In this camp," he sharply rebukes me, "you will always walk like a soldier, not like a lazy pedestrian taking a stroll in the city with his hands in his pockets!"

The thought comes to my mind that I am anything but a soldier. More than being a term I have come to dislike, it is inaccurate. If anything, I am a conscripted member of the National Service who has been forced away from his family and job without even the courtesy of a notice. How can such a person proudly call himself a soldier? Shouldn't that term be reserved for men and women who volunteer to fight for their country? I resent that my service has been forced upon me without choice.

Perhaps he sees some part of this struggle in my face. Or maybe he understands how hard it is to stay mentally engaged all the time, but whatever the reason, he doesn't deliver the usual punishment. Instead, he orders me to assist the administrators with their paperwork during my free time. I realize then that he must know a little about me personally. He knows about my education and my accounting degree, as this is the type of paperwork I am asked to do.

After a little while, they ask me to do more. Rather than resenting them for it, I'm grateful, as the job helps keep my mind occupied. Still, it does little to lessen my homesickness and worry. Or my impatience with this place, its people, and the reasons for our being here.


Our final task of the day before being dismissed is to line up for roll call. This usually happens near dusk, and since there is no electricity, there's nothing for us to do afterward but settle onto our blankets for the night once we are released. But now, after so many months of training together, our bodies stronger and leaner and more resilient, few of us succumb to exhaustion as quickly as we once did. We're supposed to remain silent, but it's hard to wind down, especially since it is one of the few chances we have to truly relax. Eventually, someone begins to speak. Soon, more join in. Listening to their voices drift past me, I can't help but feel closer to these men. They are like my brothers. We have endured so much together already. We will endure so much more before it's all done.

Among those I am closest with are a half dozen or so whose backgrounds are similar to mine. We're all over thirty years old, married, and have families. We're all Christian, except for Mahmood, but that has never been a problem for any of us; there is no judgment between us. Besides, Mahmood grew up in Keren with catholic friends, so he is comfortable inserting himself into our discussions, even when religion is the subject. We have found common ground in our beliefs. We all place our faith in one divine being, whether God or Allah, and we know He will see us through this ordeal.

In my culture, children are given a secular surname at birth, which generally acknowledges the father. A given first name, usually religious, is provided at christening. Before the arrival of our second child, Wudasie and I made a list of possible baptismal names. Not knowing whether we would be blessed with a boy or a girl, we considered both. Now that our daughter has arrived, the next major milestone in her life will be choosing this name. We have a little bit of time, as girls are christened in our faith on the eightieth day of life. Had she been a boy, I would have had only half that amount of time to choose.

My friends are eager to help me pick. Given their faith, many of their suggestions come straight from the Good Book. It's an easy point of reference for us all. Of course, I would much prefer to be having this discussion with my wife, but that is impossible given my current situation.

My friends pester me for days about it, asking me every chance they get if I have chosen yet. Eventually, I break with tradition and my wife by settling on Natsanet. The word means freedom, and was a popular girl's name during our armed struggled with Ethiopia. I think it's especially appropriate now, not because I equate our current struggle with the last, but because the freedom we should have been given remains so elusive. By picking Natsanet, I am placing all of my hope in my daughter and her generation, that they will be wiser than their parents have been in managing our nation's legacy. It is my hope, just as it was my parents', that our children know the blessing of true freedom from bondage, whether it's from foreign governments or our own.

Tonight, I tell my friends what I have chosen. Tomorrow, I will write to my wife and let her know. My friends express their support with a quiet cheer, immediately eliciting a stern warning from our trainer to keep quiet. We obey, even though sleep is still far off. None of us wishes to be called out of our beds for punishment.

*Natsanet*, I whisper. *Natsanet*. Freedom for my little girl. Freedom — *true* freedom — is all I ask for us all.

One by one, the others drift off, and I am soon surrounded in a chorus of snores. Then, seemingly moments later, the whistle blows to start the next day. And still Natsanet whispers in my ears the promise of her name.

*One day*, she says in a woman's voice, *we will truly be free.*


After sending Wudasie my name suggestion, I anxiously await her reply. If she doesn't approve, then I will have to choose something else. At last, I receive her response. With shaking hands, I open the letter and find that she loves my suggestion, as do the other members of our families. Even my friends here admit they like the way it sounds, although they still tease me for not picking a name from the Bible. For a little while, the letter helps me forget my dreary existence. It gives me the strength to face the final few weeks of training.

It doesn't take long for reality to destroy my good mood. That same afternoon, our instructors unexpectedly order the entire brigade to assemble for an announcement by our commander. We stand at attention for so long that it is a wonder no one passes out from the heat. We don't know why we have been called, but we have our suspicions. A rumor has spread through the camp that some people escaped. At last, the commander comes out.

"Several days ago," he says, his voice booming across the desert, "three soldiers left their unit without permission." He pauses to let this sink in. He knows their desertions have been the subject of rampant speculation throughout the entire camp. Some of us have been silently praying the men make it home safely; others, resentful of their freedom, wish them to be caught and brought back to finish their training.

The missing men are all part of the Rashaida group I had noticed earlier on the boat to Assab. Most of us hadn't been surprised to hear the rumors of their desertion, as they are a nomadic people and tend not to assimilate well with others. They keep to themselves and speak their own language.

The commander slowly sweeps his gaze over us before he continues. "I'm sure you will be happy to know that they have been found."

There is no sound from the formation, nothing but the soft hush of the wind. We're all anxious to hear about their fate. Will they be sent to prison? Will they simply be returned to finish their training, as Mahmood had been?

"As we expected," the commander continues, "they were trying to make their way to Assab. They did not make it. They are dead."

The news sends a ripple of anguish through us all. This time, there is an audible gasp. How did they die? Were they shot? Beaten? Were they defeated by hunger and dehydration?

"They fell asleep in a riverbed. A sudden flood drowned them and swept their bodies downstream, where they were found."

The skepticism the explanation creates is palpable. How could this be possible? Those men would have known better than to make their camp in such a vulnerable place. And when had it rained enough to cause such a flood? We wait for an explanation, but no more details are given. Instead, the commander begins to shout crossly at us.

"This should never have happened!" Spittle flies from his lips. He raises his fist and shakes it, and his face twists with anger. "Why do you think they deserted? Is it because this is too hard for them? You are soldiers! Of course this is hard! Fighting for your country is never easy! Is it because you are being treated unfairly here? War is not fair! Your enemy will not treat you fairly! Are you afraid to die? Well, those men were afraid, and now they are dead because of this fear!"

It's hard for me to listen to what he is saying, even if I know it's the truth. All I can think about is the men's bodies. Were they truly drowned? Were their bones broken on the rocks by some improbable flood? Or were they broken by sticks wielded by their fellow countrymen? I feel terrible for them and their families. I feel terrible for myself and my own family, too.

"Those people grew up in the desert," the commander reminds us, "and yet they did not survive very long there. How do you think you would have done, if it had been you?"

Nothing but silence meets his question, but we all know the answer. We know why he is asking us this. He wants us to imagine our own failure, so that we don't try it ourselves.

"This will not happen again!" he screams. "If anyone here thinks he is being treated harshly, then he is invited to report it to me. My office is open to everyone. You are all welcome to tell me in private what we can do to make your stay here more pleasant."

He steps away and returns to his office.

We all know what he is really saying. He isn't inviting us to make suggestions, but warning us to stop thinking about freedom. To do so will only get us killed.

One day, there is a sudden disturbance in the camp. One of the squads from our battalion is abruptly taken away to a different block. We don't know why or what they are doing to them. No one is allowed to see them. Soon, a rumor spreads that some of the trainees might be infected with a contagious disease and that the camp administrators decided to quarantine them to prevent it from spreading to the rest of us.

The news is both a relief and frightening. After the desertions, everyone is nervous, so we are glad to know the isolation is not for disciplinary reasons. Still, medical quarantine is a serious matter. Here at the camp, we have no ready access to health professionals with more than a basic level of training, and the closest hospital is thirty kilometers away. We are all vulnerable to injuries, but we are especially scared of illnesses that can spread easily from one person to another. We continue to worry, both for the welfare of our fellow trainees, but also for our own.

Some members of the National Service are provided basic first aid instruction. The training these *agar hakim*, or "combat medics," are given is mostly limited to treating battlefield wounds. Here at Kiloma, our daily medical needs are seen to by one man sitting beneath a tree with a bag of simple medicines, which he dispenses to us after listening to our complaints and guessing about their causes. He is not a doctor. And the medicines are only good for minor maladies and skin ailments. As an example, he has been unable to cure me of my digestive problems. And when I ask for help with a chronic skin condition, the best he can offer is some ointment from his personal supply that does nothing for me.

Even our instructors are helpless. Most times, if they send someone to the hospital in Assab, the condition is already very grave. Some of the conscripts sent there don't come back. We always hope for the best in such cases, but fear the worst. For the men now in quarantine, we pray it doesn't come to such measures.

There is a well-worn story passed among the men here, one that had begun to be shared even before we arrived. It claims that several trainees died in the previous cycle. At first, we didn't believe it. Or rather, we didn't *want* to believe it. We were convinced it was meant to scare us into doing only what we were told to do. Now, we know it must be true. There are so many ways one might die out here, and so many chances as well. As for the story, the trainers would never confirm or deny it.

A day after we learned about the quarantine situation, Teame tells us the trainers had confided in him that some of the isolated men are in critical condition and are being transferred to the hospital. Again, we have no way of knowing if this is true or made up simply to frighten us. Either way, it does.

We are in the middle of weapons training a week later, this time learning how to handle old American-made M-14 rifles, when the entire quarantined group unexpectedly rejoins the unit. They arrive with a new rumor, and we are not quite sure what to make of it. They say our training is finished weeks earlier than expected, and we are to be assigned to our units.


There is no ceremony, no recognition of our achievements or the abrupt end of our training. This raises new worries. Ahead of us will be a long, hard journey back north. Then the possibility of going straight to the frontlines of the fight. Why else would they cut our training cycle short?

We gather to hear our fate, but the trainers blandly announce that everyone has passed their tests. We are ordered to wait while the army puts together our assignments.

Of course we must wait. What else can we do? This is the way the military operates.

Speculation abounds. Some people believe we will be sent back to Sawa first, Eritrea's main training center, to receive our assignments. Others claim we won't have to wait that long to find out. They believe our assignments will be decided here and now. Regardless, we all agree on one thing, that none of us wants to remain in the middle of this wretched desert so far away from our families another minute more than we have to.

The seconds slowly tick away. Then the minutes turn to hours, and the hours pass just as slowly. The day ends, and still we have no news.

The next day passes in similar fashion. We grow restless, anxious, afraid to hope for the best. In this limbo, we can only imagine the worst. We don't know what is happening to the war. Could the fighting be over? Are we being released?

Or is the war growing more deadly?

Three days after being told to wait, the entire brigade is ordered to assemble. A hush falls over us as we spill out of the buildings and line up. The sun is blinding, here in the center of the camp, as if the attention of the world is focused on us beneath a giant lens. The heat burns our skin, sears the insides of our noses, brings tears to our eyes. The air buzzes with anticipation.

"Make your lines!" we are told. "Listen carefully!"

Finally, the commander of the brigade appears. He has papers in his hand. He crosses the yard and comes to a stop before us. His skin shines with sweat. It drips down his cheeks and darkens the collar of his shirt. He pauses to gather his thoughts.

The Eritrean military has three branches — Air Force, Navy, and Army — and any soldier within the EDF is called a *wetehader*. Many of the former freedom fighters, *tegadelti*, hold permanent, paid positions within these three branches, often filling positions of command. National Service members, once required to serve for only eighteen months but now conscripted indefinitely, are initially assigned to the Army Ground Force, or *Agar Serawit*. Some individuals, depending on their skills, are then transferred onward to serve in the Air Force or Navy. It's a complicated process choosing who goes where, and one shrouded in mystery for those of us waiting to hear our names.

"Congratulations," the commander says. "You have all performed well. Now you are ready to fight for your country."

Our hearts sink. The war is not over.

He informs us that the border issue is still unresolved, and that many tens of thousands of fighters have already given their lives to defend what is rightfully Eritrea's. He sucks in a lungful of the hot air before bellowing out, "Half of you will remain here in Kiloma! You will be part of the zonal command in the south! The rest will head north towards Kebessa."

There's a ripple of unease and numerous groans. The southern command is a major war front, one of the bloodiest of both wars. The Ethiopian army nearly broke it before, but we held on. Does growing it mean the conflict is getting worse? Or does it mean we are close to victory and don't want to lose our advantage? The questions swirl in my head, but all I can think about are the rusted and burned out trucks and tanks we saw on the road from Assab. I think about how many bodies the sands conceal. I can only imagine a future where more will soon join them.

"Wherever you are sent," the commander continues, "you must be ready to accept whatever assignment you are given. Only in this way can we defend our country and win!"

My throat constricts. I try to swallow, but my mouth is as dry as the dust beneath my feet. I know that I am not the only one praying to avoid this terrible assignment here in the south.

He doesn't say anything for several moments, just lets us stew in our worry. Finally, he announces the companies that will remain here in Kiloma. The remaining units will be heading back to the highlands. I heave a sigh of relief when I realize that I will be going with them.

I know that I'm in for another long, hot, tortuous boat ride, and yet I don't dread it as much as I should, despite knowing how difficult it will be. After nearly six months, I will be returning to the highlands, which is what the commander meant by Kebessa. I may get a chance to see my wife and daughters, including the daughter I have never met, Natsanet.

That is all I care about right now. Whatever happens to me afterward, I will worry about later.

# Kebessa

MAYBE IT'S BECAUSE WE KNOW what to expect this time around. Or maybe our minds and bodies have been toughened by our training these past several months, but the journey north, under conditions no different than those we experienced during our previous trip, is easier to endure. Mostly, however, I think it's because of the bonds of friendship we have developed with each other. They nourish us during the wretched journey up the Red Sea to Massawa. This time, we share the experience together, looking out for one another, supporting each other rather than suffering alone.

For me, it helps to know that I am heading back to the highlands, back to where I will be closer to my home and my family. When at last we dock at Massawa after two hard days at sea, I step off that boat in better spirits than I have felt in a very long time.

After debarking, we are instructed to line up. "Keep quiet," they shout at us over the din of the waves and machines and the harsh cries of the seabirds scrambling for scraps along the shore. "Listen for your names," one man commands. He points at a small group standing to one side. "These men are representatives from different military divisions. When you hear your name, you will go with them."

With each roll call, our group grows smaller. Each representative checks his tally against the paper in his hand. Then the men are led to trucks waiting in a nearby parking lot and driven away. I'm sad to see my friends go. I pray for them, as many of them are assigned to ground force units and will be heading straight to the frontlines to fight. Mahmood is among them.

The fate of the rest of the group remains uncertain. I can't help but notice that many of us are high school and college educated; the rest have construction skills. I don't wish to speculate that we will be lucky to be assigned to one of the administrative departments, or *kiflitat*. What if I am wrong? So I wait, just as impatient as all the rest, yet also dreading the finality of the decision. We all want to get this part of the journey over with, but we fear something worse awaits us.

At last, we're told that we will be heading to the headquarters of the zonal command's administration at Adi Keyh. And again, fear flushes through me. At a hundred or so kilometers south of Asmara, Adi Keyh is no closer to my family than where I am standing right now. In fact, it's far closer to the Ethiopian border, where the heaviest fighting is being waged. Even if we are there in some sort of support capacity, it's still very close to the fighting.

The war our country fought for freedom, the war that took the lives of more than sixty-five thousand of our countrymen and many more civilians, was a justified war. Most Eritreans believe this. But very few believe the same about this new conflict. What have twenty thousand more Eritrean deaths gained us? When it's finally over, will we be any- more free than we already were?

I worry it will be just the opposite. I worry that our own leaders will find a way to oppress us as we have become so accustomed to before. Perhaps even more so. I don't want to believe this, but I can't find it in me to deny it, either.

If I am told to fight, I will have no choice. Doing otherwise would mean losing all that our *tegadelti* won. But the thought of killing another man sickens me. I'm no longer sure who the enemy is. Most people still blame the government of Ethiopia, but ours is not totally innocent, either. Both sides had many chances to resolve the crisis through peaceful means. Both sides chose to fight instead.

I am among the last few dozen to leave Massawa. Although I'm glad to see it behind me, I'm not looking forward to what lies ahead. But there is little time to dwell on the possibilities, as the trip is much shorter than expected. We soon reach Nefasit, where this whole ordeal for me began. A flood of emotions fills me as the memory of that day returns. I can't believe it has only been five months since then. Already so much has happened to me and my family. Knowing how much we have missed makes me sick.

After Nefasit, instead of continuing west toward Asmara, the truck heads south to Dekemhare on the Asmara-Adi Keyh road. It's the same road I traveled on when I returned from Addis Ababa at the end of the war nearly a decade ago. This time, I am no longer a free citizen. Now I am a soldier, forced into compulsory service. And instead of heading home, I am leaving it behind.

It tears me apart knowing how physically close I am to my family. It makes me sick not knowing if I will get to see them anytime soon. I curse the leaders of both countries, Eritrea and Ethiopia, and pray they will open their eyes soon and realize we are no longer fighting for something meaningful, but for petty trinkets and useless pride. We are like two brothers whose hatred for each other is stronger than our love.

When we reach Adi Keyh, we're taken to a military compound a couple kilometers east of the town. There are a few buildings here, but no fence or gate to prevent us from running away. What would be the use of trying? We would be caught. Our families would be torn apart, sent to prison, and tortured.

The driver takes us to one of the buildings, where we disembark. "Remain here, outside," he instructs us. "Do not go anywhere until we have your orders."

Once more, we wait. Hours pass with no news. Evening comes, and no one tells us anything. We are resigned to spending the night sleeping on the bare ground, just as we did in Sawa and Kiloma. Here, however, it's much colder after dark. Adi Keyh has the highest elevation of any city in Eritrea. Located some twenty-five hundred meters above sea level — nearly eight thousand feet — it is hundreds of meters higher in elevation than Asmara. Over the past several months our bodies have become acclimated to the blistering heat of the Dankalia Desert and the mild nights so close to the Red Sea. But while we have been toughened by all we endured, the cold and the dampness here quickly seep into our bodies, chilling us to our bones. As we did in Sawa, we cover ourselves in plastic sheets to keep the dew off of us, and we huddle to conserve body heat. The cold is bad, but it isn't intolerable. What prevents us from sleeping is the continued uncertainty of our futures.

No one comes to talk to us the next day. We are still forbidden from leaving the camp, but that evening, when it becomes clear we will be spending a second night in the cold open air, three of my companions grow restless. They talk about sneaking out and try to convince me to go along with them. Eventually, I agree. We slip away without being challenged and make our way to a small eating establishment nearby. It's as far as we dare to go. There, we drink coffee like free men and momentarily forget that we aren't.

"Let's take a picture," I say, as we make our way back. "In case we're separated after this and don't see each other again."

We stop at a small shop where photos can be taken, and we go inside. The moment is a solemn one. As we pose in our soldier uniforms, each of us must be wondering the same thing: Which of us will survive the coming days? We stand together, arms locked, and look into the camera. By habit, we smile, but this isn't a joyful moment for any of us, simply a meaningful one. We are brothers now — Tesfalem, Tedros, Samson, and myself — and it pains us deeply to know that tomorrow we may never see each other again.

I tuck the photograph carefully into my pocket. Then we return to the base to await our fate.


At last, we receive further details about our assignments and are relieved to learn that none of us will be going directly to a combat unit. The group, nearly thirty of us in all, is split in half. One part is assigned to a construction outfit, and they leave as soon as their names are called. I'm glad we had a chance to say our goodbyes last night.

The rest of us are being held back for *kiflitat* assignments to the Zone 3 Core Guard Unit known as *Halewa Maasker*, which is headquartered in Asmara. A heavy weight lifts from my soul. Not only is there a very good chance I won't be near the frontlines, but I could be assigned close to my home and family. It isn't a guarantee, as the Zone 3 Command covers a lot of area. It's possible I might be deployed onward to another, more remote post. Still, it's more hope than I have allowed myself to feel in a long time.

We are taken to the administrative office in town to be processed. The mood is significantly lighter, almost jubilant. The only thing tempering it is the guilt we feel for our less fortunate friends. While waiting, we enjoy a nice, although modest, meal. There's even fresh tea and soft drinks. I eat quickly, eager for us to be moving on.

Finally, we are loaded onto trucks and taken to Asmara. I am in such a good mood that even the ride there energizes me. For the first time since my detention in Nefasit months ago, I'm on an official military truck without anyone to watch us like prisoners. I'm not told where to sit, nor ordered to keep quiet. I am able to chat freely with the other soldiers and can move about if I wish. I feel like a member of a team, an equal to my fellow brothers-in-arms, rather than a conscript. My only regret is that the circumstances of my return to my hometown and family are not as a free man.

Soon after arriving at the command's headquarters, we are told our final assignments will be coming soon. I pray I will be able to remain here in the city. They need people at the old military installation called Tseseret, the site of a former Italian military base. I'm anxious to see my family and meet my new daughter for the first time. My mood bounces between joy and sadness each time I remember I have missed her first moments of life.

It is customary in Eritrea for fathers not to be allowed to attend the delivery of their children. We are expected to be present in the hospital, if possible, but we must wait in a separate room until both mother and child are judged to be recovering well. So it was for the birth of our first child, Titi. When the doctors and nurses wheeled my wife out to take her to the maternity ward, I was able to hug and kiss her. It was a moment I will never forget, seeing her happy but tired face. And there she was, my daughter, the smallest, most perfect little person in the world. When I bent down to kiss her forehead, I could never have imagined such soft, delicate skin or such unblemished beauty.

This had once been my dream for our second child, but that chance was stolen away from me the day I was ordered out of the minibus in Nefasit. No embrace for her mother for her hard labor; no kiss for the child for the miracle of her arrival. Instead, on the day little Natsanet took her first breath, I was a thousand kilometers away.

I vow to make up for it the first chance I get.

# Tseserat Army Base, Asmara

ALL THAT REMAINS of the original Italian base in Tseserat are a few intact wooden barracks located in an area the size of two soccer fields. After World War Two, the Ethiopian army occupied the installation, even adding a number of large warehouses. Now the barracks and other structures function as the headquarters for various segments of our military command. The warehouses are owned by the Red Sea Trading Corporation, which was formed by the People's Front for Democracy and Justice— formerly, the EPLF, and now the nation's sole political party. Red Sea Trading is the largest income generator in the country, so politics, the military, and the economy are all tangled up together, especially in places like this.

On our way to Asmara I'm told I could be assigned to the platoon responsible for guarding the camp. If so, it would be a poor use of my education and skills, but I won't complain. I will be happy if I'm able to stay in the city. "Your duties begin as soon as the paperwork is processed," they tell me. Unfortunately, this means more waiting in limbo and more uncertainty before I can contact my family. I'm frustrated that this aspect of my service has not changed. Everything is still hurry up, then stop and do nothing while someone somewhere decides my fate, then hurry up again. Nobody tells us anything ahead of time; we are just expected to follow orders immediately, exactly as we did in training. Even now, asking questions is discouraged. We must wait patiently and quietly for someone to tell us what to do, and then we must act quickly to do it.

Finally, we're taken to where some of the other soldiers are being housed. It's a single-story L-shaped structure that looks thrown together without much of a plan. The roof is corrugated metal, the only protection from the rains. The floor is bare dirt. It looks more like a horse barn than a place where soldiers live. There are partitions, with each "room" holding three beds, each consisting of a simple metal frame, thin mattress, stiff sheets, and a scratchy blanket. Personal items are stored underneath.

After being introduced to the other members of our new unit, a pair of *tegadelti* and a dozen or so ENS members, we are invited to take our lunch meal with them. This is part of our induction, and it isn't possible to say no, despite my eagerness to break away to call my wife. Nor am I the only one with such intentions. I can see how difficult it is for the others to contain their impatience. We all have family we wish to speak with.

At last, lunch is finished and we're taken to a telephone stand. With shaking fingers, I dial home and hope someone answers.

How is it possible for two hours to pass so slowly? How can it take my family so long to arrive from home, when they already live so near? Don't they want to see me?

Finally, I'm told by the guard at the gate that I have visitors. I must pass through to see them outside, as they aren't allowed to enter. To protect the base from car bombs, visitors must park a safe distance away and wait. I have marched through searing desert heat carrying heavy loads for hours at a time, but I can't remember a walk as long or as hard as this one.

I see them before they see me, standing in the distance beside my brother-in-law Dawit's car, waiting in the heat of the day. Wudasie looks over. She seems to be confused. Suddenly, I'm afraid. Why isn't she excited to see me? I want to call out her name. I want to run to her. And yet I'm scared that if I do, she will run away. I quicken my pace, but only slightly. I want to see her joy for the reunion. But there's still no expression at all on her face.

Only when I finally draw closer does it occur to me why she isn't reacting. I am dressed in a military uniform, not the clothes she is used to seeing me wear. And I have lost a lot of weight. My skin, now much darker from the desert sun, pulls tight against my bones. Then there is the way I move— more slowly, deliberately, without the same energy I once had. My body is tougher now, but it's also ground down by the

116

abuse. I have been chronically weakened by digestive problems. These changes in my appearance and bearing are nothing new to me, but my wife is seeing them all for the first time. In less than half a year, I have become a complete stranger to her.

Dawit is the first to recognize me, or at least to accept that it really is me. I know the exact moment he does. He quickly turns to Wudasie and says something, and a look of complete disbelief creeps into her eyes. She doesn't want the man walking toward her to be her husband. I see Dawit raise his finger to his lips, signaling her not to make a scene. It isn't the time or place for such a display. But his warning can't stop the look of shock and horror from her face. She covers her cheeks with her hands, as if she can push her emotions back inside and hide them. But at least she doesn't run away. She keeps moving forward, and suddenly the space between us evaporates. We are both silently weeping when we embrace.

After a while, when we are able to draw apart again, only then do I see the effects the past several months have had on her. Her exhaustion is far deeper than mine. She is a proud woman, strong, but she can't conceal how much the responsibilities of the shop and two very young daughters have weighed on her. She doesn't speak of these things, or of the stress of trying to find care for Titi's medical issues without me to assist her. They have taken as much of a toll on her as my conscription has taken on me. What I have physically experienced, she has experienced emotionally. In that moment, I remember the weeping mothers and children of the men on the side of the road in Nefasit, knowing their lives are about to get so much harder. I remember the elderly parents who begged for special consideration. I recall how dismissive the soldiers were, how they ignored all of them. And I curse them for their complicity in this crime, even though I know they were helpless to stop it. This war demands so much from us all; it takes without regard to the holes it leaves behind.

The real reunion with my family is a rush of emotions and images: Wudasie returning with the children; our newborn daughter nestled in her arms; three-year-old Titi clinging to her mother's leg beside her, hiding her face, as uncertain about me as I am about myself. It startles me to see how much my little angel has grown in such a short amount of time. I bend down, and she lets me pick her up, but only because her mother encourages her. I squeeze her close to me. She resists at first, before finally relenting. I never want to let her go. I never want to forget how this feels as long as I live.

Because I can't leave the base, we have to find a place where we can talk. Our words tumble out of our mouths, get tangled up in our haste to catch each other up on all that has happened in the last six months. When Wudasie tells me some of the things Titi said during my absence, how she felt like I abandoned them both, it crushes me. I struggle to hold back the tears. I hate how much my absence has hurt them, and I can't help but feel responsible, even though I know it wasn't my fault.

It's a blessing that children can forgive so easily. Soon, Titi is sitting on my lap like old times, refusing to leave me. But it isn't exactly like old times, either. She can't stop staring at my face and hands. She seems profoundly affected by the physical changes in me. She doesn't like the uniform one bit and demands I change back into my old clothes. My fellow soldiers try to reassure her. They buy her treats. But like someone with years more wisdom than she should have, she wants none of it.

When it comes time for them to leave, Titi begs me to come home with her. "We will give you a bath," she assures me, as if she thinks what has happened to me can be washed away as simply as dirt. My heart breaks seeing my precious little girl so worried for her father. It crushes me to have to convince her to go home without me, especially knowing how our last separation affected her. I promise to come home later, as soon as I am able.

I am restricted to the base for the next three days. On each of those days, I request a pass, which would allow me to walk freely about the city. The slip of paper is proof that I have been granted this right, in case I happen to be detained while not in uniform. This is especially important now, as there are random checks all the time, not just near the ends of the training cycles. The government is rounding people up for conscription every day.

My family visits me daily at the base. My parents come to see me, too, as do my siblings. Friends arrive as soon as they hear I'm back. I see the disbelief in their eyes when they look at me for the first time. I can hear the alarm in their voices. I had managed to acquire a small mirror for shaving while in Kiloma, so I know the changes as they have occurred on my face. But tracking such incremental changes each day is not the same as seeing them all at once.

I'm finally granted a pass on the fourth day of my arrival, with permission to spend the weekend with my family. All I want to do is sleep, but Titi is even more adamant this time that I take a shower, so that is what I do. After I'm finished, I step in front of the mirror and see my whole body for the first time in many months. Now I understand the look of shock on everyone else's faces, because it now fills my own. The man standing before me isn't the man who last left this place the previous May. The man in the mirror is an imposter, a frightening skeleton who moves and sounds nothing like the man he replaced.

It terrifies me that my family may never get him back.

In contrast to all I have been made to endure over the previous six months, the next several days are remarkably placid. I quickly slip into a quiet routine. One week soon passes into the next. A month passes. Two.

I'm grateful for being able to see my family on a regular, although fleeting, basis. I want to be more involved in their lives, but my duties prevent me. I take whatever they are willing to give me, but nothing will ever make up for what I have already lost. When Wudasie tells me she had to give up our minimart, it comes as little surprise. I knew instinctively that it would be impossible for her to singlehandedly manage the business, hold a job, and raise two very young children, even though I clung to the hope that she would somehow find a way. I know it isn't her fault we have lost our entire investment. It makes me angry, but I can't forget how blessed I am now to be so close to my family.

And so far from the warfront.

Little by little, my health begins to improve, thanks in part to the food Wudasie makes for me while I am at home, as well as the supplements I can now access. In Kiloma, lentils and flat bread, *kitcha*, was the standard fare. Here, I can go back to my old diet. And I no longer worry about my sugar intake. Also, now that I'm no longer subjected to the constant, grueling assault of the training on my body, it slowly grows stronger. My scars fade, although they don't disappear. But it is the nourishment of my family that has the greatest impact on me. It heals my spirit. I no longer resent my conscription. I forgive the army and the men who captured me. Instead, I wake up each day and remind myself how lucky I am. I think about those who have been taken away to fight, and I pray for their safety and a quick end to this war. My only wish is that we could all go back to the way things were immediately after we won our independence and start all over again on a new path.

The younger and more able-bodied soldiers here at Tseserat are as accommodating as the men I knew during those backbreaking days at the start of my training, when I was forced to pull weeds and cut down trees outside Sawa. Even here, they are willing to take the more physically demanding task of patrolling the camp perimeter, leaving me in charge of manning the guard post at the gate. It's an odd feeling I have as I stand here in my uniform, armed with a Kalashnikov I hope I will never have to fire. I feel like a man only playing at being a soldier and hoping the game will end before it's my turn to roll the dice. My heart and mind are simply not in it. In truth, most of us here feel the same way.

The relatively easy duty at the gate is not entirely risk-free. Violent attacks against the military by dissenters are on the rise all across Eritrea, particularly in Gash Barka, the administrative region stretching from the Sudan border to just south of Asmara. Although we receive daily reminders to be vigilant for threats, we are inadequately trained on how to recognize them. It's always a scary situation, when a car races by near the entrance to the camp, especially at night. It would be easy for someone to ram through the gate or explode a bomb in protest. There have been similar such attacks elsewhere in the world, like the recent US embassy bombings in Kenya and Tanzania. If anything were to happen here, the gate is the most vulnerable target.

Besides guard duty, there is always something for us to do. For example, we're tasked to provide physical and logistical support to the administrative staff. Most of the time, this means moving supplies and equipment, including food and other consumable items, into and between the various storage facilities. In addition to a number of warehouses, Red Sea owns dozens of metal shipping containers scattered about, both inside and around the camp. A handful of them are assigned for military use, one of which is placed conspicuously apart from the others. As I have never seen it open, I'm naturally intrigued by what it might hold.

One night, I raise this very question to my duty partner, Hagos. It's a quiet night, and I'm struggling to keep awake. The question had been on my mind for days, but this is my first opportunity to ask it.

"That one?" he says, turning to glance at the lone container sitting silently beneath its own spotlight. He is several years younger than me, but he has been assigned to this post for three years, so if anyone knows the answer, it will be him.

I wait for him to answer, but he doesn't right away.

Save for the occasional shout drifting over from the base club, which is a popular gathering place for off-duty soldiers, there is little to break the silence of the night.

"That's our prison," he finally says. He raises his eyebrows at me, as if he is surprised I hadn't already known that.

At first I think he's joking. The box has no windows, no ventilation, no electricity or other utilities. It's just a metal box locked from the outside. During the day, the sun beats down on it so that you can't touch the metal without getting burned. Even in the morning, when the air is still chilly and turns your breath into mist, the insides of those containers can quickly become unbearably warm as soon as the sun hits it. I know this from my own experience over the past few weeks moving supplies into and out of them. Just a few minutes inside one, even with the doors propped wide open so the cooler air outside can replace the trapped heat, is enough to soak my shirt through with sweat.

At night, once the sun goes down, the air can chill to near-freezing. The insides of those boxes must get as cold as a freezer. How can any man survive inside?

"Is that the truth?" I ask. Such cruel practices as these were common during the time we were under Ethiopian rule, but surely we wouldn't adopt them for ourselves, would we?

121

Hagos nods. The solemn look in his eyes tells me he is being sincere. "Wait a little while," he tells me. "Watch. You will eventually see for yourself."

A few weeks pass before I do.

I'm off duty and drinking coffee in the club with a couple of soldiers from my unit, when a commotion on the other side of the room catches our attention. Someone is shouting. A bunch of people gather around him and try to calm him down. As we make our way over, I see that the shouter is a member of the National Service assigned to another military division. My friends try to convince him to leave peacefully, explaining that the consequences of getting arrested for being disorderly can be severe. But he's too drunk to reason with, and he refuses to heed their warnings.

One of the female staff members manages to catch the attention of the guard on duty, who arrives with more men hoping to talk some sense into him. Again, the drunken man refuses to listen. Instead, he becomes more belligerent. He starts shouting louder and angrier. But nobody can understand him because his words are too slurred. Nobody knows what made him so upset in the first place. And the harder everyone tries to reason with him, the more belligerent he becomes.

Out of nowhere, a punch is thrown by one of the bystanders. The drunken man's head rocks backward. He stumbles, crashes against a wall, and bounces off. It barely even fazes him. Two more men join in, trying to knock some sense into him. They beg him to leave, but he still refuses. After several more minutes, the guards finally wrestle him into submission. Since he is from another camp, they demand to see his pass, which everyone but the highest ranking soldiers are required to carry. When they see that it has expired, they haul him away.

I watch as they drag him over to the shipping container and lock him up inside. He shouts for a little while, then goes silent, likely passed out from his intoxication. The next morning, when he's allowed out to use the bathroom, his expression is subdued. He apologizes to the National Service member assigned to watch over him, and he seems genuinely repentant, but his punishment is to remain in the box for three full days. I can't imagine how terrible the torture will become, when the sun reaches its peak in the middle of the afternoon.

Out of pity, some of the National Service members assigned to the base sneak him food, drinks, and cigarettes. This is against regulations, but it doesn't stop some from helping. If they are caught by our superior officer, a seasoned, no-nonsense ex-liberation fighter, they risk being put inside the box, too.

By the third day, the soldier is weak and severely dehydrated. This time, when he emerges, his head hangs down low against his chest. He says nothing. All the fight has been drained out of him. I hope he has learned his lesson.

After this incident, I learn that similar containers, both above ground and buried, are frequently used by the military to imprison and punish those who break the rules or who fail to show discipline. Not just here, but all over Eritrea. It leaves me shocked, bewildered, and angry. How could we do this to our own people? It's torture, plain and simple. If the world knew, they would not let it go unchallenged. On the other hand, who is going to tell them, when it is clearly an effective deterrent for misbehavior? The alternative is to be taken to prison and tortured.


There is a corner of our camp where many of the martyrs of this new war are buried. Some died while fighting on the front. Others were wounded and survived long enough to arrive at our hospitals, but were either too badly injured or the care was too inadequate for them to be saved. One of the soldiers' duties at Tseserat is to lay these men to rest, a task that is assigned by the command's representative. It's a heartbreaking job, and for reasons I can only guess at, it seems to fall most often on the same small group of service members. The holes are dug nonstop, often by civilians, in expectation that they will soon be filled. The bodies are brought and laid to rest by ENS members. I'm lucky enough to avoid this chore altogether, but it still affects me deeply, as I know it does us all. Whenever we pass by the spot, it's hard not to stare at the open holes and imagine the men and women whose bodies will fill them, or to ponder the fresh mounds of dirt and wonder if their deaths made any difference.

The men who perform this grisly chore want nothing but privacy after it has been done, or to drink themselves to forgetfulness. The actual burials are done under cover of darkness, when most people in the camp are asleep anyway. The bodies arrive in covered vehicles, usually from Denden Military Hospital out at the former US army base at Kagnew, and are interred without ceremony. We are advised to avoid the burials for reasons of morale, but there's something shameful about the whole arrangement, something deceitful. It's a betrayal of honor. Even the family members have no chance to attend, as so few, if any, are ever notified their loved one has perished.

I mourn for all those who are killed. I mourn that their sacrifices are hidden away, like a shameful secret. I mourn the families, too, who must only guess at what happened when the letters stop coming.

Nearly all of the sixty thousand who died during the first war were buried on the battlefield where they fell, with little ceremony, far from their homes and families. They died never knowing the gift they gave to those they left behind. But *we* know. We listened and mourned as their names were recited to us over the radio. We heard them fall from the lips of friends returning from the front. We didn't hide from their deaths then, so why do we hide now? Is it because we don't know why they died? If we acknowledge their sacrifice, we have to explain what it was they died for, and I'm not sure anyone will be able to do that to our satisfaction, so the solution is to avoid it altogether.

A year after Ethiopia's Mengistu fled, our new government commemorated those sacrifices by marking June 20 as our official Day of Remembrance. Each family who lost a loved one was sent a Martyr's Certificate, which we proudly and prominently display in a place of honor in our homes. That paper is both testimony to, and a constant reminder of, the price our people paid for independence. It is a promise that we will never forget that price.

But less than ten years later, we have already broken that pledge.

This time, our new martyrs fall away from us in silence, like leaves from a tree deep inside an empty forest. They are buried behind a veil of darkness. Some of those killed are *tegadelti*, unable to elude death a second time. Some are the children or siblings of those who passed in the earlier war, bringing new trauma to those families all over again.

Just as the relatives are never notified, we on the base aren't told the names of the buried, either. But their names still find their way to our ears. I hear by word of mouth that some buried here were my fellow trainees in Kiloma, men I knew and grew close to during our time there. I think of the children and wives they left behind. I'm devastated to learn that my friend Mahmood is among them. He had feared so deeply the uncertainty of ever seeing his two children and wife again that he risked his life and freedom by trying to escape his training. He was such a nice person to many of us and a dear friend to me. It was he who taught me so many words in his native language of Tigre. After my daughter's birth, he shared so much in my pride and joy that he began calling me *Abo Natsanet*— father of Natsanet. Father of freedom. The day I learn of his death is *amEl Selam*.

In Tigre, it means it is a sad day indeed.

Late in the spring of 2000, both countries are deep in talks regarding a peace plan that will post UN troops along our border. There have been prior attempts to end the fighting, but this time I am cautiously optimistic that our leaders are serious about a ceasefire. Ethiopia has already agreed to the plan, and everywhere there are rumors of peace. We have been at war for two years, almost to the day. I have been a soldier for half of it, and yet it feels like so much longer.

I'm impatient for an end to my National Service duties, so I pray every day the talks lead to a permanent resolution to the conflict. Just six more months and I will have fulfilled my responsibility under our nation's draft of the Constitution. The timing could not be more significant, as Wudasie has finally found a surgeon willing to fix Titi's heart. She's now almost four years old, and we have been living in the shadow of this terrible diagnosis for far too long. After numerous failed attempts to locate a doctor in neighboring countries, we finally have a chance in the United States. The hospital is even willing to pay for the medical costs. Unfortunately, the war has made it next to impossible for us to act on the offer, since it's very difficult for anyone to leave the country, much less afford it at all, so we pin a lot of hope on our leaders' ability to negotiate peace.

In the midst of this ceasefire, I request leave from my superiors. I reason I can do more good to my family and my country by being at home. But instead of granting my request, they assign me to a new unit on base. It's a disappointment, although if I'm being honest, I hadn't expected to be released anyway. The transfer, however, comes as a surprise.

Wudasie worries my new role could make me more valuable to the ENS, which would make it harder for me to escape the service in the future. I am more sanguine about the move. At least the new job will allow me to finally put my accounting skills to good use.

My new unit is responsible for overseeing the distribution of supplies to the various leisure and recreation clubs on the army base, mainly cigarettes and beverages, but occasionally alcohol, food, and other consumables, such as batteries and writing pads and pens. The facilities range from bars to game rooms to coffee shops. The more established military bases operate such establishments as centers of community for their soldiers, many of whom are originally from far away and so have no family close by. The game rooms include pool and ping pong tables; others offer BINGO. Many are operated exclusively by ENS members, although some employ civilians on occasion, especially the larger ones in big cities.

One club on base has a dozen billiards tables and is a popular hangout for off-duty soldiers. If we aren't playing, we're betting on those who are. Because gambling money is against the rules, the prize is usually just a sandwich or drink instead. This particular club is run by a *tegadalay*. Other ENS members serve as cashiers, storekeepers, and janitors. Civilian girls are hired to prepare drinks and sandwiches and to wait on the customers. While the club is open to all, military and civilians alike, it mainly caters to service members. The walls are bare and the decor is plain, perhaps intentionally to discourage civilians. In any case, it doesn't attract the same rowdy crowds as the bars in town.

It's a relief not to have to pull guard duty anymore. The change in responsibility also means I won't have to carry a Kalashnikov around, as I did while patrolling the base. As a soldier, I am still assigned a weapon, but it now leans against a wall in a corner of my office, like an umbrella waiting for a rainy day I pray never comes.

I also don't miss the physical labor of hauling supplies off trucks into storage containers and back out again. My body still suffers from long term effects of the abuse it received in Kiloma, and at my age I am beginning to realize it may never fully recover. Instead, my new duties include managing the accounting books. Of course, I would much rather my skills be applied to my family's benefit. When I complain to Wudasie about this, she wisely tells me I can't dwell on things that are out of our control. What is done is done. We just have to make the best of it.

On the afternoon of May 29, 2000, I'm standing outside the main club with two of my unit members, when our conversation is interrupted by a thunderous roar overhead. We duck and cover our ears as a pair of MIG jets pass low and fast over the base. Believing they are our own, we share a nervous chuckle and jokingly curse the pilots for alarming us. But our amusement turns to horror when the ground shakes a moment later from several explosions in the direction of the airport. Did one of the jets crash, or are we under attack again? How can it be the latter, when we are so close to a ceasefire?

If it is Ethiopia, then the attack comes in complete disregard of the conventions of warfare, as they must know about the International Red Cross and other humanitarian aid organizations currently assisting the estimated half million Eritreans now displaced by the fighting. But it would not be an isolated event for them. Their Air Force has a history of such reckless and unlawful acts. Just yesterday, for example, their jets bombed and damaged our Hirgigo Power Plant outside of Massawa on the Red Sea coast, raising international outcry. The newly constructed facility is not a target with military significance. It was built to supply electricity to civilian populations in Asmara and other cities. Ethiopia claims the electricity is used by our military.

This is what they do, attack us all, civilian and soldier alike, by claiming they are targeting only our fighters. Last year, they bombed our Harsile reservoir, which supplies the port city of Assab. Tens of thousands of civilians rely on that life-saving water, but Ethiopia argued the attack was meant to disrupt the training being conducted in Kiloma.

But this game of misrepresenting the facts is played by both sides. After the previous bombing of the airport in 1998, our state-run media withheld the truth from us by reporting only that the Ethiopian shells landed on the base with limited effect. Only one building was destroyed, and a small number of people were injured. Two civilians were taken to the hospital with unknown injuries. Later, we learned that the extent of the damage was far greater. An Aero Zambia cargo jet was ruined, and nearly thirty civilians were injured. One person died. In retaliation, our own Air Force struck military targets in Mek'ele, Ethiopia, which our state-run media reported took out five of their jets. What they neglected to say was that a schoolyard was also hit. Ethiopia claimed that forty-four people died and well over a hundred were injured. Eritrea accused them of lying.

As always, the streets of Asmara fill with frightened and angry residents seeking answers and demanding retaliation. Others urge calm. Rumors swirl that people are injured and there are fatalities. My own thoughts go out to my friends and family within the city. I pray that no one, most importantly any noncombatant, has been hurt.

In the aftermath of the attack, the United States recalls its citizens from Eritrea, but Ethiopia sends more of its jets screaming over Asmara as soon as the next morning, hoping this time to completely destroy our Air Force. They fail, yet again, and another bombing run is planned.

This time, the international community demands restraint, and the attack is postponed to allow the last of the fleeing foreign nationals to leave. But I cannot go. I am stuck here in Asmara, and my family remains behind because there's nowhere else for them to go.

After this, fighting intensifies all over Eritrea, resulting in some of the worst casualties we have yet seen in this war. New rumors begin to spread that our forces are becoming so depleted the army is now considering adding *kiflitat*, non-combat ENS members from administrative and finance departments, to the ground units. That would include me.

Whenever fighters visit the base, the *kiflitat* members are the subject of their scorn. We see how they look at us— with envy and resentment. They come in dressed in tattered, filthy, faded uniforms, rifles slung over their shoulders. It's a terrible thing to see, and we sympathize with them. We offer them whatever small comforts we can give — a cigarette or drink, or even just a few words of encouragement and a prayer for their safety — but we know we're only trying to assuage our own guilt. None of us has any desire to take their place.

Each soldier is provided a khaki bed sheet, similar to the ones we were given in training. They offer protection from the chill at night. But they also serve as death shrouds to cover the bodies of the slain. Sometimes, I feel like a hypocrite by offering the soldiers so little, when they sacrifice so much. I paste a smile on my face to mask the dread that fills my soul for their safety. I wear it like a charm to ward away danger to my own.

One day, I find myself at the Alla Military Hospital southeast of Asmara. The entire facility is filled with wounded soldiers, many with thick bandages wrapped around their heads, necks, hands, and feet. How many more bandages are hidden away beneath their uniforms or underneath their bed sheets? Some of the injured are able to walk unassisted, others only with the aid of crutches. How many more will never walk again?

The *agar hakim* tell us that many of those wounded on the battlefield arrive dead, while others die after reaching the hospital. Many of those who survive their injuries and surgeries will forever suffer from some disability. All will be permanently traumatized by the violence of war, even those with relatively minor injuries. Those who can fight are forced to return to their units.

On my way out, I stop to chat with one of the guards. A familiar haunted look fills his eyes, which I mistake for battlefield fatigue. But he tells me he isn't stationed on the frontlines. He only sees the casualties after they are sent here, the victims of our Third Offensive. He mentions their sacrifices, then confides in me how regrettable it all is. "I don't understand at all why we are fighting," he says. "I don't believe the sacrifice is worth it anymore. Every day, the wounded come in. Sometimes, they arrive on military vehicles, but more often I see them coming in on civilian trucks and city buses, too. It is happening everywhere. There are too many, and it isn't slowing down. It's only getting worse." Then he points to a hill nearby and tells me that it has been turned into a burial ground, and I finally realize where I have seen that look in his eyes before. He is one of the soldiers responsible for placing the dead in their graves.

Even though I have been aware of this, seeing it with my own eyes makes a big difference. Now I am able to see the truth about the war. There are more hospitals just like this one in all of the cities spread out across this country. They, too, are filling up. I wonder if the only thing that will stop this fighting is when we run out of people who can hold a gun.

But then, just as the situation seems most dire, a breakthrough is reached in the negotiations. Fighting eases, although it doesn't completely end. That only happens when a new ceasefire agreement is finally reached in early August, a few months later. This time, it seems to hold. As weeks turn to months, we cautiously allow ourselves to hope. It's like the sun coming out after a long spring rain has ended.

And like a flood slowly receding after a terrible storm, the hospitals begin to drain of casualties.

During this time of relative peace, the base restrictions at Tseseret are relaxed. I'm now permitted to spend more nights at home with my family. It's a treat to be able to join them at dinner once more, although there are constant reminders of how much things have changed since I was conscripted. I bring my uniform home to be washed, but Wudasie refuses to let me hang it in our closet with the rest of our wardrobe. More than reminding her of a war we never asked for, the uniform represents the hardships my involuntary service has brought to our family. My black sandals, *shidda*, she won't have in view of company or the children inside the house. I must instead leave them outside, away from the door, as if the very sight of them implicates me directly in the unnecessary deaths of our new martyrs. And instead of discussing our individual day-to-day routines, Wudasie insists we speak only about the future, of the day when we can once again forge our own path. We had plans once to become independently successful; she says it's still not too late to happen.

On one of these visits, I mention that I will have to leave for a few days to take a short course on basic bookkeeping as part of my new duties.

"Why do you need such training?" Wudasie scoffs. "You already know enough about the subject. You should be teaching the course. Did you tell them you already have college education in this area?"

She doesn't understand how the military works, so I try to explain to her that I don't wish to upset my superiors. Duties and rank are not based on educational level and work experience, but rather by seniority and connections. A soldier may possess certain skills or knowledge, but he cannot expect such things to reward him with special treatment or offer any protection from certain unwanted assignments, no matter how illogical they may seem. One must accept orders as a matter of course, without complaint or discussion. Any questioning of rationale is considered an act of disobedience.

"And if I refuse," I explain to her, "the consequences can be severe." Although such consequences wouldn't be as harsh as I have experienced or witnessed in the past — which I have never spoken about to her — I still wish to avoid them. "It's a small sacrifice," I tell her, and add that it's better than risking offending someone, especially if I am to have any hope of an early release. "And it won't hurt me to get a refresher."

I have two instructors, both members of the ENS. Although they seem relaxed and comfortable with each other, I sense they resent having me in their class, undoubtedly because they know I have advanced knowledge in this field. But they have also worked in finance departments in other government-run institutions, so they should know at least as much as I do.

There is one other service member who has similar credentials as mine. Tewelde is ten years my junior and also attended Asmara University. The instructors tell us both that they want us to help out, but after they assign us menial tasks, their intentions become clear. They only want us to stay away from the rest of the students. They fear we will embarrass them. Unfortunately, they can't find enough trivial chores for us to do. We are back after being gone only a few hours.

The course is taught in Tigrinya, but the bookkeeping terms are mainly in English. This makes it difficult for those participants unfamiliar with the language to learn and understand the material. Many of the students lack even a high school education, when they would have been taught English. The instructors are forced to rely on our assistance to help explain in layman's terms what they cannot. This quickly leads to new problems, although not of the type they had expected.

On the second day of the course, I offer to clarify some confusion on the meanings of debit and credit, when a couple officers in attendance warn me to keep my mouth shut. "Stop interrupting, and let the instructors finish their job!"

The outburst confuses me. But then I learn that they were also ordered to attend the class against their wishes. They clearly feel they don't need the training and resent being here. They just want the instruction to end as quickly as possible, ideally ahead of schedule, so they can go do other things. They don't care if they learn nothing. They care even less if anyone else does.

After this, the instructors tell me and Tewelde not to attend. But because we can't return to our units in Asmara, we are reassigned to providing "logistical support," which simply means more menial tasks. The next day, for example, we're told to travel to Adi Keyh to purchase groceries and goats to feed to the students. I think about what my wife would say if she knew how this has turned out for me. I'm sure she would simply shake her head in disgust, but all I can do is shrug it off and be patient.

At last, the ten-day course finally comes to an end, and the instructors have a party to celebrate its successful completion. But I don't feel successful, only relieved. I am no more knowledgeable than I was before.

When I return home this time, I'm surprised to find that Wudasie has had a change of heart and now agrees that it was wise of me to comply without argument, even though I learned nothing. When I press her to explain what changed her mind, she confesses that a friend from college, Tsehaynesh, shared a relevant story with her while I was gone.

Tsehaynesh's husband was conscripted into the National Service while on a visit home from a master's degree program at a university in Europe. Instead of being allowed to finish his studies abroad, he was forced into becoming a guard at a military post. Every other weekend, an acquaintance of his in the ENS would deliver news about his wellbeing to the wife, which is how Wudasie learned of his situation. One day, Tsehaynesh asked the friend, "How are you able to visit so often, when my husband hasn't been allowed to come home even once? What's the difference between you and him?"

The man replied, "I have a higher rank. Low-ranking members don't have such privileges."

"But he has many years of university education!" she countered. This surprised the man, who hadn't been aware of this.

"All this time," he said, "I assumed your husband was just another conscript in the National Service, like everyone else. It's only because he is always so polite and cooperative that I'm happy to bring his messages to you."

"Now that you know," she told the man, "maybe you can help him find a position that is better suited to his training."

"I will see what I can do," the man replied.

But even though he was able to get the man transferred to one of the bases in Asmara, Tsehaynesh's husband was never given any special consideration for his education. He is still a guard checking people's paperwork as they go in and out through the gate. It proved that what I had said before was accurate, that the army doesn't care about my education, so it wouldn't help to raise this point. The best thing for me to do is to make as little trouble as possible.

Since Wudasie was forced to return the shop we leased, she has had to find other work to make up for the lost income. She now has a fulltime position in the government. Although she is paid better than I am, our combined incomes are still not enough to cover the cost of a planned trip to the United States for Titi's heart surgery, so she proposes exploring other income-generating opportunities in the private sector. She is more determined than ever to get our daughter's heart fixed, and she works tirelessly and saves every *nakfa* to help pay for it. Unfortunately, there's nothing I can do to help in that regard, other than to support her as much as I can. It has been six months since the Algiers Peace Agreement was ratified, and so far the president has given no indication he will allow any ENS member to be released.

The first thing Wudasie explores is the business of importing goods for resale, not by us personally, but rather by merchants with established clientele. She has been allowed to travel with a friend and new business partner. On one trip, they go to Dubai, where they procure women's shoes, dresses, and jewelry. They make a separate trip to Sudan, except this time to assess the market there for such goods. On both trips, Wudasie used the opportunity to inquire about heart surgery options, but neither panned out as a more practical option than the one in the US. Still, she remains optimistic, and I can't help but marvel at her dedication. Once, our greatest limitation was ourselves, but now it's our leaders. Their whims change as frequently as the direction of the breeze. Seeing my wife press onward makes me yearn to forge my own path, but I'm trapped by my conscription. Everyone is considered too valuable for the army to let go. This gives us little assurance that the government is fully committed to peace. In fact, we are still constantly accusing Ethiopia of violating some miniscule aspect of the treaty, or they are accusing us. It's as if the two presidents are searching for any excuse to resume attacking each other again.

Wudasie's previous worries seem to have been justified, as there is a growing need for my bookkeeping skills in the government, especially now that the party is taking over more of the commercial operations of our country. This keeps me very busy. One day, I'm unexpectedly transferred to the Finance Office of the Zonal Command. It's a promotion of sorts, although it doesn't come with better pay, only more responsibility. Rank in the National Service — and, by extension, pay — is determined strictly by years in service, rather than one's abilities or job. The pay is a pittance at all levels, not much more than pocket change, which tends to discourage hard work and leads many to shirk their duties as much as they can get away with. But I have always abhorred idleness, and I would rather work harder for little pay than not work at all. I take particular pride in always doing my best. My father taught me that a job done well and thoroughly is its own reward. That being said, I have never heard anyone complaining of being overpaid.

By now, I have achieved the rank of lance corporal, the lowest of the noncommissioned officers. It's lower than the four men I oversee on the team, who are also National Service members, but who trained in earlier cycles. My new supervisor confides in me that he thinks I should be higher up in rank than I am, especially given the work I do. But while he tells me he will try to change this, I know there is little he can — or will — do about it. I have witnessed enough by now to know that that is just not how the government works.

In my new role, I now have access to the accounts for all the income-generating clubs, farms, and shops within the division. I also oversee the *tekoratsi sidrabet*, or money transmittal service, which the government uses to send payments to the families of soldiers and National Service members. Finally, I handle certain special assignments and audits handed down by the head of the Zonal Command Office.

The income-generating entities my team reviews are supervised by the commanders of the divisions, all of whom are former *tegadelti*. They typically look unfavorably upon members of the National Service, but they are particularly dismissive of *kiflitat* conscripts. They also feel my team and our activities are unnecessarily intrusive.

I can understand this feeling of protecting one's own operations, so their treatment of us is not surprising to me. Nor is their resistance, despite the mandate to provide us their full assistance. But sometimes they are overtly hostile toward us, which makes my job all the harder. But I have my orders, and I am nothing if not thorough in carrying them out, even if it means antagonizing someone in a position of considerable authority.

To ease the tension, I try to work with them. I suggest new ways to help make their jobs easier in the future. For example, I will oftentimes show them strategies to make their financial recordkeeping more efficient. But few of my recommendations are ever taken seriously.

The work can be challenging in other ways, often because so much of the accounting methods they applied is a mathematical nightmare. In some cases, I suspect this is entirely intentional. The harder it is to track discrepancies and their causes, the more difficult it is to separate negligence from criminal activity. More importantly, it makes fixing the issues nearly impossible. I try to explain this to my own superior, but my team is offered little guidance. We are expected to stay on schedule. Sometimes, all I can do is submit the results of an audit and wait to see what happens.

In some cases, our conclusions are clear and critical, and people end up receiving discipline. For the worst cases, the punishment can be severe. Some people end up going to jail. While I am sure some of them deserve their fate, I'm equally as certain some aren't guilty of wrongdoing, only of being incompetent. In one instance, for example, we uncover a large cash shortfall that leads to charges of embezzlement. I will never forget the distraught look on the face of the man in charge, when we deliver our findings. Like me, he is a National Service member, and like so many in the ENS, he had been forced to take on a role he was never adequately trained to perform. It's my belief that he is being punished for someone else's negligence, possibly even their misdeeds. I have no doubt the person being protected is a former freedom fighter, but I have no proof of it.

In another case, charges of misconduct have already been filed before I'm asked to investigate. The accused supervisor, a *tegadalay*, is in prison when I conduct my audit. I'm assured my conclusions will be used to determine his sentence. But the other members of his team remain faithful to him and sabotage my work in as many ways as possible. The audit ends up being much more complicated than we expected, requiring me to interview the friends and family of the man suspected of embezzling the money. The investigation drags on for several months. When it's over, I'm relieved to be able to hand in my report. I never hear about his sentence, but I am more confident of his guilt than almost any other case. But not long afterward, I learn he has already been released from prison. I can only assume my report was completely ignored.

Since the cash transmittal unit is not income-generating and cannot be as easily abused, auditing it generates far fewer headaches for my team. As a result, this work is much more pleasant for us, and the cooperation we receive from the units is better. The negative side is that it requires me to travel away from Asmara more frequently than I would like. There are other, unique challenges, as well. For example, on one occasion in the southern part of the country, I'm loudly interrupted by a man demanding his son's monthly National Service stipend be put under his personal control, rather than his son's wife's. Naturally, I tell the agent overseeing cash transmittals within the subzone that this is not possible. Out of curiosity, I ask him why he thinks the father should have this right over his son's wife, and the agent tells me, "Because he thinks his daughter-in-law is cheating on him with another man. He doesn't think it's right that she's able to get her portion of his monthly stipend, only to spend it on her boyfriend."

"And where is this man's son stationed?"

"He is on duty at the border with Ethiopia."

"And what proof does he have of infidelity?"

"Only that the daughter-in-law is well dressed and being with the wrong crowd."

I try not to express my impatience. I want to explain that this man's suspicions prove nothing, but the subzone commander tells me the man's situation is not all that unusual. "Many parents in this part of the country are very much involved in the lives of their children, especially now that so many were taken from their homes at an early age. And I don't mean just the finances, either. Prearranged marriages are common. Later, if problems arise because the son is in the military, the parents take charge of the divorce process."

"But this is none of our concern."

"Yet issues like this demand the majority of my attention. You have to understand how different things are here. Traditions are different. It is hard for a father to see his daughter-in-law out in public, while his son fights far away, risking his life. It doesn't matter the reason why she is out in public. Maybe she is dressed nicely and looking beautiful for some other purpose. But these men think that their sons' wives should stay home under close supervision and not dress up, except in plain clothes. If they look pretty and walk around, then they must be trying to attract men."

"But that is only their opinion," I say. "And it's still not our concern."

"I am sure some of these women deserve such judgment; others don't. But innocent or guilty, their in-laws are going to decide for themselves what is the truth. The older generation thinks differently than these younger people. Do you wish to fight a whole way of thinking?"

I don't answer.

The subzone commander shrugs. "Ultimately, the outcome is always the same. When the accusation spreads, the woman is mistreated afterward, so it becomes a bigger issue than it started out as."

"So, your solution is to break the rules?"

"No, I am saying that it's sometimes best to listen and patiently explain the social consequences to the parents so they don't interfere, rather than just telling them the government rules."

"And does it help?"

He shrugs.

I try to imagine my own parents thinking this way, and I remember how my own mother used to try and decide things for me, as if I were still a child. Parents can't help being overly protective of their own, sometimes to a fault. The war hasn't changed this about us. The government won't either.

Despite the problems I encounter in my new position, it turns out that my greatest challenge is boredom. With few exceptions, my unit's investigative activities require only a fraction of my work hours, leaving me with little to do with the rest of my time, which is especially hard when I am traveling elsewhere in the country. I don't enjoy being unproductive, especially when I think about how I can't be using the time to help my family.

My situation is far from unusual. With the pause in active hostilities, many of the National Service members find themselves idle. We would all rather be home, but we can't leave, so we end up spending much of our downtime at the club or sitting in the barracks watching television. At this time, Eritrea has only one TV station, and being state-run we have limited viewing options and restricted access to information. The shows are mainly local and generally focus on the war, which everyone is fed up hearing about. We are constantly barraged by nationalistic songs and interviews, unnecessary reminders of what we supposedly fought for and what we stand to lose. The similarity of it with the propaganda Ethiopia forced on us years before makes many of us uneasy. Our leaders tell us the reason we must remain vigilant and ready to fight at any moment is because "those crazy Ethiopians might decide to attack us again."

On the rare occasion that the television fare is not war-related or nationalistic, it is usually highlights from the British Premier League soccer. And once in a great while, we are treated to a full game. It sometimes feels like this simple pastime is the only thing our leaders don't feel threatened by.

I try to read as much as possible, but new and interesting materials are hard to find. It has been two full years since all of the privately-owned newspapers were closed down. The owners were either run out of the country or taken to prison. Imported magazines and books are very rare. They are confiscated at the airport and removed from our mail.

By now, Wudasie and her friend have leased a small dress shop where they can sell the imported goods they procure from outside of the country. But it is far from easy for her, given that this is a second job. And each day, it seems the government finds new ways to make it harder for us. But she never stops, never rests. When she isn't working at either job, or managing the household and family, she continues to look into treatment options for Titi's heart, as the government still won't grant them permission to travel to America for the surgery. Thankfully, the sponsor there has been patient while we work it out here.

Wudasie's mother helps out as much as she can. She divorced her husband years ago, so she lives alone and welcomes the opportunity to see the grandchildren. My parents are getting old and frail. I visit them every weekend and try to get over to their house at least once during the week. This makes them both happy, especially my dad, who is now bedridden from a stroke. He cherishes our talks and presses me for news about everything that is happening. Between my visits and those by my brother Yebio, my mother has time to check in on other relatives and friends who are unable to come to her. She has a list of people who have lost loved ones during the conflict to whom she delivers condolences on behalf of our family.

My eldest sister, Saba, comes for a visit from her new home in northern Europe. She has always been very close with our youngest sibling, Ellen, who is stationed in the highlands some sixty kilometers from Asmara. Ellen manages somehow to convince the battalion commander to grant her a three-week leave to visit. But all too soon, the family reunion is over before it even seems to begin, and both sisters are saying their goodbyes. They are in tears, which result from the uncertainty hanging over us all. They don't know when — or if — they will ever see each other again. I try to reassure them, but the same fear has been infecting my own thoughts of late. How much more uncertainty can we endure?

There is an Amharic saying that seems especially relevant now. It refers to difficult times, such as the one our country is going through at the moment. It describes one's life under troubled times, when you are "growing downward like a carrot." For a country that so recently won its independence, we should instead be growing upward into the light.

This is truly how I feel about our situation. After so many years of false starts and setbacks, since long before I was captured on the road to Massawa, we still have nothing to show for ourselves as a people. All we have managed to do is grow even deeper into the darkness below.

One morning in March of 2003, the telephone in my office rings. It's Wudasie.

"Have you read today's newspaper?" She directs me to an advertisement posted for an open job.

"What about it?"

"It fits perfectly with all your qualifications."

I still don't understand why she's calling. She knows I can't switch jobs. I'm still conscripted in the ENS — nearing the end of my fourth year, in fact — and there's no indication the government has any plans to release anyone anytime soon. But when I remind her of this, she urges me to apply for it anyway.

"How on earth do you think I have any chance of getting it?"

"I think you should just start the process, and if they offer you the position, then you can ask for a transfer. Who knows what will happen."

"I know what will happen," I tell her. "They will think I'm out of my mind, something I am beginning to wonder about you."

She laughs at my joke.

"Wudasie, the hiring office is a government entity, so the moment they find out I am in the National Service — and they will find out — they will automatically disqualify my application. I cannot hide that fact. And unless I can provide paperwork showing I have been released from service, there's no possible way they will consider me."

"I'm not asking you to hide anything. In fact, I'm saying you should tell them everything right from the start. Ask them to take you on as a National Service member. It's a win-win situation. They get a highly qualified person without the burden of having to pay you a big salary or provide other benefits, and you will be much happier by working a more challenging job in better surroundings. How can they refuse?"

"I'm not sure it's possible," I tell her.

"If it works, you will be able to wear civilian clothes again," she goes on. "And you will get to work with people who actually enjoy the job they're doing."

"I wish it could be like you say," I counter, "but you know the chances of this happening are zero. No company, even one owned by the party, will want to take the risk of hiring a National Service member like that. There would be no incentive for me to be loyal to them. And the government could pull me out at any time."

"But you are loyal! You are a hard worker with very good skills. And—"

"They don't know that, nor do they care. And besides, how can I ask my superiors for special treatment? This would be completely out of the norm."

We go back and forth like this for a while, but she is like a train engine running downhill without brakes. She is unstoppable, and it's foolish of me to try. Before we hang up, she asks me to just think it over. I promise her I will, because I know she won't let it drop. I expect it will be the subject of conversation as soon as I get home.

I can't help but wonder where she came up with such a crazy idea. Or why she's so adamant about pushing me to do it. I have never heard of such an arrangement before. I know that some people are able to get better assignments because of their connections, but I have never played that game, and I feel too old to start now.

As expected, Wudasie won't let me rest until I finally agree to try it her way. If the process goes nowhere, then nothing is lost. But before I submit my application, she suggests I visit the hiring office first and meet with the manager. At least then I will get a better idea whether her plan is even possible. She also solicits the help of her uncle, Habtom, who isn't just well-connected, but knowledgeable in ways to work a system that doesn't always strictly follow the rules. He was one of the *hafash widib*, the secretive network of civilians who aided the freedom fighters, so he is well known and regarded by many of the *tegadelti*. Working from inside the Ethiopian government, he was able to recruit sympathizers to the resistance movement. In fact, he was caught by the Derg and sentenced to prison for ten years, where he was regularly tortured. After his release, he returned to Asmara, where he resumed his campaign to assist the fight against Ethiopia until we finally won. It is he who finds out who is in charge at the hiring office, and he who takes the lead when we go to pay the man a visit.

Habtom greets the manager by warmly clasping the stranger's arms in his hands as if they are long lost friends. They chat at length, ignoring me. I start to get the feeling that I'm wasting my time, when Habtom skillfully shifts the conversation. He introduces me and mentions the reason for our visit. The hiring manager listens patiently. When the pitch has been made, he doesn't dismiss the idea outright.

"I will be honest," he says, "I am intrigued, although I have never heard of such an arrangement before. I wouldn't even know how to make it work. Are there even procedures for such a situation?"

One thing he doesn't do is discourage me from competing for the job. In fact, he welcomes the opportunity to review my qualifications. And if I happen to be the top choice, then he promises to try and figure out how to make it happen. He emphasizes that it will still depend on me getting the proper paperwork for such a transfer from the Ministry of Defense.

I submit my application, just beating the deadline. Then I wait.

It has been years since I last interviewed for a job. It isn't lost on me that the last one put me on the road to Massawa and got me conscripted. To prepare myself, I brush up on my accounting knowledge. I ask a friend who works for another ministry office to advise me. He has hiring experience and is familiar with such procedures. He coaches me through answering the most common interview questions. I'm finally asked to come in. I can't remember the last time I was so anxious. I take it as a sign that I really want this to work. At the same time, I keep thinking that it is all for nothing. There is no possible way the ENS will allow it. But a week later, I'm shocked to receive a notice that the job is mine.

That is, assuming I can get the release from my superiors.

My commander informs me that to get a transfer from an active duty role to this kind of assignment I will need authorization from none other than the Office of the President, and to secure that I will have to follow the proper chain-of-command. My heart sinks, as I know what this means. It's basically a coded message telling me not to bother. The leaders of our country will not be distracted by such a small concern.

I make the mistake of telling Wudasie, who refuses to let it rest. She pushes me to keep trying. I don't yet understand that she has her own reasons for doing this, and that they have to do with getting me free of my conscription. Reluctantly, I submit the requests and somehow manage to secure an appointment with the Office of the President.

"Do you have proof of your acceptance from the department willing to hire you?" they ask, when I show up.

"I do," I say, and produce the document.

I'm stunned when they provide the letter of transfer, no questions asked. Next, I'm instructed to present it to the Office of the Zone Command— my supervisor's boss. It all seems too easy, and I begin to think I have been foolish for questioning every step of the process.

But then I'm proven right to be skeptical. The Office of the Zone Command tells me I have to take my case up with the Office of the Ministry of Defense. They are the ones who make the final decision.

And sure enough, that's where the process stalls. A month passes. I make frequent visits to the Ministry of Defense to see if there is a problem. The answer they give me is always the same: "Not yet. Be patient. Come back next week." I start to think they are never going to push this through. They never had any intention of it.

Once more, Habtom comes to the rescue. Together, we find a senior official in the Ministry of Defense who also happens to be a close friend of my wife from years back. He promises to look into the matter and help move the paperwork forward. When I thank him, he dismisses it as unnecessary. "You are Wudasie's husband, which means you are family."

Then I wait.

Just as it seems like I'm doomed to failure, I finally receive my permission to transfer. Now, all I have left to do is get the Chief Administrator of the Zonal Command to sign off on it. Since the order comes from the highest levels of the chain-of-command, this last step should truly be nothing more than a formality. Nevertheless, the Chief Administrator, a former *tegadalay* now in his fifties, stalls. Each time I ask about it, he makes excuses. Finally, he admits that he can't afford to lose me. We have always had a courteous working relationship, and I have considered us to be, if not exactly friends, then something between that and professionals who respect each other. But after giving him my dedication and trust for more than two years, he suddenly treats me no better than a stranger. If this is how he rewards me for my hard work, how can I not feel bitter?

It isn't in my personality to stir things up. If there is one thing I have learned about myself in the years since I once brashly considered joining the resistance as a teenager, it is that I don't like confrontation. But this time I can't just sit back and let someone take advantage of me. I realize that if I don't act now, I will be stuck in this role forever. So I continue to pester the Chief Administrator until he finally relents and signs my transfer papers.

It is the strangest of feelings, being able to leave the camp for what will hopefully be my very last time, to walk away from the regimented routine of the military. Of course, I am technically not free of it entirely. I could still be pulled back at any time. And my new job is awarded to me strictly on a contingency basis. Should our conflict resume, I would have to return to the ENS immediately.

Nevertheless, it is a moment of personal validation— for me, yes, but especially for my wife, whose strength and determination made this all happen. Without her, I would never have even considered the possibility. Without her, I never would have tried. It's not the first time I relied on her support, and it certainly won't be the last. In fact, as time will tell, we will need every last bit of her strength and determination to see us through some of the most difficult and heartbreaking times of our lives.

# PART THREE

Falling Apart

Eritrea, 2003 - 2007

# Asmara

DECEMBER IS ALWAYS A FESTIVE MONTH in the capital, even during times of conflict, as long as we aren't under attack. Christmas is one of our most revered holidays, so the weeks leading up to it are always filled with as much joy as we can manage. But this year in our house, the mood is driven by a new development in my daughter's medical case. My little angel, now a little girl of seven years, has finally been cleared by the government for travel to the United States. Not only will she be undergoing heart surgery during the holidays, but our family will be separated. Only her mother is allowed to accompany her. It crushes me, both because I won't be there to help ease their worries or see them through the recovery, but also because Natsanet is still too young to fully understand why her mother and sister will soon be leaving us.

For the past several weeks, our attention has been focused on securing the proper visas, one to exit our country, another to enter into the United States. Initially, our own government wouldn't allow anyone else to accompany Titi, suspicious that once out of Eritrea, they would never return. One would think that no human being could be so heartless as to use a child as leverage to secure a parent's loyalty to their homeland, but that is the kind of thinking our leaders have adopted. Even the Americans are guilty of it, denying Natsanet's entry visa for exactly the same reason, that with both of her children with her, my wife would never return. It was only with persistence, wile, and connections that Wudasie was finally able to win permission for herself. At times, she was even forced to employ the system's own illegitimate practices against itself in order to achieve our own personal goals. But the bribes have depleted our meager savings, much to my dismay. We are learning that there is always a steep price to be paid.

It's a constant wonder to me how my wife manages to keep moving forward in the face of such obstacles. Every time she reaches one wall, she finds a way to go over it, usually to be met by yet another, and another. But now there are no more walls before her. Not yet, anyway, and we hope it stays that way. We rush forward with the preparations fearing the situation could change without warning. We must get Titi and her mother on their way before another wall goes up.

I have tried to be of help during this period, but my new job has had its own challenges. It keeps me much busier than I have been in recent years. Although we expected this, and so cannot complain, the pay is no different than before, a pitiful stipend that can't cover our expenses. And since Wudasie will have to take leave from her government job while they are gone, I will be the sole wage earner and the sole parent to Natsanet. For this reason, we hope the surgery and recovery take no more than a few weeks.

Natsanet is now four years old. She suffers from her own medical issues, although they are much less serious than her sister's. Some unknown ailment has afflicted her, destroying her already small appetite. She has always been a fussy eater, but the more she grows, the more malnourished she appears. Other than that, she is healthy, thank the Lord. It is a lot of responsibility for me to bear alone, even if only temporarily, but my wife's example gives me the strength to take it on.

All too soon, the eve of their departure arrives, and we pack for what promises to be an eventful and difficult experience for us all. The surgery itself is scheduled very soon after they arrive, but then there will be weeks of recovery to follow, even if all goes as well as we hope it does. God only knows how long this will take, or when Titi will be strong enough to return home again. Secretly, I worry they will decide not to. The seed of doubt had been planted in my head by our own government's paranoia.

My wife says I am being foolish entertaining such thoughts. But I know I'm not the only one. Her own mother expressed to me the same worry. But Wudasie says there is no question in her mind that they will come back. After all, this is where our home and families are. She has always told me there is nothing more important than these two things, and I know this to be true. Everything she has ever done has been for the benefit of the family.

Also, we have always been fiercely proud of our homeland, and we always will be. Nothing can ever take away the pride we felt when we won our freedom a decade ago, and that pride still dwells within us. Not even an unnecessary war or an increasingly repressive government can diminish it. But if one follows the trajectory of our country over the past decade, it becomes easy to see how much worse things could get if nothing changes. We hear more stories of people sneaking out of the country across the border to escape the conditions here. We are becoming once more like the Land Rover, as my Ethiopian colleague Meseret once observed, back when it was Ethiopia driving us away. We are once more a people fleeing to all corners of the world, except this time it is to escape our own government. In response, the government cracks down harder on us all by tightening the borders and restricting legal travel. There was a time when people left the country simply to avoid the violence. Now, they risk violence and death just so they won't have to spend their lives in unending conscription, stripped of the freedoms we thought we had earned.

But I am not ready to give up hoping for better days. I still believe we can turn ourselves around. Some might think I am a fool for thinking this way. I am Eritrean. If that means I'm a fool, then so be it.

One thing I am not blind to, however, is the knowledge that someone might still try to stop Wudasie and Titi from leaving. So, on the day of their departure we sneak away without any fanfare. I have never seen my wife so anxious before. Some of it is worry over Titi's impending surgery. She's also upset about leaving Natsanet behind, still asleep in her bed with her grandmother watching over her, and her regret that she could not tell her. We were afraid our little girl might tell someone else by accident. This is how distrustful we have become. It will be up to me to break the news to her after she wakes.

I'm filled with so many emotions — anticipation, hope, worry, sadness — that I am numb as we get in the car for the ride to Asmara International Airport. Wudasie frets the entire way there, certain something will go wrong. She encountered such incredible resistance over the past several months by people she thought she could trust, so now she finds it hard to trust anyone. As hard as it is to believe, some people are so heartless that they would try to stop us, whether out of jealousy or spite. And the way things work now, some people have the authority to act on their whims. This is why we leave in secret. And why only a handful of family members even know about this trip.

All too soon, we arrive at the airport. The terminal building is busier than one might expect for its small size and the amount of travel the airport sees. But because the main gate is close to the bus station, there is a lot of foot traffic in the area. Scattered among the crowds are people saying goodbye to loved ones. I wonder what trips they are taking, to which unknown destinations and for what unknown reasons. Considering our country's political situation, it isn't hard to believe that some of them are leaving their homes for good. What I witness could conceivably be their final goodbyes.

Since I can't pass through security, we hug each other tight and say our goodbyes outside. I try not to let my emotions show. The men in my culture, particularly those in the army, are supposed to exhibit only strength. We aren't supposed to express our fears or show despair. We don't break down in tears. I'm determined not to cry, not simply because of this, but also for Titi's sake. I can't let her think this is anything but good for us all. She is excited about the prospect of the trip, at least until she realizes I won't be going. Then she starts to cry.

Wudasie hurriedly pulls her away. I wait until they disappear from view before turning around and heading back to the car. Once more, I'm filled with numbness. I barely notice the crowds. I barely notice the traffic or pedestrians on the road. I just let my brother-in-law drive me home. In my mind I keep hearing the questions Natsanet will undoubtedly ask after she wakes and finds her sister and mother gone: *How could they leave without saying goodbye? How long will they be gone? Why couldn't I go with them?* She doesn't know about her big sister's heart problem. I will simply have to tell her that she has gone to see a doctor far away and will come back after they have finished taking care of her. I hope it will be enough for her. I won't tell her that we did try to send her, too, but she wasn't allowed. She wouldn't understand why.

Most of all, I hope she doesn't raise the possibility that they won't come back. I'm not sure I would be able to mask the truth from my face that this is my fear as well.

It's disconcerting to realize how easily we settle into our new routine after such a big change. The chores of daily life quickly fill in the holes created by Wudasie's and Titi's departure— not entirely, as nothing could, save for their return, but enough so that I dare to believe it will all be over before long. As they say, life moves on. By necessity, so must I.

Wudasie's mother is a big help, and despite living alone and having to deal with her own health issues, she helps more than I could ever ask her to do. I am deeply grateful for all she does, just as I am thankful at how much Natsanet looks to her as a surrogate mom. She picks her up after school every day and cares for her in the afternoons. I try to stop by as much as I can in the evenings, but it isn't always possible. I'm sometimes only able to take her home on the weekends. After so many years depending on Wudasie to take care of so much, I realize how much of my daughter's upbringing I have missed. And how much I am still being denied because of my duty to the National Service.

I leave at dawn for work each day, so most mornings I'm often already gone long before Natsanet wakes. I hate that I can't be with her to be sure she eats her breakfast. I try to return during lunch, but sometimes I can't. When I do, the time we spend together is usually filled with her chatter. Before, she would talk about her toys or the friends she likes to play with. Now, the subject is always about her sister and mother.

On the day before the surgery, out of the blue, Natsanet asks, "What time is it in America?"

"Nighttime," I reply.

"That means Mom and Titi are asleep then."

"Yes. But after they wake up, they will go to the hospital to make your sister better. That's a good thing, isn't it?"

"Uh huh." I can't tell if she is agreeing with me or just acknowledging that she heard. I'm not even sure she fully understands.

"How long will it take?"

"The surgery? Not long, I think. A few hours, maybe." I don't want to think too much about it, or the recovery time, which I fear could take longer than a few weeks.

"And they will come home after that?"

We have been through all this before. Both her grandmother and I have tried to explain why Titi had to go so far away, and why she has to stay afterward. Yet Natsanet continues to ask, as if testing us, seeing if our answers change.

"There are better doctors in America than here," I say. "We want your sister to have the best care she can get."

It's a hard thing to explain to someone so young and who doesn't have anything to compare it with except for her own limited experiences. For her, far away is a two-hour drive. And a visit to the doctor is usually a rather brief affair. The only exceptions to this that she has personally experienced regard my father's stays at Halibet Hospital in town, some of which have lasted a few nights.

The next day, Wudasie calls to tell us what we have all been anxious to hear. "The good news is, the surgery to fix one of the holes went smoothly. Titi is awake and in good spirits."

"*One* of the holes?"

"The doctor found two. They fixed one, but there's too much of a risk trying to fix the other. It's small, and he thinks it could heal on its own. He says she will be as good as new very soon. In fact, the hospital is discharging her tomorrow."

"Already?" I ask, surprised. "You are coming home already?"

"She needs a couple of weeks to fully recover."

*A few weeks*, I think, still trying to understand what that means in light of the news about the second hole. Waiting a few weeks isn't as good as coming home right away, but the last thing I want is for them to return before all of the medical issues are resolved, since we won't have another chance like this. I want my daughter to be completely healed, so she can have the best possible future.

"Don't worry," Wudasie tells me. "The time will pass quickly."

I tell myself I can manage a few weeks. I have no doubt my wife can, too. After all she has been through to get to this point, she could practically survive anything.

It took her nearly six years of hard work, of unwavering focus and a steady determination as she searched every possible option. She had to fight a system that seemed more concerned with arcane policies and isolation than with the wellbeing of children. Half of that time was while the country was at war and I was away in the National Service, but the other half has not been any easier. Even after I returned to Asmara, I couldn't help out as much as I would have liked. On the few occasions I was able to join her as she pleaded Titi's case to any medical professional willing to listen, I came to appreciate how lucky I and my children are to have such a strong woman on our side.

We learned that our daughter isn't the only child with severe medical problems in need of surgery, nor is she the only child in our country with such a serious heart defect. There are far too many of these children here, and far too few of them have an advocate like my wife. I would be lying if I said I don't put the blame for much of this tragedy on the government. They have done little to help its own citizens. In fact, they have only made things more difficult by dictating to our doctors how and when they can perform their duties and by discouraging outside agencies from offering assistance. It has been a great frustration for all but the privileged few.

I once commented to a doctor friend about his graying hair, to which he replied that it was "better white than green." He was referring obliquely to the government's practice of conscripting doctors, then dictating their practices. This was especially true when we were actively fighting, although it continues to be a problem today. Very few people are able to practice their trade without the government interfering.

On Christmas Day, Wudasie's sister, Akberet, and I take Natsanet out to lunch at her favorite restaurant. Naturally, there are all kinds of goodies to eat at home, but I have been worried about my daughter's mood. She has been so unhappy lately that I hope the change in scenery distracts her from the fact that we will be spending the holidays without Mom and Titi.

The subject is always on my mind, too, but I'm hoping a busy restaurant, colorful decorations, and the happy shouts of children dressed in their best outfits will help us forget about it for a little while.

At first, the crowds only seem to further discourage Natsanet. Luckily, a table quickly frees up for us, and her mood begins to lift. Like a flower opening up in sunlight, her face brightens. She starts to smile, then laugh. It fills my heart with joy to see her this way, and I silently pray that her good mood persists beyond today.

The outing continues at her aunt's home, where Akberet treats her to her favorite dishes. Then she gets her hair and nails done up. She's only four, but she has seen Wudasie and Titi receive similar such treatments, and they make her feel like a big girl. Later in the evening, we all go downtown to see the Christmas decorations.

New Year's Eve offers another easy opportunity to distract Natsanet from her feelings of abandonment. We walk downtown and head over to the Cinema Impero, where we happen to run into some of my friends. Natsanet has met them before, and immediately her mood lightens, because she knows she is in for more treats. My friends are familiar with our situation at home, even if they don't know all the details, so they can't resist spoiling her. Before long, Natsanet is sipping cappuccino and digging into a large slice of cake. Someone has promised her gelato, too, which she won't let them forget. My friends ask if we will be staying for the fireworks at midnight. I'm not so sure Natsanet will be able to stay awake until then, but she begs. The fireworks always draw thousands of people. In years past, Wudasie and I would bring the children to watch them, if we could. For a moment, the memory saddens me. I tell Natsanet we will see how we feel later.

We spend much of the afternoon strolling along the city's main avenues and admiring the holiday decorations, most of which are sponsored by the Asmara Municipality and individual business owners. Christmas songs play from speakers, and bells ring from the tower of the Church of Our Lady of the Rosary. Harinet Avenue — also known as Liberty Avenue — is especially delightful during this time of the year. Towering palm trees line both sides of the road, and brightly colored lights, happy sounds, and delicious smells bombard us from every direction. Some of the same shops I remember from my teen years are still here, while others have changed. We pass City Hall, and the Bar Impero, the cathedral, and the Ministry of Education, and we keep on walking until we reach the FIAT Tagliero. We Asmarinos forget how special these buildings are, how beautiful their Italian architecture. It isn't until we can see them with fresh eyes, or hear about them through a visitor's account, that we remember how wonderful this place truly is.

As we walk along, Natsanet suddenly pulls herself tight against my side, and it takes me a moment to realize why. Passing among the decorations is yet another reminder of these troubled times: soldiers. They aren't doing anything particularly scary, just walking along and enjoying the same sights and sounds that we are, but their presence has always upset Natsanet. Seeing them makes it hard for me to maintain my happy mood, too.

In our culture, at least since the time of the European occupation, men have traditionally been the wage earners, while women have tended to the household responsibilities. This has been changing for a while, most certainly helped along by the War for Independence, when women volunteered to fight alongside men. My wife has always been one of the most progressive women I know, so I have come a long way since my bachelor days in western Ethiopia, when I didn't even know how to cook an egg for myself. Now that she isn't here, I am even more thankful for having learned these domestic skills. And all the more appreciative of everything she has done for the family over the years. These days, my weekends are filled preparing meals for the rest of the week.

On one particular Saturday afternoon in mid-January, I'm cooking one of Natsanet's preferred dishes: battered and fried fish. We typically go to the fish market at the *Mercato* in the morning and I let her choose which one she wants. Then, after cleaning it at home, she likes to help me prepare and cook it. I guess I have come a long way since my bachelor days in Jimma, because she says it is her favorite of all. It's one of the few dishes she will actually eat without making a fuss.

We will soon be joined by a young friend of hers, a neighbor from next door. Like her, young Hanibal has a poor appetite and is just as particular as she is about what he eats. But when they eat together, they are both less picky. Because of this, Hanibal's mother, Azmera, and I have arranged to alternate hosting their meals on the weekends. It's my turn this week, and I'm still in the kitchen when they arrive. The moment Hanibal runs in, Natsanet's mood improves, and she treats me to the first real smile of the day.

I can hear them jabbering away on the veranda, and I step over to the door for a moment to observe. Between mouthfuls, they joke and laugh, and the sound warms my heart. I wish my little girl would laugh like that all the time, but she's too easily overcome by sadness these days.

After they finish their lunches, while I pick up the dishes, Azmera positions herself behind Natsanet to braid her hair. It's something I have tried to do myself and failed miserably at. I just don't have the touch. Azmera only has a son, whose hair is cut short by a barber, so she takes every opportunity to fuss over Natsanet like the daughter she never had. This time, however, as soon as she touches her long hair, Natsanet pulls away and complains. I know it's because she misses her mother's touch, and she resents anyone else taking her place. She snaps at Azmera to be careful.

"Of course, my dear," Azmera says, pretending Natsanet's words don't sting. She talks softly to the children to distract them. At last, Natsanet allows the braiding to begin. Then, partway through, for no apparent reason, she bursts into tears. I step over to comfort her, but Azmera waves a hand. Once more, she calms Natsanet down. When she finishes, I quietly thank her for her patience and help. I try to explain that Natsanet deeply misses her mother's attention, but Azmera shushes me. She already knows this, and even if Natsanet resents her for trying to fill in for her mother, she still needs a mother's touch, even if Azmera isn't the one she wants.

It is yet another reminder of how important it is to have our family together again, and I'm eager for the next few weeks to be over so we can all be reunited.

Later, after Azmera and Hanibal have gone home and I'm cleaning the kitchen, I notice that Natsanet is not with me. She doesn't answer when I call her name. I find her on her bed weeping. All I can do is try to comfort her with my presence. She doesn't acknowledge my touch, only calls out for her mother. I wish I could take her pain away. After a while, she quiets. I lift her up and hug her close. I tell her that things will be all right. I insist that we will only have to wait a few more weeks. Then we talk about everything we'll be doing over the coming days. "Tomorrow is Sunday," I remind her. "That's our downtown day. It will be fun."

She smiles through her tears, and tells me she's okay. Sometimes, all it takes is a good cry to flush away her sadness and reset her mood.

So, with another crisis averted, I return to my chores. I have so much yet to do before going back to work on Monday, and the weekend is passing swiftly by. Once, weekends were for rest, but now they are just as busy for me as the weekdays. First, there's the laundry to do. We're lucky enough to have a small, portable machine, a combination washer and dryer in one unit. I gather the dirty wash and take it out to the courtyard and begin a load. Natsanet joins me, along with three of her young friends. I spray water on the colorful tiles, and they play in the puddles, laughing and chattering. When the wash is done and ready to rinse, I use the soapy water to scrub down the floors in the corridor and courtyard. The children help me mop and rinse. Afterward, Natsanet brings out some of her toys for everyone to play with.

Satisfied that I can leave her alone, I tackle the bathroom. I'm midway through cleaning it when the children's laughter drifting in from the courtyard turns into shouts of anger. By the time I get there, Natsanet is crying again, and one of the girls has disappeared. The other two rush to explain that there was an argument over one of the toys. The missing girl, Luna, kicked Natsanet in anger, then ran home. Because of my daughter's poor eating habits, she's smaller than the other children, which they sometimes use to their own advantage. I have to stop myself from pointing this out to her each time I try to get her to eat more. I know it isn't her fault. Luna is a couple years older and should know better.

I spend the next half hour holding her and rubbing her back before she's calm again. I remind myself that her mother and sister will be home in just a few weeks and everything will be better then. But for now, this is our new normal, bouncing between highs and lows, averting crises as best as I can.

Wudasie calls to tell me that they're going to need to stay longer than expected. I immediately think something has gone wrong and that Titi's health is at risk. Did something happen with the unrepaired hole? "There have been no setbacks," she assures me. "The doctor just wants to be sure Titi gets the necessary follow-up, and he doesn't think she will have them at home. Leaving the US now is not what's best for her."

It seems the surgery is only the first step to making sure my daughter gets better. Even if there weren't a second hole to think about, there are more treatments needed to make sure the repair heals properly. We all want Titi's heart to grow stronger. Thankfully, the medical visa is good for six months, although I pray we won't need the whole time. What I don't expect is when the doctor says Titi will almost certainly need regular checkups for much longer than that, possibly even for the rest of her life.

I don't dare ask what this means. I'm not sure I want to know. But for the first time since they climbed aboard the airplane and left us, that irrational fear that they aren't coming home doesn't seem quite so irrational anymore. Especially when Wudasie tells me she has decided to enroll Titi in school.

Over the next few weeks I listen carefully to what she says — and how she says it — to try and guess what she might be thinking. I don't want to ask the question outright, both because I'd rather she not think about it, but also because I can't be sure someone else isn't listening in on our conversation.

We have never talked about emigrating to anywhere else, and I know she has never given it any serious thought in the past. I certainly haven't. Not even when my friends Gebru and Weldu asked me to go with them to Kenya all those years ago in Addis Ababa before the War for Independence officially ended. Or when Mahmood told me of his own attempt to flee his training at Sawa in hopes of seeking a better life for himself and his family. Or when other people I know decided to leave. We both know what other countries have to offer — we have both traveled internationally for business — but we are Eritrean. This is our home, and nothing will ever make me feel any differently about that. The whole idea of leaving here feels like a betrayal of strongly held beliefs. Oddly, I never once felt this way about those I know who chose to leave— my childhood friends, my sister now in Europe, or Wudasie's sister in the US. I have always felt that it is a personal decision to make. For me, there was never any question of staying.

But now I sense my wife beginning to question it. And I know that once she gets the idea in her head, then I have to be prepared to consider it, even if that idea is that living in America might be what's best for our children. I know that she will continue to mull over the possibility, study it from every angle, then make a decision. And if she decides yes, then she will spend a long time figuring out how to go about doing it, and whether or not it is even possible.

But like a seed after it's planted, the thought slowly takes root in my own mind, too. How would I be able to get out of my National Service commitment? Would the government allow it? After all the difficulties we experienced just getting Wudasie's travel visa and the denial of Natsanet's, it seems highly unlikely we would be allowed to leave. But who knows? Anything is possible. Also, assuming we were to apply now, how long would it take to get permission? I don't want to go through the torment of trying, if it means being separated from my family for many years.

These and other questions plague me, but I share them with no one. I can't take the risk. There is a saying here: *"Ms kolia aytmker; ms kelbi aytithabae."* Keep your secret to yourself; it is your strength. I think this is good advice, especially in such times as these.

Most of all, I don't dare tell Natsanet, and it's not because I'm afraid of who she might tell. I don't want to raise her hopes, especially if they are just going to be crushed.

\* \* \*

Over the next several weeks I continue to struggle with the idea of emigrating. Am I being unreasonable by wishing my family would just come back? Am I being selfish?

I try to think objectively about what exactly my wife and daughter would be coming back to. This is their culture, their language. Their family and friends are here. And Eritrea itself has many beautiful places to see, and centuries upon centuries of history. But the list of positives quickly reaches an end. The list of negatives is far more extensive.

Despite the ceasefire agreement, we are technically still at war. Everything is on hold. Ten years after our Constitution was written, it remains inactive. Our president alone decides what is right for Eritrea and Eritreans. So, more of our youth are being forced into national service; no one is dismissed. The border issue remains unresolved. We are not actively fighting, but neither are we acting as if there is peace. The employment situation is depressing. The government owns or runs nearly everything, so it alone determines who works and who doesn't. We are denied many basic conveniences— private automobiles, cell phones, the internet. And there is no reason to believe anything will change anytime soon.

The government is the source of all our frustrations. President Isaias Afewerki, once our hero, has become even more autocratic and isolationist, and it has only gotten worse since the ceasefire. We have never had a totally free press, especially after 2001, and there's no indication we ever will. Anyone who speaks out against the regime risks being imprisoned, deported, or executed. The same fates have befallen his former allies in the government who later challenged him. There has been talk of presidential elections, but they never happen. Corruption abounds. How long can we persist in our hope and optimism when there is so much to be pessimistic about?

For so long now I have ignored the complaints of those who speak out against the country, especially those of the younger generation. But now I realize how stubborn I have been dismissing their grievances simply because I didn't want them to be true. Now, for the first time, I have to think about it in terms of my own children's future. They are still very young, but within the blink of an eye they will be grown up. What do they have to look forward to here in Eritrea? The promise of being shipped off to Sawa to complete their high school education? Or possibly some place far worse, like Kiloma. Forced into military training. Forced to fight. Forced to shoot at someone who tries to escape over the border or torture someone in prison. I can't stand the idea of them being taken away from their home and family at such an early age, to finish their childhood among strangers. And especially among boys and men who think nothing of abusing women. Now I understand why so many youth talk about escaping. Now I see why so many are willing to risk their lives to sneak over the border. What kind of father would I be if I demanded my own daughter return to this, when a far more humane option exists for her?

Thinking about Titi makes me realize the gift she was given by the opportunity of going to America. I understand now how she never would have received such care here. But it is more than that. I once dreamed Eritrea would be the land of opportunities, but that dream has been smothered. What is left for us here?

In America, Titi will continue to get healthy. She can grow up in relative peace, safe from the constant worries of war. Safe from the whims of an oppressive leader and his followers. How could I expect her to come back to this? How could I expect Natsanet to stay? Shame fills me for even considering asking Wudasie to return. How could I sentence them to this?

The next time we speak, I tell her I have made up my mind. I don't have to tell her what I mean. It's better if we don't say it out loud. And the timing for them is right, anyway, since their medical visas will expire soon, and she will have to make a choice when she applies for an extension.

After that comes the long and difficult process of figuring out how to make it work.


Each year, on the twenty fourth of May, the Independence Day celebration rises across the Asmara and coalesces at the stadium, where President Afewerki, high ranking government officials, diplomats, and other dignitaries gather to give their speeches. Others lucky enough to get tickets, including civilians, are allowed to attend. The stadium, built in 1938 by Italian businessman Francisco Cicero as a soccer venue, fills up beyond its capacity of six thousand. Everyone is eager to view the national parade. Units for each branch of the Eritrean military — Air Force, Navy, and Army — as well as local police units, are on full display. The event is televised live on state-run ERi-TV and picked up by international stations. As it is in other authoritarian regimes, the parade is highly militarized, and the accompanying music and pageantry are broadcasted as a show of might to discourage foreign powers from entertaining imperialistic ideas. The speech by the president to his people is meant to be positive, forward-thinking, and rousing. I used to believe the words he spoke. Now I wonder why it took me so long to see how hollow they are.

This year, in contrast to previous years when I attended in person, we are staying home and watching the events on television. When Natsanet asks me why we don't go, I tell her it's because of the large crowds, but the simple truth is I can't raise much enthusiasm for the celebration. It tears me apart to remember how optimistic I was after the War for Independence, a feeling I long for again, yet believe I will not find until our leadership changes. And as we sit and watch, I realize from the looks on the faces in the crowds that I am not alone in my unhappiness with the situation. Nobody protests outright, but there are fewer smiles than I remember. Somewhere along the way, when I wasn't paying attention, the days of celebration, of song and dance and hope, were being replaced with doubt, anxiety, and quiet pleas for better days. More and more, instead of praising our leaders, we pray for them to come to their senses and reverse this downward spiral we are in. Not everyone feels this way, of course. There are still devoted followers of our president. I wonder what it will take to open their eyes to the truth.

It's now early September, more than eight months since Wudasie and Titi left for America, and I have had a while to adjust to the idea of leaving Eritrea behind. In those few months, I have taken full stock of my feelings on the subject, studying rather than suppressing them. I try to be careful not to let my growing bitterness at our country interfere with our lives or taint my daughter's opinion about her culture. There is so much about our people and history to be proud of— our resilience and generosity, our fierce nationalistic pride, our boundless optimism, even in the face of terrible oppression. I still believe Eritrea will someday become the great nation it was always destined to be. I just can't risk it happening *after* my children have grown up and I am very old.

We are celebrating Natsanet's fifth birthday. Her aunt and our neighbor, Azmera, have volunteered to help me with the party. The house is decorated with colorful balloons and a giant poster that reads *"Happy Birthday"* in English and Tigrinya. It also has a photo of her in the middle. In the center of the room is a table, and in the middle of the table is a birthday cake with five glowing candles. It is dwarfed by stacks of gifts from friends and family. There is also *himbasha*, a celebratory sweet bread, soft drinks, popcorn, and candies. We wait for Natsanet to come out in the blue dress Wudasie sent her from the US. At last, she emerges and takes her place on the sofa, sitting beneath the handmade poster. Everyone sings the birthday song. Then she cuts into the cake. I glance around the room, at my family and friends and all the kids in attendance. So much warmth, excitement, and joy fill the room, and I'm happy to see it reflected in my little girl's face. But beneath her smile, I know there is still pain. I can tell she feels her mother's and sister's absence especially keenly today. She makes me proud with her brave face, but also a little sad.

After the party, when everyone has gone home and it's just the two of us left, Wudasie calls to speak with her. This time, Natsanet doesn't try as hard to mask the loneliness she feels inside. When her mother asks if she likes the gifts she got from America, she quietly says, "Yeah, I like them." Tears fall from her eyes. I have no doubt she likes the presents, but they aren't the ones she wanted.

Later that week she shows me some photographs from her birthday celebration at her kindergarten school. All of the September children are honored with one big party on the same day. The kids wear decorated party hats, and the tables are full of treats. I can tell that they are having a good time, even Natsanet.

She recounts for me what everyone is doing, what they are eating, the songs they sing. She tells me their names and describes each child. This is the daughter I love to see, the little girl who beams with excitement and talks until she runs out of breath.

She surprises me by placing another stack of photos into my hands. These are from another celebration at school, except this time they are from her sister's seventh birthday. I didn't even know she had them. Natsanet presses herself against me as I look through them. I can tell she's picturing herself in the photos. When I'm finished looking at them, she extracts one from the pile and holds it to her lips. I don't know what to say. I have to choke back my tears.

Natsanet wakes one morning and tells me I need to buy a red car.

"Why?" I ask. We are waiting for her grandmother to come over to walk her to school.

Natsanet jumps off the couch and spins around. She's wearing the same color uniform her sister wore to school when she was the same age, and the dress flares about her ankles.

"So I can ride to school in a red car, like a princess," she says.

I marvel at how quickly she is growing up. Blessedly, the days when she breaks down in tears are coming less frequently, but this is a bittersweet observation for me, as it means she is missing her mother and sister less. I don't want her to forget them.

"How about I get one as soon as I'm released from the army?" I say.

"When will that be?" she asks.

"Soon, I hope," I assure her. But in truth, only God knows when that day will come.

Despite our unsettled living situation, Natsanet excels in her schoolwork. Her reading skills far exceed her teacher's expectations, and she amazes us all when she starts reading the local newspaper, which is printed in Tigrinya. She also loves reading her children's books to her grandmother. I'm especially proud at her grades in math class, since it's my own field of study. She's also eager to learn English, which I both encourage and assist whenever we are at home together. I don't tell her why I want her to learn it as much as she can, but she will need to know how to communicate when we move to the United States.

*If*, I solemnly remind myself. *If* we get to the US. It's far from certain.

Her grandmother has begun telling her stories about her own childhood growing up in a rural village before they moved to Ethiopia. Natsanet always listens to these tales with rapt attention, and afterwards she will often pull me aside to recount them to me. I have already heard many of these stories before, but even when she uses the same language and copies her grandmother's mannerisms, it's like I am hearing them all for the first time. The biggest difference is that she will often incorporate her sister and mother into the tales in little fictitious ways. I believe she does this to keep them alive and fresh in her memory.

The stories resurrect memories of my own, tales told to me by my own parents about their years growing up in small rural villages south of Asmara. This was during the Italian occupation, when very few Eritreans were allowed to live in the city, and so much of the surrounding area, particularly the fertile and easily farmed regions, had been seized by the Italian government under the principle of *'domeniale'* property and handed over to white settlers. Farmers and herders who had lived and worked the area for generations upon generations were pushed out and made to settle in less favorable lands.

When my mother was very young, her father died from an unknown illness, leaving her mother, aunt, and grandparents to raise her and an older sister. As was customary during the time, both she and the sister were married off by prior arrangement to men who happened to be living in Asmara. Raising us while my father worked, she was the disciplinarian of the family, and she had very high expectations for all her children. But she loved us all and protected us fiercely, especially when she saw us straying too far from our roots.

My father, like my mother, was born to a peasant family. He spent his childhood tending his family's cattle and farming a small plot of land. When he was old enough, he was hired off to an Italian-owned farm outside the village. It would be his first experience with industrial-scale farming techniques of the age. Today, those same methods would be considered both inefficient and abusive. One of his duties, for example, was harvesting by hand acres upon acres of alfalfa, which would be used for cattle feed. It was backbreaking work. He would spend the entire day cutting the grass with a sickle, the unrelenting sun searing his bare back, then gather it up into sheaves to carry and stack into great heaps. The native farmers never had need of so much. They produced only what they needed to survive. The Italian landowners were profiting mightily off the backs of the people they had essentially enslaved.

As soon as my father was old enough to strike out on his own, he left the farm for Asmara, which the Italians called *Piccola Roma,* or Little Rome. They were gone by that point, expelled after their defeat in the Second World War, but the name stuck. *Piccola Roma* had grown into a modern city by then, and it was still growing. Aboy was a part of a migration of locals from villages to inland and coastal cities seeking work.

There was a lot of it then, too. Asmara's rapid growth created a high demand for manual labor. My father worked a variety of jobs under both Italian expatriates and the British caretakers who remained here after the occupation. After Eritrea was annexed to Ethiopia, he found moderate success as a small business owner. Long known for his generosity and kindness, he worked diligently for years to transplant youngsters from the villages to the city. He often provided financial and material assistance from his own savings, all while encouraging the youth to get as much education as possible. Both of my parents believed deeply in this philosophy of helping others, although my mother was typically more prudent, whereas my father would give the last coin in his pocket to a total stranger in need without a second thought. He was a jolly man who rarely went about without a smile on his face and a joke to tell. And he never laid a hand on anyone in anger. These were values they instilled in their own children. They taught us to be kind, careful with our money, yet also generous. They taught us to study hard and work harder, and to respect tradition while keeping an open mind about others.

Aboy had always been a healthy and physically fit man, despite the hard labors of his youth. He seldom employed public transportation to get around, preferring instead to walk or ride his bicycle. He continued to work hard late into life, rising at dawn and finishing long after dusk. A stroke at the age of eighty finally did what no farm owner could. Although paralyzed and weakened, his mind remained strong. The irony is that the stroke finally returned this hardworking man back to us, his wife, children, and grandchildren. Now, it is we who must give back to him all the care and love he provided his entire life.

My parents are very old now, and my mother is growing frail and is finding it harder to tend to his needs like she once did. I do what I can to help, visiting them as often as I can. But the phone calls come more frequently, sometimes in the middle of the night, and the medical emergencies are more serious than they once were. After ten years in bed, his body has withered away. His heart is failing. Who knows what else is wrong that we don't know about? Yet his mind remains as strong as ever. We have that blessing to be thankful for.

I don't know how I am going to tell them that I am contemplating leaving them.


Early one morning at the beginning of November 2004, almost a year since half my family went to America, as I am walking to the bus stop to catch the service minibus to work, I'm passed on the street by a half dozen or so military trucks filled with soldiers. I would normally not give them a second thought, since so many of our youth are now in the military, but for some reason it troubles me on this day. Something on the faces of the soldiers and drivers strikes me as especially ominous. A vague sense of unease settles over me and sticks for most of the morning, but by noon I have forgotten what caused it.

While on my way to my mother-in-law's house to visit with her and Natsanet during lunch, the bus I'm on is abruptly stopped in the middle of the road. Since all of the seats are occupied, I am standing in the aisle, squeezed in tightly with other passengers. I try to see out the windshield, but my view is blocked. Through the window beside me, I can see a large gathering of people milling about on the street. My first thought is that there has been an accident. Others are wondering this, too. I don't hear any sirens, and there aren't any emergency vehicles yet in sight.

A loud banging comes from the front of the bus, and when the driver opens the door, a young soldier sticks his head inside and orders everyone off. "Quickly!" he shouts. "Line up there, on the side of the road!"

I'm one of the first to hand over a National Service pass to the soldier demanding our paperwork. The age for exemption had recently been raised to fifty, so men older than that turn over their identification cards instead. The soldier collects everything without checking any of them. He separates us by gender, and tells the men to remain where we are. The women are ordered back onto the bus.

My thoughts immediately go back to the roundup at Nefasit, which started me on this path to unending National Service, now five-and-a-half years ago. Visions of the military training camps at Sawa and Kiloma come back to me. I have since mostly recovered from the physical abuses I suffered all those years ago, but it hasn't been long enough for the painful memories to lose their vivid edges. I remind myself that if this is another training roundup, then at least I will be spared from the indignity— or at least I should be. But whether it is or not, the fact that they are even stopping us like this raises an even more disturbing thought: Are we gearing up for war again? Or is there another reason for this?

Ten minutes pass. Each one seems like an hour. I'm used to the lack of information provided to us by now, but it doesn't make the wait any less stressful. Finally, the soldiers call the older men out of the lineup, hand their identification cards back, and tell them to go back to the bus with the women.

Some of the men still waiting in line try to ask what's happening, but the soldiers either ignore them or tell them to keep quiet. The crowd grows. I see people of all ages, young and old, women and men and little children. Some sit quietly in cars, which have been ordered to pull over to the sides of the road. Others sit astride their bicycles or on the ground. I find our compliance infuriating. Why do we allow this to happen to us? Why don't we speak out and stop it?

Those of us in the National Service carry what is known as a Yellow Card, proof that we are already conscripted. The paper allows us to travel with relative freedom about the country. It does not, however, exclude us from being detained. The government can call us up at any time, for any reason, if it requires our service. I hope this isn't one of those times.

My first thought goes to Natsanet. I can't bear the idea of leaving her alone, parentless. Instinctively, I scan around me, before realizing it would be foolhardy to try to escape. Anyway, there is no chance.

The soldiers mill about, guns strapped over their shoulders and thin wooden switches in their hands, tapping their legs. They act as if they are waiting for someone to come and tell them what to do. The rest of us can do nothing but wait to hear what our fate will be. More cars and buses are stopped, and the lineup of men beside me grows larger. I lose count after a few dozen. We must now number in the hundreds. Our minibus driver grows impatient and asks for permission to leave. When he gets it, he wishes us good luck and wastes no time pulling away.

The soldiers grow restless. We flinch each time they walk past us, sure they will suddenly bring their sticks down on our backs and shoulders. We don't say anything to them; we look away. *This is freedom?* I wonder. It's clear by our Yellow Cards that some of us are already in the National Service, so what good does it do to hold us?

A full hour passes, and at last they hand our cards back and let us go. No explanation is provided, and no one waits around for one. What would be the use of that? It would only invite trouble. Is this what we have become? Are we no different than when Ethiopia was in charge? The oppression we once fought to free ourselves from is now being wielded by the same people who led that fight.

Because of the delay, I reach my mother-in-law's house much later than usual. She reports having witnessed a similar event nearby, which caused her and Natsanet to worry about me. My daughter is very sensitive to the military, and she doesn't like to see the soldiers. Even though she was born after my conscription, and she was too young to remember the worst parts of what I was made to endure, she knows how difficult it has been for all of us, so she associates soldiers with negative thoughts. She worries about me more than any five-year-old should, and always asks me if I have my Yellow Card with me whenever she sees a military patrol. I know part of her current attitude has to do with her mother going away; she's terrified of the prospect of losing me, too.

I spend much of my remaining lunch break assuring her that I will be fine. Then I send her off to play with her friends. Her grandmother tells me that the other children are also worried for their fathers. More and more lately, children everywhere are living with the fear that they will be abandoned.

The entire public transportation system has been paralyzed, as the soldiers are stopping taxis as well as all of the buses, so I decide to ride my bicycle back to work. I risk becoming part of another roundup, but I have no choice; if I fail to report to my job, there would be consequences, and that could lead to even more trouble, which could expose my plan to go to America.

After I arrive, I expect to be asked for an explanation for my tardiness. Instead, I find half the offices empty. A few more people trickle in after me, but it seems that many simply decided to take their chances by staying home. Those of us here are still expected to put in a full day's work, however. We get no sympathy from our bosses. They pretend that there is nothing unusual happening across the city.

Over the next couple of days, more details emerge about the roundups, the worst so far in Asmara's thirteen year history as the capital of independent Eritrea. We learned that the army held the entire city captive, not only stopping vehicles, but raiding houses. Every man caught out in public, whether student, active or demobilized ENS member, and even *tegadalay*, was stopped. The *giffa* never went away entirely after independence, but they've never been as widespread or as ruthless as this, either. In the past, we simply had to show our passes to be excused and allowed to go on our way. This time, many people were never even given the chance to explain themselves or get any explanation for why they were being detained. Instead, they were simply harassed. Some were physically beaten. Some were even loaded onto trucks and taken to Adi Abeito prison on the outskirts of Asmara for no obvious reason. Only later would we learn that some of those taken were targeted for religious reasons or suspected of associating with known dissenters of the regime.

A coworker of mine tells me that his son was on one of those trucks to Adi Abeito when it flipped over. Although no one died, many were injured, some seriously. The army transferred them all, untreated, to another vehicle and took them into detention. "This really is unacceptable," he tells me. It's the first time I have ever heard him speak critically about the government. He has always been a staunch supporter of our leaders and their actions, so this is a new development.

Like so many of our prisons, Adi Abeito has earned itself a notorious reputation. It is where, years earlier, over two hundred Eritrean refugees were brought after being forcibly repatriated from the Mediterranean island nation of Malta. Human rights organizations begged the UN to stop the move, arguing that the returnees would be persecuted for illegally fleeing their homeland. These claims were summarily dismissed. Then, just as predicted, many of these people, including children, were tortured. Some who attempted to escape their imprisonment were sent to Dahlek Kebir Prison on the Dahlek Archipelago. The conditions there are even worse, and the stories of those who managed to get free since then are filled with examples of truly abhorrent treatment.

In the days that follow, we hear an equally disturbing rumor that the army had taken so many people to Adi Abeito that a supporting wall collapsed beneath their weight. During the chaos that followed, dozens of detainees tried to escape. Guards opened fire, killing some. Many others were beaten into submission. The government, condemned by the international community, maintains that there were only two casualties. But more reliable sources, including eyewitnesses, insist the real number of dead is greater than twenty.

My coworker's son is eventually released. Sadly, his father has reverted back to supporting the government and still views anyone who speaks out against it as a traitor. He isn't the only one who thinks like this, just as I am not alone in thinking our leaders have lost their way. Our country is being torn apart from the inside, split between those who blindly follow our cruel leaders out of some misguided idea that this is how our country must be, and those who believe that this is wrong. Unfortunately, the divide is only getting wider.

* * *

172

Our country's economy is crumbling.

In its report published in February of 2005, the International Monetary Fund cites "the adverse impact of the widespread use of administrative controls, the expanding role of the state into commercial activities, and the lack of a transparent regulatory environment" as the main drivers for Eritrea's economic stagnation. It states that we are one of the poorest nations on earth. Our annual per capita earnings are just US$130 (€105). Naturally, the government refutes these claims and instead blames private business owners for boosting prices out of reach of most Eritreans.

It wasn't always like this. In the years after we won our independence, most basic necessities were in ample supply. Many of these products were manufactured in the country; the rest were imported. But this situation changed when the Eritrea-Ethiopian War started in 1998. Life became more difficult as necessities grew scarce, and the situation has only gotten worse since the cessation of active hostilities two years later. Now, inflation, drought, and the depletion of able-bodied farmers through forced conscription have taken their toll. Imported goods are either unheard of, or are very expensive to buy, mainly because the government places heavy restrictions on what can enter the country.

In an attempt to stem rampant inflation, the government begins to ration certain basic necessities, a move that is criticized as regressive by international financial institutions. Comparisons are made to the times of rationing under the Derg, but our leaders dismiss them as inaccurate. They argue the steps they are taking are necessary for ensuring the survival of a market-based economy in Eritrea.

In May of 2005, the government-owned and run Hidri Distribution Company begins selling essential items — including flour and lentils, coffee, tea, sugar, and cooking oil — through *Dukan Rithawi Waga*, or so-called "fair price shops." These commodities are sold at below market value, some discounted as much as fifty percent. As a result, many private shops already selling these goods are forced out of business.

To control who purchases what and how much, we are given coupons from the local district's administrative office. Need is determined solely by the number of family members, rather than income, which draws even more criticism to the program, as no distinction is made between the rich, who can afford the food without them, and the poor, whose situation is already desperate. Any adjustments to these numbers, whether as a result of death, birth, or marriage, must be reported immediately to the administrative officials. Failure to do so is a crime.

This places me in a terrible bind. If I claim only myself and Natsanet, it will alert the government that Wudasie and Titi still have not yet returned from America and trigger an investigation into why, which could expose their intention never to return, and I am not yet ready to do that. *Ms kolia aytmker; ms kelbi aytithabae.* I must keep my plans secret for now or else lose any advantage I might have toward reaching our goal.

On the other hand, if I am discovered collecting rations for people not living here, I would almost certainly be imprisoned.

I decide to take my chances and pretend my wife and daughter are home. It is a hard thing for me to do, as I have an aversion to deceit.

While some items, such as pasta, cooking oil and sugar, are mandatory to take, others are optional, such as millet. Very few people turn anything down, however. Even if they don't plan to use something, or they find themselves with an excess, as I do, there are better options. In some cases, we collect the produce and give it to those who need it more, since the coupons aren't transferable and expire at the end of the month anyway. Many of these excess goods inevitably make their way to private sellers, thus creating a whole new and unintended black market system.

The process of collecting our rations is not an easy one. We are allowed to go only once per month. Since I also collect my parents' supplies for them, the bundles are much too large for me to carry by hand. Instead, I am forced to borrow a stronger bicycle than my own, one that can carry the extra weight. It's not easy balancing it all. Thankfully, the Dukan Hidri distribution center assigned to my administrative district is less than a mile from my house. The queues there are long, and latecomers must often wait the entire day to get their supplies, sometimes only to learn that certain items have run out. As a result, people begin to arrive earlier and earlier. One month, people line up hours before the sun comes up. The next month they arrive the night before and sleep on the street, all to ensure they get enough of the limited supplies to feed their families.

Electricity is likewise in short supply. It's expensive and unreliable. Petrol, too. In the days when the refinery at Assab was supplying all of Eritrea's and Ethiopia's needs, we had plenty. Now it must be imported, so the Ministry of Energy rations that, as well. Much of our cooking and heating is done using wood, just as it was once done long ago. Others use kerosene. Long lines form at every petrol station for the fuel. People bring every container they can carry, from glass jars to jerry cans, sometimes dozens at once. More often than not, the people waiting are elderly and infirm, or children and pregnant women, as so many of the men have been taken away. Oftentimes, those in line are forced to sit or stand for hours in the baking sun, regardless of whether they wish to purchase just a few liters or several dozen. The stations frequently run out of supply or are forced to stop distribution when ordered by some government official. The moment this happens, there's a mad rush to get to the next station. People get trampled, lose their money or belongings. They cross the street in traffic and cause accidents. I have personally witnessed all of this and experienced much of it, too, now that I have only myself to gather everything I need to keep me, Natsanet, and my parents alive.

Almost overnight, our personality as a people changes. Once, we were tolerant and cooperative, but the long lines and limited supplies have eroded these virtues and turned us into something much less civil. Patience is easily lost. Arguments break out with greater frequency. There are more physical altercations. Just trying to survive in the city is becoming a challenge. I find myself growing more and more impatient to leave. No longer do I have any doubts about my decision. But each day that passes finds the likelihood of it ever happening even more remote. Meanwhile, Natsanet grows older and the memories of her mother and sister are fading quickly.

Desperate for a quick resolution, I begin to contemplate options I would never have in the past.

\* \* \*

Another year passes, and there is still no possibility of the National Service releasing me from callback, much less allowing me to leave the country to rejoin my wife and eldest daughter in America. Wudasie continues to work from her end to bring us to the US, or even just Natsanet to start, but every diplomatic option she tries fails. She mentions the possibility of returning to Eritrea instead, but I tell her it's completely out of the question. If she were here and could see what I see, then she would understand why.

One day in the middle of summer 2006, while having coffee at a downtown café with some old friends I have kept in contact with from Tseseret, one of them tells me a heartbreaking story about a female National Service member who happened to be captured with her brother trying to cross the border into Ethiopia. Her name is Salem, and even though I didn't know her very well, I do have some memory of working with her in the Zone Command. It's enough of a connection that I am deeply saddened to hear of her fate. One thing I remember about her was that she always talked about starting a family. I recall telling her once that I hoped the army would release her soon so she could.

"What happened to her and her brother?" I ask, afraid I already know the answer. The storyteller, Tekesete, confirms my suspicions when he says the siblings were imprisoned and interrogated for several weeks. Interrogation is just another word for torture. What information they hope to extract from prisoners is either irrelevant or of secondary importance; the torture is meant to punish them for trying to escape and to discourage others from attempting it as well. She is apparently still alive and being held at one of the military prisons in our own command. I don't want to think of her baking inside one of those shipping containers, but I can't stop the image from filling my mind.

"She was tired of waiting for the army to let her go," Tekesete says, and the others with us — Alem, Temesgen, and Semere — nod sympathetically. "Now she will never have children. She voluntarily joined the National Service in one of the early training cycles, and she served her country faithfully for many years. But seeing no end to her commitment, she chose the only way she could see to getting free. And now it has cost her everything."

I feel terrible for her and her brother. My heart also breaks for her parents, for now they have lost two more of their children to our government's ruthless ways.


Shortly after Titi's surgery, Wudasie's sister invited them to move in with her family in Illinois until the doctors were finished monitoring her heart. Since deciding to stay in America, they have moved into their own apartment. Titi continues to receive regular medical checkups. Because of the time zone difference and the frequent problems connecting by telephone, we have taken to using email. It is one of the few allowances our government grudgingly gives us, although I suspect it might be a way for them to more easily keep tabs on our communications. Cell phones, too, although they are still uncommon. For this reason, we are always careful what we write in our messages, just as we are when we speak. I prefer hearing her voice, but the calls are expensive. Wudasie insists they are doing well. She says life is good, although she admits that it isn't easy. She has no money and no easy way to earn it. She has always been fiercely independent, and it pains her to have to depend on her sister's family for so much.

After each call, Natsanet asks when her mother and sister will be coming home. I can only tell her that I hope we will be together again soon. I don't dare say anything about our plans for fear word will get to someone we can't trust.

One day, she doesn't ask, and the omission breaks my heart. On the other hand, it is a relief not to have to lie to her about it.

Work consumes me. And raising a little girl alone overwhelms me. Even with the help I receive from my mother-in-law and, occasionally, other members of the family, I still feel like I can never catch up with everything that needs to be done. Natsanet was a fussy eater when her mother and sister left for America, and this still hasn't changed. Nothing I say or do can convince her to finish what I put before her. I warn her that her mother won't like how skinny she's getting. Upon hearing this, she gets defensive and yells that her mother doesn't care. "If she did, then why isn't she here? She is never coming home!"

I tell her that it isn't true, but even I don't believe the part about them returning.

We continue our routines, and before I realize it, we are approaching our third year apart. Natsanet is now six years old. I continue to go to work, and she continues to ask every so often when we can all be together again. Meanwhile, the situation here in Asmara grows harder by the day.

Despite our difficulties, the decision to leave Eritrea continues to weigh heavily on me. I don't doubt it, only regret that it has come to this. Asmara is my home. I grew up here. And even when I was living in Ethiopia, I missed the familiarity of this city and its inhabitants. I even enjoy the job I have now, which suits my abilities much more than before. The idea of living so far away, in this place called Illinois, where everyone is supposedly rich and each person owns one or two cars and a big house, and everyone is rushing everywhere, unsettles me. How could I ever fit in in a place like that? I can tell that Wudasie hasn't found her place, either, but is it because she's waiting for me to join her? Or would we find our situation no better than it is here?

I struggle with this every day, wishing I could see into the future. I know it must have been a terrible thing for Wudasie to contemplate leaving our home behind. She wouldn't have proposed it without first giving it serious thought, so I have to accept she has already decided it is worth the sacrifice. And still does.

Another Christmas comes and goes, the third since they left for America. Natsanet is in the second grade now. Titi, now in fifth, is learning everything in English and picking up American customs. More and more, I feel them slipping away from us. I secretly suspect Natsanet already believes they are gone forever.

Wudasie pushes me harder to act on our plan. She insists that I try again to request my formal discharge from the National Service. I tell her the timing couldn't be worse. The government is growing more isolationist, more repressive. The economy has almost totally collapsed. Dissent is criminalized— even the hint of dissent is not tolerated. And there is renewed anger in Ethiopia over a boundary commission's conclusion that Badme, where the conflict began, truly does belong to Eritrea, which does not bode well for a permanent peace treaty.

I apply again for Natsanet's exit visa and it is denied once more. Out of desperation, I try a third time, this time visiting the consulate in person to plead my case.

I don't know what else I can do.

Without warning, the department I have worked for since 2003 is shut down. Instead of being released from the ENS, my personnel file is sent back to the Ministry of Defense, and I'm ordered to report to the Office of the Administrator for reassignment. I receive a letter of transfer, which I must also present. When I report, the clerk tells me to check back for a status update in a couple of days. The next time I do, they tell me to return again a few days hence. After two weeks of this, I am still not assigned a new position.

With Natsanet's visa request demanding so much of my attention, I lose track of the time. A week passes between visits to the Ministry of Defense. Then two. Nothing happens. I'm still not assigned. Another week passes. Then it's a month before I remember to go back.

This time, an administrator informs me I will be disciplined for not reporting to duty. I desperately try to explain what happened, but he accuses me of evading reassignment. He isn't interested in listening to my excuses. Everyone these days, it seems, is angry about something.

Now I'm terrified of what they will do to me. It's all too easy for anyone with any level of authority to make any claim, no matter how flimsy, that can get someone imprisoned. And they would have a valid claim against me. I have heard of people being taken away for the most minor of infractions, so I decide I need to get some advice. I visit a close family friend I can trust, Abraham, who also happens to be a long-time member of the National Service, having served in it since it was first established. He works in the Administrator's office, so if anyone can help me, he can.

He listens to my case and my explanation of why I stopped reporting. When I'm finished, he tells me he can't help with reassignment, since that is outside of his jurisdiction, but he introduces me to someone who can. Abraham provides them only enough information regarding my situation with Natsanet for them to sense the pressures I'm under, but not enough to raise any suspicions of my personal motives. For all they know, I wish to send my daughter to be with her mother, but I don't have similar plans for myself.

My friend's contacts act quickly to intervene, and they manage to alter my record to make it look as if I have been reporting all along. They also provide me their telephone numbers and encourage me to contact them directly so I don't have to continue to report to the Ministry of Defense in person. They will notify me when this status changes.

The arrangement seems suspicious to me, but Abraham is certain nothing bad will happen to me now. He assures me his friends have made it clear to him that they have done him a big favor, which they intend to make good on. "It also means I now owe them," he says. He chuckles when he sees the look of dismay on my face. "Don't worry, Yikealo. This is just how it all works now. National Service members help each other out. One day, I need a favor. Another day, they do." He also lets me know that it is customary to offer some form of tip as recognition of the assistance.

By tip, he means a bribe.

It isn't the first time I have been asked to offer some sort of payoff. Before this is all over, it won't be the last.

I have been trying for months to get all of the paperwork for the American consulate in Asmara for Natsanet's trip there, but as the relationship between our countries grows more strained, my chances of succeeding feel like they are receding farther away every day. Appointments at the US Embassy are nearly impossible to get, and when I finally do get one, they tell me they can't do anything until I first get permission for her to leave the country. In the meantime, Natsanet's passport has expired, so that is another hurdle I must overcome.

When Titi's medical trip to the United States was approved four years ago, it was much easier to get passports. Now, the government issues them only grudgingly. The exit stamps have always been subject to the whim of the government, and it has grown much less inclined to grant them. Before, working with our Immigration Services was like climbing a very tall ladder. Now, it's like trying to climb that ladder all the way to the monastery at the top of Mount Bizen.

Certain legitimate workarounds still exist. Eritrean consulate offices in countries such as Kenya or Egypt are generally more amenable to issuing passports and exit visas. Unfortunately, while travel between Eritrea and these nations is theoretically possible for some people, it is completely out of the question for me. Until I am granted my discharge from the National Service, I will remain a prisoner in my own country.

This seemingly never-ending series of obstacles is dispiriting. Nevertheless, Wudasie and I agree that our best option for initiating Natsanet's travel paperwork remains an outside consulate, so we decide to ask Wudasie's mother to go in my place. At her age, she is already far too old for National Service, and government travel restrictions for the elderly are much looser. But this raises a whole new set of problems, the greatest of which is her inability to speak in any language other than Tigrinya and Amharic, neither of which would be helpful in Egypt or Kenya. Still, if there is a chance of it working, we must try.

When Wudasie tells her sister about our plan, Aster is incredulous. "Are you kidding me?" she says. "This is a crazy idea. Our mother would be lost in a foreign country with a foreign culture and a language she can't understand. If you gave her a map of Africa, she wouldn't even know where to find either country on it."

Wudasie's mother, bless her soul, never gives it a second thought, even though I know the idea of traveling to another country terrifies her. She loves her granddaughter and has witnessed firsthand the pain Natsanet has suffered over the past three years missing her mother and sister. She would sacrifice anything to help her be happy, no matter how scary it might be for herself, even if the outcome means never seeing any of them ever again.

While we search for someone in Egypt to assist her after she arrives there, another relative of my wife raises a third option we hadn't considered, which is the consulate in the United Arab Emirates, where he believes he will be able to find assistance through his own personal connections.

Before long, we have Natsanet's renewed passport in hand.

Obtaining an exit visa to leave the country can be a challenge under the best of circumstances. It's always helpful if you know someone who can speed things up. Foolishly, I believe I can do it all on my own. After all, we are talking about a child who just wants to see her mother again. What more could they ask for?

For one thing, proof that Wudasie and Titi left the country legally.

And for another, an explanation for why they have remained in the US for more than three years without coming back. Specifically, they are challenging our claim that Titi needs to have continuous follow-up care, since the surgery fixed the hole in the first place. And the original medical visa expired years ago.

And finally, they want documentation from the American side showing Natsanet is allowed to migrate there. This shouldn't be a problem, as we were all cleared for permanent residency status by the US when Wudasie applied to extend her stay beyond the original six months.

I am instructed to coordinate with the Eritrean Embassy in the US to obtain these documents. Within days, Wudasie is able to get everything faxed to the Eritrean Office of Foreign Affairs in Asmara, which I hand carry to the Immigration Office. Once more, I am confident we now have everything they need to issue the exit visa.

And once again, I am wrong.

Three more days pass before they inform me the doctor's note is unacceptable, as it wasn't written on the proper forms and lacks specific information from the hospital they deem necessary. These seem like arbitrary complaints, but when I point this out, the woman processing my request, a *tegadalit* in her mid-fifties, deflects from the accusation by claiming the documents are forged. She completely ignores the attached letter from our own embassy in the US accepting the doctor's letter as valid. In dismay, I ask what else I can do to convince them.

"We need a letter from our Ministry of Health proving your daughter is under medical care," she replies in a sharp voice.

"*Ayteredeanin*," I beg. "Please explain, because I don't understand."

Instead of clarifying, she simply repeats her previous response, word for word. She speaks slowly, as if I am a child.

"But—" I begin, but she doesn't let me finish.

"No buts. No more discussion. Bring me a letter from the Ministry of Health."

When I don't move, she snaps her hand in the direction of the door, as she would shoo a fly that is bothering her. *"Wtsaley!"* she says, ordering me to leave.

I know what to expect at the Ministry of Health, and my suspicion is confirmed when the secretary there tells me my request makes no sense. "How can we comment on a medical procedure that took place in another country?" she asks.

Back in Immigration, the woman who sent me to the Ministry of Health tells me, "I can't help you until you give me that letter."

This time, she doesn't give me a chance to explain why I can't get it. She tells me to leave or she will call for security to take me away. Knowing this could land me into detention, I have no choice but to obey.

Another two weeks pass, and I need to find a way to break the impasse I am in with Immigration. For the first time, I consider looking for a "backdoor facilitator," someone with enough influence or connections inside the government's bureaucracy to make things happen. It's an option I have resisted in the past simply on principle. I dislike admitting that this is what our country has become, a place where the corrupt fare better than those who play by the rules. But I am growing desperate, and this seems to be the last option left to me.

I become a regular visitor of some of the city's more notorious bars, where I have heard people can be hired to help in situations like the one I'm in. I pay for dozens of meals and drinks but gain no leads. Once more I'm about to give up when someone introduces me to a well-known *tegadalay* and member of a popular EPLF musical group. Given his broad appeal and his connections with high level officials, it's easy to understand how he could be the one to negotiate a quick resolution to my problem. Furthermore, he has a reputation to uphold, and I don't think he would jeopardize it by cheating me, so I tell him what I need. He listens carefully and agrees to help. We settle on a sum of twenty thousand Eritrean *nakfa* — roughly $1,350 — an almost impossible sum to procure in a country where the average person earns one-tenth that amount in an entire year. He requests half in advance, "to pay the right people."

I am to give him the balance once he has delivered the exit visa to me.

Wudasie wires me the money. Two days later, I turn over ten thousand *nakfa* and the necessary documents.

Over the next two weeks, we meet or talk over the phone six more times, and each time he reassures me that he is meeting with the immigration people. He tells me not to worry, that there is a certain process and that it takes time. I emphasize that time is one thing I don't have. But then I hear nothing from him for several days in a row. He won't answer when I call, not until I use a public phone with an unfamiliar number. When I ask him why he hasn't been answering, he tells me that he had to take an unexpected trip with his musical group. He offers an apology, then suggests we meet in an hour at the bar where we arranged the deal. "Be patient," he tells me again. "I'm still working on it."

It's hard not to take note of this man's extravagant lifestyle, or the number of people who come to the bar to hire him for jobs similar to mine. But instead of assuring me, I begin to doubt his intentions. So, instead, I find the man who introduced us and tell him I want my documents and money back. Not surprisingly, he tells me the cash is gone, allegedly spent on bribes. I don't believe him, but I have no recourse for getting it back. I'm furious that I have been made a fool, but it is the delay that hurts most.

Seeing my despair, a coworker at a part-time job I picked up offers to speak to her husband on my behalf. He has a friend in a branch of the Immigration Office and might be able to help. The man reluctantly agrees to get involved, but only if we communicate with each other indirectly. This is a clear signal of a bribe. When I ask the price, he tells me it will be ten thousand American dollars. I choke. That is more than seven times the amount of the deal that fell through.

How am I going to get that much money? Angry, I tell Wudasie, but she says I can't focus on the amount. "How much are you willing to pay for your daughter's freedom?" she asks.

It isn't the amount that concerns me, but rather our ability to come up with it.

"If he can guarantee the exit visa," she says, "then tell him we can guarantee the payment. But pay him only *after* it's done."

I relay the message, and he agrees to the deal. He instructs me to draft a new application, which will be submitted to the supervisor of the woman who threatened to have me thrown out of Immigration the last time I visited. He informs me that it will be edited by the unknown third party before it reaches her desk. I don't know exactly what this means, and I still have serious doubts this will work, but at least this time no money will change hands until the deal is finished, and no money will be lost if it fails to work.

Three weeks later, I receive word that the committee has reviewed my request and decided to grant Natsanet's exit visa. I'm happy, but still doubtful when I return to the Immigration office the next day to face the woman. This time, however, she is pleasant and congratulatory. She shows me the approved document.

Once more, Wudasie wires me the money, and I exchange it for the stamped passport, no questions asked. I'm even able to negotiate the bribe down to half. At this point, I'm immensely relieved and thrilled to be one step closer to reuniting our family after nearly four years apart. It's a major victory. On the other hand, at what price has it come? I have enabled a corrupt bureaucracy in an oppressive government, encouraging more illegal behavior at the expense of people like me, all for personal gain. It doesn't make me proud, but neither does it make my decision to leave Eritrea behind any easier. It only deepens the sense of betrayal I feel.

With passport and exit visa finally in hand, there is just one last hurdle to overcome before Natsanet is cleared to go to America, and that is getting her entry visa stamp. Wary that the process will play out much as it did with the exit visa, I visit the consular at the US Embassy in Asmara with a healthy dose of skepticism. When the agent, a professional-looking white man dressed in a suit and tie, sees the passport with the exit stamp inside, he expresses disbelief. He knows that we have been trying to get it for a while. He tells me not to worry, that he will make it happen, even though the consulate has been told to refer any such visa requests to offices outside of the country. I keep waiting for him to mention money, but other than the official processing fee, he doesn't. "This will only take a few days," he promises.

That Friday, I receive a call from the US Embassy. They need to conduct an interview with Natsanet present. My heart begins to race—not with anticipation, but with apprehension. They tell me to bring her in on Monday. "Don't worry," the man says, perhaps hearing the panic in my voice. "This is just a formality." I manage to get my emotions under control, but I spend the entire weekend in a cloud of anxiety.

On Monday, the consular agent asks Natsanet if she wants to go to America. He speaks in English, and she has trouble understanding everything he says. I translate for her, but the moment I say the word America, she nods excitedly. The man smiles and nods back. "Come back again in three days," he tells me. "Your daughter's passport will be ready then."

The relief is so great that I can't stop the tears from coming this time. The agent seems to understand exactly how I feel and takes my hand. He nods sympathetically when I tell him thanks. "At last," I manage to say, "my little angel will finally be able to be with her mom and sister."

As we leave his office, he urges me not to wait too long to make travel arrangements, as the exit stamp is good for only a month and will expire soon. He gives me a knowing look, as if to say the longer we wait, the greater our chances that something will happen to stop us.

But I don't care about any of that for now. I have more urgent matters to consider. Now that it's a near certainty that Natsanet will be leaving me, how do I let her go? I have already sent one daughter away, along with my wife, and the holes their absences have made in my life have remained unfilled. This time I won't have anyone left to help me cope or remind me daily for what I am fighting. I'm not sure how I will manage.

These worries soon become secondary as the days pass and I begin to feel the urgency of preparing for the departure. It will be a long flight, and Natsanet will be on her own. Given that she is a minor, the airlines want to make sure an adult will accompany her, someone we can trust to hand her off to her mother. This is not something I can ask her grandmother to do. And I don't want to simply leave it up to the airlines to take the responsibility.

But then, almost as if to offset the heartache and frustrations of this whole experience, I find out that a sister of a friend of mine from the National Service has come to Eritrea for a visit from the United States. She tells me she will be returning within a week and can accompany Natsanet, if we can get her on the same flight. Even more improbably, it turns out that she lives in Chicago, close to where I will be sending my daughter. When we are introduced, she tells me she knows my family— knows Wudasie very well, in fact. She is more than happy to accompany our little girl and make sure she is delivered safely into her mother's arms.

I can't believe our luck. It seems too good to be true. I keep waiting for something to happen to make it all come crashing down again. I tell Wudasie, and she immediately makes the flight arrangements to match my friend's sister's. The date of travel will be right before Natsanet's exit visa expires, so there is absolutely no room for error or delays. Although I don't want her to leave me, I almost wish she could just go now rather than waiting. Every day that passes is another day in which her visa could be revoked for any reason by anyone who thinks she shouldn't go. Every time the phone rings or a knock comes at my door, my heart races with panic. Each morning, I wake from a restless sleep filled with dreams where we are somehow thwarted. I start each day with my nerves more frayed than the night before.

But the day arrives in the blink of an eye, and we make our way to the airport, once more in secrecy. We aren't stopped. We aren't questioned or challenged. The sun is bright and the sky is cloudless. It's a fine day, an exciting day. But for me, it's also a terribly sad day.

Watching my little girl, so tiny and vulnerable, walk away from me at the gate is heartbreaking. At eight, she's nearly the same age as Titi was when Wudasie took her away. But poor Natsanet will not be traveling with anyone in her family this time. Although she is with someone I can trust, this woman is still a complete stranger to my daughter. Natsanet turns to wave, and suddenly she begins to cry out. She doesn't want to go. Her screams tear through the air, and I am openly weeping now, too. Gone is my stoic facade and my resolve. Ever so gently, my friend's sister leads my precious little girl away. They disappear into the crowd, but I can still hear her cries of anguish cutting through the noise.

And suddenly, my world feels so unbearably empty that I am sure it will crush me into nothingness. I have no guarantee at all that we will ever see each other again.

# PART FOUR

Putting It All Back Together Again

∾

**2007 - 2010**

## Asmara, Eritrea

THE HOUSE IS SILENT AND COLD when I return from the airport. As I stand in the doorway, my hands twitch restlessly against my thighs, already missing the feel of Natsanet's tiny fingers wrapped up in mine. For a moment, I'm stuck there on the doorstep, unable to venture further inside, unable to back away. Everything in our modest home reminds me of all I have lost— not the items that remain, but the empty spaces in between and the quiet that fills them. I can almost hear Natsanet's voice echoing throughout the rooms and the courtyard outside, and I wonder how my life came to be at this point. I just want everything back— my family, my freedom, my hopes and dreams. And my country.

I remind myself that I will get back what I can. The rest will either return to me or it won't, but either way, it's all out of my hands. All but the part where I find my own way home.

Natsanet's departure is only the first step to recapturing all I hold dear. The next step is getting myself free of this situation. It won't be an easy task. As challenging as the last four years have been — as terribly difficult as the past few months have been — I can expect far worse before I'm finished. Accepting these truths finally completes the shift in my way of thinking. For too long I have clung to unrealistic notions about how the world is supposed to work, despite being proven wrong time and time again.

I glance into the gloom, at the few possessions my family has accumulated over the years— the modest table with its four matching chairs, our two couches, the bookcase with our books and collected trinkets on the shelves. Despite all the hardships our situation has imposed on us, I realize while making this inventory of my adult life that I have somehow managed fairly well. We may never have been prosperous, but we have done better than most. Better than might be expected, in any case, given all of the challenges we have had to face. So much of it is to

Wudasie's credit. She is the hardest working person I know. I also thank my parents for the discipline they instilled in me.

By the same token, I know that life in America for Wudasie has not been as easy as she lets on. She doesn't complain about how much of a struggle it is, only hints at it. She hasn't had the best luck finding enough work to support the family on her own. She hates being dependent on her sister's family— or anyone, for that matter. She dislikes receiving assistance from the government. And Natsanet's arrival will only add strain to her finances. What will my own moving there do? She tells me not to worry about any of that. She is completely convinced that a modest life as immigrants in the United States will be far better than the miserable life we would have here. Either way, there will be a cost. The question is, how much are we willing to pay?

But I know the time for worrying about costs is long past. It's time I found my own way to America, back to my family.

While Wudasie works on my entry visa from the US, I begin the process of getting permission to leave Eritrea. The restrictions our government imposes will make it difficult, if not almost impossible. Still, I am determined to exhaust every legal option first. So far, in spite of the bribes we have paid, all we have accomplished have been through the official, if not entirely proper, channels. I am determined to try my luck with them in hopes that the system continues to work for us. That way, I won't burn any bridges. Someday, I will want to come back.

It doesn't take long for me to figure out the system is too badly damaged, perhaps even fatally. Diplomatic relations between Washington and Asmara have entirely broken down, and the American Embassy has essentially stopped operating. Migrant visas for Eritrean citizens are now being handled in Cairo, Egypt, while all other, non-immigrant visas are being processed in Nairobi, Kenya. Being unable to leave the country legally to go to the consulate in Cairo, I'm left with only the illegal option of sneaking across the border.

The fear of capture fills me with dread. I might be shot and killed trying to leave the country. I could be caught and sent to prison, where I could easily spend the rest of my life. The guards will torture me until I die or confess the names of all those who helped me.

But my need to be with my family is so strong that once I decide to do it, I'm ready to go immediately. The voice inside my head urges caution. I remember the Bible verse from Ecclesiastes: *Do not be foolish and die before your time.* Wudasie also tells me not to be rash, since I can't come to America until they have granted my application to enter anyway. So I force myself to wait. I don't know how long it will take. I only hope I can hold out long enough.

One day while downtown, I run into an old friend, Kiflezgi. I haven't seen or heard from him in a few years, but in that time he has aged noticeably and now walks with a stoop. His clothes are worn and tattered and hang loose off his withered body. I ask where he has been and what happened to him. He tells me he was held at Dahlak Kebir Prison. Seeing the shock on my face, he explains: "My daughter deserted her National Service post and tried to cross into Sudan. She was captured."

"Why did she go?" I blurt out. The answer is obvious, of course.

He sighs. "Same reason so many of the country's youth are trying to escape. They see no future for themselves here, only a future in the National Service, and that's no future at all."

"But why did they take you?" Again, there is only one answer to that question. As her father, he would be suspected of helping her. But usually they don't take family members to Dahlak Kebir.

"Why do they take anyone?" he replies. "They accused me of arranging her trip and financing it. When I denied it, the secret security service took me in a truck with other prisoners to the coast, one body piled flat on top of another, stacked up like logs. Then they shipped us out to the prison. They held me there for six months, and I was tortured. Have you heard of the helicopter method?"

I nod. By now, everyone has.

"They did this to me."

"I am so sorry."

"There were six of us in the cell. They fed us half-cooked bread and thin lentil soup. One open toilet in the middle of the floor. It was humiliating. Two blankets to share between us all. The only reason they let me go is because they needed to make room for new prisoners."

I know better than to ask him if he actually did help his daughter. Any parent would if they could, and asking would only make him suspicious of me. Now, like Ethiopia did nearly twenty years ago, the Eritrean government has its spies everywhere, so it's hard to know who to trust anymore. Like these times, former acquaintances have grown uncertain. The worst thing I could do for our friendship right now is pry. And the worst thing he could do for himself is say more than he should.

It saddens me to see how our leaders are turning their own citizens against each other, even those who are friends. I feel terrible for him, a man in his late fifties, for the torture he endured. The same metal shipping containers we used to punish soldiers in Tseseret have become employed even more throughout the country. On Dahlak Island, the daytime temperatures inside such a box could easily kill a healthy man in under an hour without intervention or relief.

"You are lucky to be back home with your family," I tell him. "You are lucky to be alive. The government has no right to take people without evidence, charging them for crimes and locking them up without a trial. Far too many are innocent."

"But not all," he acknowledges, before stumbling away with a promise to come by sometime and visit my father.

I have heard too many stories like Kiflezgi's over the past few years. Until recently, I tried to ignore them. If I am considering illegally crossing the border, then I can't allow myself to be distracted or paralyzed by the possibility of failure. But that night, as I lie awake in bed, I can't stop the stories from coming to mind. Each one is like a warning to me, drawing me back away from the edge of a cliff I am ready to jump off.

The radio plays one of our country's most beloved singers, Yemane Gebremichael, whose songs celebrated love and hope and liberation. Before he died nearly a decade ago, he was revered for his generosity. Now, as more stories like Kiflezgi's come to mind, I wonder what Yemane would think about what his beloved homeland has become.

Among the most heartbreaking story of capture I have heard is the one of Semira, whom I knew ever since she was a baby. She grew up to be tall, beautiful, and athletic, and was always the center of attention in any setting. In high school, she threw herself into a summer work program called *Maetot*, a civil agricultural organization established in 1994 to reforest land devastated by the war. I had heard she was conscripted soon afterward and sent into the National Service.

The next time I saw her was some years later. Much of her beauty had been beaten out of her by then, and the vibrant light in her eyes was nearly extinguished. When I asked her how she was doing, her response left me deeply saddened.

She had been sent to Wi'a, a detention center a few kilometers south of Massawa, for not reporting back to her command at the end of a break. The name of the prison would come up again and again for its horrific abuses. Most recently, in 2006, an especially vicious *giffa* was conducted in the Anseba region, where every student seventeen years and older was rounded up and forcibly taken for conscription. There was an immediate public outcry, because of what had happened a year before, when more than one hundred and sixty youth were similarly rounded up and taken there. They had tried to escape, but failed. According to rumors at the time, the president, made furious by the news of their attempt, had them all rounded up and shot dead.

"It was stupid of me not to go back to my unit," Semira told me, "but I just couldn't face it anymore."

With some coaxing, she had eventually confided in me that the conditions for women in the service are brutal. They are constantly subjected to sexual harassment by men in command, and are raped on a regular basis. The assaults are rarely reported, and when they are, the attackers are seldom punished. In fact, it is the victims who end up suffering even more.

"The conditions were so bad in prison," she went on, "that I contracted some kind of skin infection. I have since been to several doctors, but they are unable to help. If you want to know what hell is like, I have been there and seen it with my own eyes."

As someone who suffered enough myself, I had no doubt she was telling the truth.

Her story validates my decision to send my daughters away. I'm grateful that they will never have to be conscripted, or risk becoming imprisoned for no other reason than simply trying to survive, as so many other Eritrean youths have experienced over the years. There was once a time when I had such high hopes for the future of our children. But as the years passed and conditions grew worse, those hopes dwindled, then turned sour. Instead of dreaming of the day when all of Eritrea's children, my own included, could enjoy the freedom their parents and grandparents fought so hard to win, I began to dread how much worse their future might be than ours ever was.

I have been alone, stuck inside Eritrea for a full two years, when Wudasie tells me the process for my entry visa into the United States has finally been initiated. It's now 2009, and I have found a job with one of the few international companies that isn't directly under the control of the government, although I'm still in the ENS database as a service member. I haven't seen my wife or eldest daughter in six years. Titi is now a teenager. Natsanet just turned ten.

"It's time," she says. This is her way of telling me I have to get out of the country and make my way to Sudan, since the first part of the procedure for being granted an entry visa requires an interview at a US consulate in another country. "You have to hurry, Yikealo. Once the appointment is set, if you don't show up in person, we may not get another chance for a very long time."

She knows that I have already tried numerous times to exit the country through the official channels. I have exhausted every possible legal option. My application for an exit visa to Sudan was flatly denied. I wish I could just purchase an airline ticket or hop on a bus, but I can't. If I were to present myself at the border, I would be stopped and sent back. The only option left to me is to sneak across illegally and work through the refugee system in Sudan. We both know how dangerous that can be.

The crossing is never easy for anyone, but for someone my age, forty-eight, it becomes so much harder. Many people, even the strongest and healthiest, perish from hunger or thirst in their attempts. Others succumb to injury or disease or are attacked by wild animals, like hyenas. If I'm caught and lucky enough to avoid being shot on sight, there is always the risk of doing many years hard labor in prison. I say many, but that's being optimistic. I don't think I would survive the torture for very long. Like so many other Eritreans of my generation, the harshness of our existence has physically and emotionally worn me down.

I could try yet again to get an official release from the Ministry of Defense, but the process might easily take another three years. Or it might take thirty. As if sensing my reluctance, Wudasie reminds me that our children need their father now, not after they are all grown up.

Still, I'm nothing if not a creature of habit, and I stubbornly cleave to principle. I don't know why I want to try the legal route one last time. Maybe it's the threat of being captured that scares me. I don't want to die. Or maybe it is the faith in my country that I continue to maintain. I don't want to betray it. It's possible the restrictions have loosened since my last attempt. Or it could be because of my parents, now ailing. If I slip across the border illegally, I will forever forfeit any right to return to see them again. The only way would be if a major political upheaval were to occur, and I don't see that happening.

I take my time composing a new letter to the Ministry of Defense. I go into great detail about the medical reasons why my wife had to take my daughter to America, and why Titi still requires follow-up care that is not available here. I mention that my youngest daughter joined them more than two years ago, because a child needs her mother. But she also needs her father. I tell them that my eldest daughter hasn't seen me in more than six years. I finish the letter by requesting a release from the National Service, in which I have served for ten years. I'm getting old now, approaching fifty. I beg for the chance to see my family again.

I present the letter in person to the Administrator General. He invites me to sit while he reads it. I study his face, but there's no expression on it to gauge his reaction, and it doesn't change by the time he finishes. It's impossible to tell what he's thinking.

At last, he sets the letter gently down on his desk as if it is made of the thinnest, most brittle glass. Then he lifts his eyes to me. He takes in my face, the slope of my shoulders, the twist of my frame. I can feel him assessing me, judging my value to the machine he helps run, this government, this country. He leans forward to pour himself some water to drink, and the parts of his chair crackle and creak. He takes a long, deliberate sip. And still there is nothing on his face to betray his thoughts. He says nothing at all for a long time.

"A release now would be in accordance with the Ministry's guidelines," I say, desperate to elicit a reaction. "I am nearly fifty years old."

He takes in a deep breath and nods. "You are not the first to apply for release from duty," he admits. His voice is stern, although I don't sense any anger or impatience in it. On the other hand, he has had years to perfect his military demeanor. "I personally receive many such applications myself. They come from men and women just like you, whose spouses and children have left Eritrea to live abroad. Why should we grant such a request, when so many others remain loyal and serve their country?"

In these few words, I finally get a peek behind the mask. I sense his utter lack of sympathy. My story hasn't moved him at all— neither my daughter's medical plight, nor the struggles we have endured since becoming separated. In fact, all he sees is my wife and daughters now living in some fantastic place called America, enjoying benefits he himself will never experience. And I am asking him to allow me to join them.

Not a single thing changes on his face, but he has already communicated enough that I know what his answer will be. He loathes me— or the idea of me, anyway. He sees me as a traitor. Dismissing me from my service obligation is the last thing he wants to do.

"I will present your case as best as I can to the appropriate officials at the Ministry," he declares. "But you should know that it could take a year or more for them to rule on it. In the mean time, you will continue to perform your duties as required. Dismissed."

In the hallway outside his office, I meet a man also applying for release. He tells me his story, and it echoes mine in many ways. I wait for him to come out of his meeting with the Administrator General, only to learn the answer he received is identical to mine.

197

"It's all a waste of time," the man tells me in a voice worn down by bitterness and resignation. "My advice, don't wait another year hoping for a different answer. It will be exactly the same as today's. Start looking for other options now." He gives me a knowing glance, then turns and walks away.

*I already have*, I think, as I watch him make his way down the hall. *Now I just have to act on it.*

From now on, I will have to be especially careful about discussing my plans with anyone. I don't know who might use my words against me, whether out of spite or for their own benefit. I have heard about people who, for a steep price, offer to smuggle someone across the border, only to hand them over to government officials, sometimes for a fee, sometimes for nothing but the simple pleasure of doing it.

Learning who to trust takes a painfully long time, and at times I feel my patience will reach its end long before I am ready to even make an attempt.


No escape from oppression ever comes without steep costs, and the least of these, yet often hardest to meet, is monetary. There is the cost to one's own emotional health, for keeping secrets from loved ones out of a desire to protect them, for the stress of knowing what you are about to do and the risks involved. Not knowing if you are putting others at risk, as well. Even if successful, there are the costs that come afterward, when the officials show up to ask their questions. Some of the detained may be lucky and avoid prison and torture. But they are still harassed, threatened, fined. Then there are the emotional costs for those people who may never know for sure whether you were successful at all, because all communication has been cut off. Finally, there is the expense to our cultural and national pride.

I am not the first in my family to seek refuge elsewhere. Six months ago, my youngest brother, Yebio, crossed the border into Sudan. Like me, he had been stuck in the National Service system with little hope of ever getting free. It was always my father's dream that Yebio would get married someday and produce more grandchildren for my parents to hold. That will never happen now. As for Yebio himself, he had long dreamed of going back to college to study for his master's degree. As a youth, he was filled with boundless optimism and energy. At the end of each year, he would proclaim that the next would be the one where everything changed. But for the past several years, he would only look back and shake his head. *"Ami-Yihayish,"* he would say, sighing heavily. "Last year was better."

Yebio's decision came after a near crisis with his position in the ENS last year. He had come home on a short break to help our mother care for Dad. Because of her own failing health, Mom has increasingly needed outside assistance, some of which I have provided. But I can't be there every day. Like so many others with family commitments, Yebio failed to promptly report back to his command when he was supposed to.

After some swift negotiating between friends of his and an acquaintance in the Ministry of Defense, he was told that there would be no jail time, as long as he reported back immediately. The official demanded a letter of apology, which Yebio submitted, as well as photographs of our bedridden father as proof. Yebio then asked for dismissal from service on grounds that our parents could no longer care for themselves. He was flatly denied. "You broke the rules," he was warned. "You are lucky we don't send you to jail. Yet you expect to be given special consideration? Get back to work!"

After returning to his post, he told me in confidence that he was seriously thinking about leaving the country. He hoped to make his way to Europe, where our eldest sister, Saba, lives with her family. I didn't realize it when he told me, but he had already been planning to cross the border with a friend for a long time. I had thought he was speaking out of frustration over what had just happened to him, and that he would not follow through.

As we have learned, very little gets done without help from people willing to take a bribe. Yebio had arranged with Wudasie's uncle Habtom, the same man who helped me secure my job transfer years before, to identify the safest route across the border. Using their Yellow Cards and a pretense of doing business in the area, Yebio and his friend, Gebremichael, made the perilous 450-kilometer journey to the town of

Omhajer. Even though Gebremichael is Christian, he is fluent in Arabic, the main language spoken in Sudan, and is familiar with the culture, which aided their escape.

We didn't hear from Yebio for several days after he defected. In fact, my parents never even knew of his plans until I broke the news to them of what happened. He and Gebremichael had made their way safely across the border, but they were caught by the Sudanese army and thrown in jail. Typically, the police will simply deport the detainee back to Eritrea, but after taking most of their money, they released my brother and his friend instead. Somehow, they managed to make their way to Kassala, where our sister Saba could send him more funds from Europe.

But after this, I don't know what they have planned. What will they do without a sponsor in another country? How will they get an entry visa? There is no guarantee Saba can help Yebio in this regard. He might essentially be stuck in the refugee system in Sudan for a very long time.

Thankfully, my brother's experiences provide me an outline of how to proceed with my own escape. And of what to watch out for. I know, for example, based on what he was required to pay, that it could cost me as much as five thousand American dollars to find someone to get me across the border. In the years since Natsanet's departure, I have managed to save a few thousand *nakfas* from my work, and Wudasie has sent much more. It is still far short of the amount I will likely need, but I can't wait any longer.

I also solicit the help of Wudasie's uncle, Habtom, and he agrees to help, but warns that it will be expensive. Every time he takes on another project, he increases the risk to himself, his family, and everyone he relies upon. "Also, there are many people in the chain," he says. "The money must be split among them according to their contribution. Some of them are needed to help you get across the border, others to shelter you. Still others will take you deep into the country and away from the dangers of being so close to Eritrea. Then you will have to navigate the refugee system once you are there."

Sudan has a much longer history of dealing with refugees, so many of the diplomatic processes and humanitarian aid networks are already well established. Still, the political situation in that country is just as tenuous as it is here. In fact, it may be even less stable, as a new civil war appears to be brewing.

"There are many ways you can get into trouble," my uncle tells me. "Educating you will take some time. So will putting all of the pieces into place. In the mean time, you must continue to live your life as if you are planning nothing out of the ordinary. Go to work as usual, carry on as usual. But be ready to leave at a moment's notice, whether it is tomorrow, next week, or next year."

The notice comes barely a month later, and I am both relieved and terrified. I'm glad because the waiting is over. The intervening weeks have been filled with such fear that I have sometimes felt too paralyzed to move. Every knock on the door is the police. Every phone call is the Ministry of Defense or Immigration. I have confided my plan only to my parents, my mother-in-law, and my sister-in-law, Yordanos, people I trust completely, and only because they each have a role to play in my escape. Every conversation, whether in person or on the telephone, is coded. We no longer mention borders or escape or American embassies and US dollars. We can never be sure who might be listening.

"Now," Wudasie's uncle warns me. "Now you must be especially discreet. This is when you are at greatest risk of being caught."

He then takes me to a coffeehouse in Asmara and introduces me to a man named Yonas, who will be in charge of my trip over the border into Sudan. Yonas has a way of blending in by assimilating with the locals. He dresses casually in jeans and a tee shirt. He has made many friendships in many towns, patiently cultured over several years using his abundant charm and good humor.

But he provides me frustratingly few details of my journey. I sense he is worried the plan will be exposed and endanger those who are helping me, if he says too much. He advises me to follow each step exactly as I am told, when I am told it. "The first thing you will do," he instructs me, "will be to leave your house on the morning of the day I tell you. You will take the bus from downtown Asmara."

"To where?"

"You will know when and where then."

My parents rent a small one-bedroom apartment in a large complex surrounding a central shaded courtyard decorated with colorful tiles. Ever since my brother's escape, I have spent nearly all of my time there helping to care for them both, so my departure from my homeland will be from there.

"Bring as little as possible with you when you leave," Yonas says. "You must give the appearance that you are only going somewhere for the day. Pretend you are only meeting someone for coffee. Bring all of your money. Hide it on your body, in case you are searched."

I feel like I have been preparing for this forever. Indeed, for months now, I have been sifting through my possessions, collecting photographs, burning papers as discreetly as I can without alerting my neighbors. Erasing all evidence of my existence from my home, or at least as much of it as I can, so that when I leave there will be no trail for them to follow. The government already knows too much about me and my family, but I don't need to help them. I hand most of the photos and papers I wish to keep to my sister-in-law for safekeeping. She will stash them away in a good hiding place. I don't bother with my clothing or furniture. Eventually, someone will come and take care of it all, hopefully long after I have gone. I can't take the chance of selling it off beforehand or giving it away. Someone might notice and become suspicious. Anyone aware of my family's situation wouldn't have to think too hard to guess the truth, that I am preparing to follow my wife and daughters to America.

I also let my brother Yebio know, because he can give me advice about how to act and survive along the way.

None of my other siblings is even aware of my plans.

On the day of my departure, a Friday, I visit my father's bedside. The right side of his body is paralyzed from the stroke, and he requires assistance using his left hand. Now he raises it to touch my face and give me his blessing. Pending either terrible luck or a miracle, this will be the last time I ever see him. I pray the police don't harass him or my other family members or friends after they discover my absence. So far, they haven't retaliated for Yebio's defection, but they may be twice as brutal to the rest once they realize I am the second in the family to escape in less than a year.

As instructed, I take a taxi cab for the fifteen-minute ride to downtown. I haven't shaved. I have allowed my hair to grow out, hoping to appear older than I am. From the station, I hop onto a minibus heading northwest. There are many roadblocks and checkpoints, and each time we are stopped, I'm certain it's because my employer has learned of my plans, or grown suspicious of my request for a couple days off work. Most of the passengers on the minibus are women or elderly, so whenever the soldiers stick their heads inside to interrogate us, I'm one of the few they naturally focus their attention on. The other men show their passes and state they are going back to their command after a break. I show my Yellow Card and say I am visiting family. The lie is not easy for me, although not as hard as it once might have been. Thankfully, it seems to satisfy them every time.

I carry a small bag containing a single change of underwear and pants and a few small items. Hidden in various pockets are twenty thousand *nakfa*. If I am searched and they find it, they will know I'm lying.

The 350-km drive takes forever, but we finally reach our destination around two o'clock in the afternoon, a small town called Tessenei near the border with Sudan. Being here makes me very nervous, for it was in this place that two of my friends, Samuel and Tesfom, were captured while waiting to sneak out of Eritrea. Like me, they were both ENS members at the time. Now, their whereabouts are unknown.

Despite worries of a similar fate befalling me, I force myself out of the bus and walk casually over to a set of shops near the station. I have been told to act as if I know the place and belong here. But as I purchase a cheap razor, comb, and some soap, I can't help but feel out of place and that people are staring at me. Then, continuing my act, I make my way to a hotel to await word from Yonas.

Somehow, I'm able to eat a small lunch, despite not being hungry at all. The food sits in my stomach like a stone. Even the coffee I drink afterward, normally the most satisfying part of my meal, curdles in my belly. I make several calls to Yonas's mobile, but he doesn't answer, and I'm beginning to imagine the worst. I try to stay calm and not panic. I tell myself to be still and act normal, but every noise outside my door is someone coming for me, every voice the voice of my captor. It doesn't help that it starts to rain very hard, drowning out all these sounds.

I wait impatiently and tell myself to calm down. I am still within my own country. I have done nothing wrong. I will stay the night, and if Yonas still hasn't called on me in the morning, I will take the bus back to Asmara.

Later that evening, sometime after eight-thirty, my cell phone rings. It's Yonas telling me he's on his way to my hotel. By now, the rains have stopped. I eat a quick dinner and pace the small room.

The moment I open the door, he slips quickly inside. Before I can say anything, he gives me a stern look and lectures me to never overreact. I tell him it's hard not to when one's fate is in another's hands.

"Just act naturally," he chides. "Imagine you are walking down the street in Asmara. The moment you start to act afraid is when you get caught."

"But I called you many times and you didn't answer."

"I accidentally left my phone at a friend's house. I only just received your messages. I came as soon as I could. I'm sorry for frightening you." He looks around him at the room and tells me to gather my things. "This hotel is too expensive. You are going to have to spend your money more wisely from now on. Come with me."

He takes me to a cheaper place, which is more familiar to him. "You will stay here for now."

"For now? I won't be leaving tomorrow?"

"No. I have to arrange with my Sudanese counterparts. When that is done, I will hand you over to my Eritrean friends, who will help guide you across the border."

He leaves me with instructions to meet him for breakfast the next morning. I spend the night wondering just how many people must get involved to sneak one person across the border. Already it seems like far too many. I guess I will find out soon enough how many more it will take.

Except I don't. We meet the next day as planned, but Yonas doesn't stay long. "I have other business to attend to."

I'm too restless to just sit and wait. So, to while away the hours, I pretend I'm in town planning to lease some farmland. I had overheard other men in the hotel make the same claim, and it seems like a reasonable cover story.

On Sunday morning, Yonas tells me his Sudanese contact hasn't responded to his calls. I tell him that I have only this day and one more of absence and that I can't wait another day beyond that. If I don't show up at my job on Tuesday, my employer will know something is wrong and guess that I have tried to get out of the country. Yonas assures me he's trying and tells me again to be calm. But the next morning, I'm on the bus again and heading back to Asmara. I still have the twenty thousand *nakfa* I had promised to give him, the second half of the forty thousand he required.

The plan has fallen through.

Before I left Tessenei to come back, Yonas apologized about the failure. "I promise I will call you the moment I have reached my people," he said. "Don't worry. It's better to try later than to risk being caught. I don't know why they didn't answer. Something happened. Things can change very quickly."

But it feels exactly like the time I paid the musician to help me get Natsanet's paperwork years back. I can't help but feel like I have been used. No longer can I distinguish who sincerely wishes to help me and who simply wants to rob me of my money and my spirit.

When I get back to my parents' house, my mother greets me with a hug and a sigh of relief. She tells me that she prayed for my safety. She doesn't act very surprised to see me, though, perhaps because I hadn't left with a lot of confidence on Friday morning. "*If* this attempt proves successful," is how I had put it, leaving open the possibility of my return.

During lunch from my job on Tuesday, I ride my bicycle to my mother-in-law's house to tell her what happened. Like my own mother, she is a deeply religious woman and makes a direct appeal to God for good fortune. She tells me not to worry, that she has faith my escape will work, but only when the time is right. "He will guide you to your rightful place at the proper moment," she tells me. "You must be patient."

But patience has been hard to come by lately. Each day I wake up feeling it will soon run out. Along with my luck.

# Tessenei, Eritrea

AFTER WORRYING THAT I HAD LOST all of my money and my chance, I get a second opportunity to leave the very next weekend, when Yonas calls to tell me to come.

Once more, I have to tell my supervisor I will need a couple extra days to attend to personal matters. He gives me an irritated look and warns me that I will have to make up for the lost time, but otherwise he doesn't seem suspicious of my intentions.

I snap awake the moment my alarm sounds at three o'clock in the morning. I dress in the darkness, then tiptoe over to my parents' room to give my father a kiss on the forehead while he sleeps. We already said our goodbyes the night before, and once more he has given me his blessing. This time, I have a very strong feeling I will never see him again. This time, I hadn't told my mother "*if* I am successful." This time, for better or worse, I know I won't be coming back.

I pause at the doorway on the way out and listen to Aboy's shallow breathing. It breaks my heart to know that I am leaving him now, near the end of his life, and that my mother will have no one left when he passes.

They have both told me multiple times that I have to do everything I can to rejoin my family. So why does it feel so wrong?

Before I exit the house, my mother appears before me like a ghost and wraps her arms around me. "God bless you, my son," she tells me. "Good luck." I think she knows, too, that this is it.

"We will see each other again," I promise. Strangely, I believe it, in spite of everything. I don't know when or how. Maybe it's wishful thinking that someday, within our lifetimes, Eritrea will manage to find its way back onto the right path, and everyone who fled illegally will be forgiven.

The second journey to Tessenei is an echo of the first. I feel like I'm living in a recurring dream. When we arrive in town, I head directly for the cheap hotel where Yonas had me stay the last time. I call him, and he answers right away. He arrives within the hour and assures me that the crossing will happen this time. "But you must be patient." It's becoming a familiar, but frustrating, refrain.

The hotel owners treat him like family and give him a place to stay. Because there aren't individual rooms, only a single large open area where the guests sleep beneath a shade, we have no privacy. We don't discuss our plans while anyone else is around, not that there is all that much to discuss just yet. In the evenings, the mattresses are brought out of storage and arranged in rows. Yonas beds down next to me, and we converse in low whispers so the other guests don't overhear. The next day, he rises early to go to work, leaving me to occupy myself as I wait. I linger in the hotel as long as I can, then spend the afternoon wandering about town reprising my previous role as a farmer interested in leasing a plot of land.

As Tessenei is a border town that receives a fair amount of traffic, there is a prominent Immigration Affairs office and multiple checkpoints for verifying identification cards and visas. There are also many more soldiers in evidence patrolling the border. I have been warned to be careful with whom I speak, as some officers dress as civilians and mingle in town to catch border crossers.

Once more, I am forced to wait for Yonas to signal that all of the pieces are in place. One day turns to two. Then three. Each day gets harder to fill, and the rain drives me indoors, where I have nothing to do. I grow more anxious. Yonas tells me that there are good reasons for the delay, although he doesn't say what they are. Again, I receive the same warnings and advice. "I have been in contact with my people in Sudan," he assures me, "and they tell me that crossing at this moment is too risky. They won't give me the okay until they can guarantee your safety."

The border between our two countries is almost seven hundred kilometers long. It's wide and barren for much of its length, especially here. It's exposed, with few places to hide. The climate is hot and dry, except during the rainy season, when it's hot and wet. Most of what grows here is grass and scattered clumps of short, thorny scrub brush too thin to conceal a vehicle crossing it, so we must plan accordingly. For all but the most desperate, walking across is a fool's errand.

"It's not a simple task," Yonas tells me. "My contacts know the landscape so they avoid getting their vehicles stuck in the mud or fall into an ambush. They must keep track of the movements of the border guards. Everything must be just right— the weather, the soldiers, everything. It could be today or tomorrow. Or it might be next week." He pauses before delivering those same words again: "Be patient, but be ready to leave at a moment's notice."

How can I be patient, when I'm supposed to report back at work the next morning? How can I not worry, when there are so many different ways I could be caught? The hotel is required to register the names of every guest staying there each night. They checked my ID the first day, so I can be traced here should anyone inquire after me. The information is copied into the register each night afterward. The register is then handed over to the local police station, so the longer I stay here, the stronger become my chances of turning up on a watch list.

But when three days turns to four, it's already too late for me to go back. Now I have no choice. I must submit my fate to God's and Yonas's caretaking. I must be patient and ready to leave at a moment's notice.

I pray no one comes looking for me while I am still here.


Hours pass like days. I'm extremely uneasy, yet I force myself to act as if I belong here. I visit the coffee shops and restaurants. I continue to act interested in farmland. I wait for the police or soldiers to show up at the hotel. I suspect everyone of being a spy. But so far, no one has approached me. The rains, like the people passing through town, come and go. But I remain in place.


A full week after my arrival, just as I feel my luck is about to run out, Yonas hands me a plastic bag. Stuffed inside are some faded but clean laborer's coveralls. "It's time," he tells me, and quietly bids me goodbye and good luck. I'm handed over to another man, who had joined us the last time we met for coffee. Like Yonas, he's Christian and dresses casually, as if he is a simple laborer. I never get his name.

The stranger hands me a hoe and takes me by minibus out of Tessenei to a farm in a nearby agricultural village called Arba'ata Ashar, the Arabic term for the number fourteen. The significance of the name is not explained to me. I assume it's not the only laborer village to be so unimaginatively designated.

The driver stops before the border checkpoint and we get off and head to a farm being guarded by soldiers dressed in olive green uniforms and carrying rifles slung over their shoulders. I pull the coveralls over my clothes, then we join the crew working the fields. There are about twenty of us, some appearing no older than their late teens, others with white in their hair. Their clothes are poor. Some wear short pants. Others are in trousers whose hems are frayed to tatters. They have plastic sandals on their feet and cheap hats to protect their heads from the burning sun. Their attention is focused on the ground beneath them. With my own unkempt hair and attire, I look more like them than the city boy I am. My guide assures me I blend in well, then moves a distance away to work the ground.

After tilling the soil for a couple hours, he reappears at my side. "See those vehicles?" he whispers, and angles his head to a spot across the way, where several palm trees line the banks of the Gash River. "Those are Sudanese trucks and buses. They transport people between here and Kassala, in Sudan. By the end of the day, you will be on one of them."

While he's telling me this, we are joined by an older man, who says it's a good time to go. Once more, I'm bidden good luck and handed over to a total stranger. This one takes me to another farm, warning me in broken Tigrinya to be careful not to speak to anyone. "Some soldiers dress as workers." We labor in the new field for some time before taking a break beneath a stand of trees.

"The border is very close now," the man tells me.

I look, but I can't make out any features that might help me identify where my country ends and Sudan begins. The Gash River runs perpendicular to the border, slicing through it rather than defining it.

There are no natural boundaries or manmade barriers to separate us here. All I see are farmed plots of land and workers dressed just like me. Am I still in the village called Arba'ata Ashar, or is it a different number here?

"We will leave now," he tells me, "but we won't walk directly to the vehicles. First, we continue north, then west. There, see? We go where there are fewer guards."

"Which ones are the guards?"

Seeing the concern on my face, he tells me not to worry. He promises to deliver me safely to his Sudanese counterparts. "You are lucky today. There is a big funeral for the daughter of one of the army officials, and it is being well attended, so there are fewer soldiers to keep watch this time."

But even his show of confidence doesn't slow my racing heart. I am about to cross into Sudan. The moment I do, I will become a refugee of Eritrea. I may never be able to come back.

"It's already too late to turn around," he says, sensing my hesitation. I wonder how many others have gotten to this point, only to wonder if they have made a terrible mistake. "You have already come too far."

I know he's right. The moment I sat down on the bus in Asmara to come here the first time, I became an exile. I had already fled my home and my country. I turned my back on my people.

*No, not my people, just our government. They turned their backs on us.*

I follow him as we make our way north, pretending that we are working the fields. After a half hour, he signals and we duck behind some bushes. From there, we head due west through the thin brush.

"Now," he says, and places a hand on my arm. "Now we are in Sudan."

# Kassala, Sudan

OUT OF NOWHERE, ANOTHER MAN APPEARS. This one is dressed in a long, white *jallabiyah*, or prayer robe. He speaks quietly to my guide in Arabic. Then, for the third time, my life is delivered to another nameless stranger. I wonder how many more times it will happen before the day is over. It's still only two o'clock in the afternoon.

My Sudanese guide takes me to an old Toyota pickup truck parked along the side of a dirt track, where a younger man waits behind the steering wheel. He opens the door on the passenger's side and gestures urgently for me to get in and sit in the middle next to the driver.

There's little conversation as we make our way over the dusty road. When the two men do talk, it's in Arabic. Occasionally, my new guide tries to explain something to me in broken Tigrinya. I learn that we are heading north toward Kassala, a city roughly a dozen kilometers inside eastern Sudan, but we stop before we reach it. There, at a small farm where a young man works a plot of land with hand tools, we stop for a break. The farmer wipes the sweat from his brow with a cloth and sets down his spade. The men exchange greetings through the driver's window. Then we park beneath the shade of an acacia tree.

While we wash our hands and feet before eating, the farmer builds a fire and prepares a quick lunch inside a small covered area filled with farming tools. Stuck in one corner is a wood stove, where the food is being prepared. After it's ready, he serves it on a large platter, as is our custom. We sit in a circle around it on small stools.

"I am Eritrean like you," the man tells me, introducing himself as Hamid. Like so many others I have seen today, he's dressed in khaki shorts and shirt and plastic sandals. He wears a scarf to protect his scalp. "But I am Nara."

The Nara are an agrarian people from the Gash-Barka region whose ancestors settled here from the Nile River Valley. They are mainly Islamic and speak their own language. When I ask him how he is able to converse so well in Tigrinya, he tells me that he was conscripted into the ENS years before, and they forced him to learn how to speak it. He left because he saw no end to his service. I wonder how he came to be helping other refugees, if he set out with that in mind or settled on it afterward. I am grateful for it either way.

While we compare stories, the two Sudanese men scout ahead for potential dangers. If I'm captured by the local military and been found to be without the proper paperwork, I will be sent back to the Immigration Affairs office in Tessenei.

The men return to tell me it's safe to continue on to Kassala. Or at least as safe as anyone can say. There are never any guarantees. Before we depart, I'm given my own *jallabiyah* to wear, so I will blend in better. My new Eritrean friend assures me I'm in good hands.

On the ride to Kassala, a deep sadness fills me again. I have left behind my home, my friends, my family. I am betraying the country I have loved so dearly my entire life, the country I wished great things for. It has only been in the last few years that my feelings have changed. I can't stop the tears filling my eyes. Will I ever be able to return? It seems unlikely.

I realize I have been neglecting my emotions of homesickness and regret, too distracted by my fear of being caught. But now I can't pretend any longer. I miss my parents. I blame myself for leaving when my father is in such poor health. I try to remind myself that he has always supported my family's decision to migrate to the United States, both through the legal channels and, when that failed to work, taking the path I'm now on. He showed a genuine interest in my progress along every step of the way. He celebrated each of our successes, felt the frustration of our every setback. The sadness crushes me and I forget where I am, seated between two Sudanese strangers in a pickup truck. I'm too deep inside myself to notice anything else.

Or to care.

* * *

213

Our sudden stop wrenches me out of the pits of my despair. Glancing around in alarm, I see that the rain has started again, but no explanation for why we have stopped. We pile out of the truck and find that the tires have become mired deep in thick mud. The driver tries to free us by spinning his wheels, but it only manages to sink us in even deeper until the mud reaches the axles. The driver has no tools, nothing but a screwdriver and wrench for minor repairs. What we really need are a shovel and some wooden boards.

After struggling for about an hour, we finally manage to lift the truck free. Now we're covered in mud, me more than the other two, as I am unused to wearing the prayer robe. The fact that these men are driving a small pickup truck through such a remote area during the rainy season without any useful means to free themselves from these kinds of situations gives me little confidence about their ability to help me. It forces me to wonder how little of the money I spent to take this journey is actually making it into their hands.

The city can't be much farther up the road, but the delay has put the driver into a sour mood. He drives too fast over the rough, slippery roads. All of a sudden, he hits a slick patch, sending us sliding toward the embankment. Someone shouts. The truck slips sideways. With a crunch of broken branches and the screech of wood on metal, we sideswipe a tree. Incredibly, the driver doesn't stop. He just keeps on going.

The other man is bleeding from a gash where he hit his forehead on the doorframe. I press the sleeve of my *jallabiyah* against the cut, until I realize I'm bleeding, too. I don't know how I cut myself. From a notebook I find on the floor of the truck, I tear out some pages to wipe away the blood and press against the wound. It isn't until afterward, once the confusion of the moment passes, that I remember how foolhardy it is to touch someone else's blood.

We continue until we reach a large house within a thick stand of trees. Without a word, the driver switches off the truck engine, gets out, and runs inside. A moment later, he reappears with fresh water and towels to tend to our wounds and to clean off the mud. After a few minutes, he takes the younger man inside. My own injuries aren't as severe as his, although they are bad enough that I risk getting an infection. Going to a medical clinic now would be out of the question.

After the sun goes down, the driver takes me to a nearby hotel. He leaves me to wait in the truck while he goes inside. A few minutes later, he returns and gestures for me to follow him on foot through the darkness to a smaller building. There, a child waits with fresh bandages to clean and dress my own wounds.

When this is done, another man appears and introduces himself as Semere, an Eritrean living in Kassala. "You will remain here for a couple of days," he tells me. After that rough ride, it's a relief to be on solid ground again and not moving. I'm also glad to be able to speak to someone fluent in my own language. "I'm a friend of Yonas," he explains. "I'm going to help get you to the next point in your journey."

Semere's house is small, but it's part of a much larger compound containing several buildings. He puts me up in an inner room that holds a half dozen bare metal bed frames. The floor is packed dirt, and paint flakes off the walls. Through a door at the other end, I see an old toilet stained with years of rust. He points out the tap, where I can get fresh water. Beneath it is a jerry can and a bucket for use in washing. Then he leaves me alone for the night.

I'm soon joined by two young men, who introduce themselves to me as Efrem and Fikru. We draw a trio of bed frames together to talk. They are in their late twenties and were both conscripts in the Eritrean National Service. They tell me they have been here a while, and are waiting for word from a man who can take them to Israel.

"How long is a while?" I ask.

"One week. It's a dangerous journey to make without paperwork, so we must wait until the smugglers can be sure of our safety."

"I don't like sitting in one place for very long," I tell them. "It's too risky."

Efrem nods, but says Semere is a close relative of his. "I trust him."

Fikru is just as anxious as I am to move on.

I tell them about my two trips to Tessenei and how I had to wait a week before crossing the border. It's strange to think that I was in Eritrea just that morning. Hearing this seems to reassure Fikru. "It's hard to be patient when you don't know what's happening," I say, and he bobs his head in agreement.

Semere returns and hands us each a pair of bed sheets. It's completely dark outside, and all of a sudden I am exhausted. We use one sheet to line the hard frame; the other is for covering our bodies. Then we take turns washing up. I left home with nothing to change into but a shirt and spare pair of underpants. I realize I will have to purchase more clothes soon.

We bid each other goodnight. After I offer my silent prayers — a wish that we will all be delivered quickly and safely to our separate destinations — I drift off to sleep. It is my first night as a free man, a refugee, and a criminal in the eyes of my country.

The next morning, Semere comes and gives me his cell phone and tells me to call my family in America, as mine won't work here on the Sudanese network. "They will want to know that you are finally safe and out of Eritrea."

It's still the middle of the night in America, and it takes Wudasie a while to answer. Before she does, I fear the phone will just keep on ringing forever. The last time we spoke was before I heard again from Yonas in Asmara, so she wouldn't have heard about my second attempt unless someone there told her. If so, then she'd have worried herself sick waiting for word.

"Hello?"

"Wudasie, I—"

She realizes it's me and she starts to talk. The questions come tumbling through the line before I have a chance to answer any of them.

"Stop and listen," I tell her. "I'm calling to tell you that I have arrived at Kassala, the border town inside Sudan."

"You're . . . okay?"

"I'm fine. I crossed safely. I am with friends, so you don't need to worry."

"You already crossed it?"

"Yes."

"And you are okay?"

"Yes. Thanks to God, I'm okay!"

I don't tell her about the accident in the truck. It isn't important. The only thing that matters at this moment is hearing each other's voices and her knowing I'm safe.

"I will be with you and Titi and Natsanet soon," I say, speaking quickly, because I have to give Semere his phone back. "I promise."

I spend a few nights at Semere's house while waiting for the next leg of my journey to begin. Now that I am in Sudan, despite the large amount of uncertainty that still hangs over my fate and the dangers that abound, I'm much more confident in my handlers and my situation, and can finally relax a little bit. Looking back on the risks that were taken, I'm thankful for those who took on so many of them to get me safely to this point. It sometimes feels like it all went too smoothly and that I'm due for a change of luck. I recall the names and faces of the people I knew who had been caught attempting what I did, and their failures leave me riddled with sadness and guilt.

During the day, I visit the nearby hotel, which is owned by another Eritrean expatriate. Many of his guests are people fleeing the oppression, drought, and famine in Eritrea, Ethiopia, and South Sudan. Some arrive under similar circumstances as mine, coming directly from the border; others make their way here from one of the many refugee camps scattered about the Horn of Africa. We are all trying to get somewhere else, and this is just one of many stops along the way. I don't know how they are able to stay here, as the hotel isn't supposed to rent rooms to people who are in the country illegally. It's why I stay at Semere's house, which I am happy for. I'm glad for the company of Efrem and Fikru.

There's a coffee bar next to the reception desk, and it's there that I spend the majority of my time waiting. It's open, breezy, and covered for shade. The ground is packed dirt, the chairs and tables made of plastic. A young woman serves the drinks. I'm surprised to hear her speak Tigrinya, even more surprised to find out that all the workers speak it, as well as

Amharic. In such a place as this, it's comforting to be surrounded by the familiar.

While I'm here, Semere helps me exchange my Eritrean *nakfa* for Sudanese pounds. The rates are fair, but as always, someone takes a share for their commission. I'm also able to purchase a new international SIM card for my phone so it will work on the Sudanese network. The service is weak and unreliable, but it's better than being without.

On my third day in Kassala, I recognize two former coworkers of mine from Asmara, Meles and Omer, asking for a room at the hotel. After getting over our surprise at finding each other here, we spend the afternoon trading stories. I learn that their adventure began many weeks before my own and that they spent time at one of the United Nations Refugee camps at Shagarab outside of the town of Showak, which is about a hundred kilometers southwest of here.

"Why did you leave Eritrea?" I ask, because while the ultimate reason is always the same — government oppression — it's the details that make the stories unique.

"There's no chance to start a business anymore," Omer tells me. He sighs with resignation and snubs out his cigarette. His trademark white pants, once kept fastidiously clean and crisply ironed, are now dirty and wrinkled. "So many opportunities exist elsewhere in Africa, but we aren't allowed to seek them in Eritrea."

I remember that both men have experience in accounting, like me. In particular, their areas of expertise are in supply chain management, hotel management, and international transactions. Our country's restrictions on trade and tourism have hit them especially hard these past several years.

"Before," Meles tells me, "it was possible to do business in Sudan, Uganda, Angola." He lights another cigarette and offers the package to us. I shake my head, but Omer takes one. Meles has always struck me as somewhat jittery, as if he's just had too much coffee to drink. When he speaks, his words come out in a breathless rush. "Now it's impossible for the private sector in Eritrea. You either work for the government or one of the government-controlled companies, you try to have your own business and are pushed down, or you starve. A close relative of mine found a great job opportunity for me in Juba, but Eritrea wouldn't let me leave, so I finally took matters into my own hands."

"It couldn't have been very easy for you."

"Compared to others who have tried, I was lucky." He tells me how his sister-in-law and two friends crossed the border on foot, led by a solitary smuggler. After walking for twelve straight hours, always on the lookout for patrols, they finally reached Kassala. Their feet were swollen for days afterward, despite their physical conditioning in the ENS.

"So, you are going to Juba now?" I ask. The city is South Sudan's provisional capital and is far from our present location. By road, it's more than two thousand kilometers, an impossible journey to make on foot. "How will you get there?"

"The same way we made it here," he answers. "One footstep at a time, if necessary."

They ask where I am going, and I tell them about my family in America, whom I have not seen in more than six years, except for my youngest daughter. My friend shakes his head. "But you have even farther to go than me."

"I don't plan to walk there!"

He smiles and nods. "And yet I'm sure you would if you had to."

I ask them for any advice they can give me about life in the refugee camp, as it will be a necessary step to my staying in Sudan. It's where I will have to register as a refugee. I also want to know about Kassala. Meles offers to call his sister-in-law, Alem, who is still in the camp. "She will take you to meet the people who can help you during your stay. They know the best way for you to process your refugee status and get you the proper paperwork."

I realize how lucky I am to have found them. It's always nice to see a familiar face in a strange place, especially so under the circumstances, but it's the advice they impart that will make my journey much easier and safer.

After a little while, Meles leaves us to take care of some business. Omer gives me a tour around the town. It's small and flat, spread out over the desert like so many other such settlements. Brownish-red is the predominant color, the color of the dirt. There is the occasional splash of faded blue and gold paint, often against a white background. A few trees lush with green leaves manage to survive the harsh conditions. In the distance rise the Tava Mountains, offering a stark but beautiful backdrop beneath a hazy blue sky. They look like giant termite mounds worn smooth by the rains.

He takes me to an internet café where I can check my email and read the news. He shows me which coffee shops are good and which are bad, and tells me other tricks to stay out of trouble. "It may not look like it, but Kassala has a population close to half a million," he tells me. Then his voice grows quiet. "But I warn you not to try to see it all. It is very important that you stay close to the hotel. If you don't, you might fall into the hands of the police."

It's the holy month of Ramadan here in Kassala, and the hotel is quiet, as many of its guests are Muslim and fasting from dawn until sunset. Only a few people sit at the tables. In fact, today is *Eid al-Adha*, the holy day known as the Feast of the Sacrifice, which honors Abraham's willingness to slay his son at God's request. After the last prayers, all the Muslim restaurants will open for the feasts and celebrations that follow the day's fasting. I am Christian, but I'm now in a land that practices Islam, so it's essential to know and respect the local customs.

The restaurant is lit only by light from the door and windows, as the electric lamps are off. A warm breeze makes its way through. The street beyond is quiet. I'm in the company of two other men eating our lunchtime meal at the hotel. Berhe and Gebray are also Christian, both young, in their twenties, and both former ENS members. Berhe is from Asmara, whereas Gebray came from Zoba Debub, south of the capital. After crossing the border separately, they were introduced to each other by the man facilitating both their trips to Israel. We sip our coffee and quietly chat while we wait for our food to arrive.

We have ordered a typical Eritrean meal of fried lentils, vegetables, and beef cooked in a variety of spicy sauces. Everything is served on the traditional *injera* bread, which we use in place of utensils to eat. The prices are reasonable. I have to be careful with the little cash I have left, roughly the equivalent of ten thousand *nakfa*. It must serve for my meals and anything else I need to purchase. For example, I'm still in need of pants, more underwear, and shoes.

We are relaxed and chatting quietly when I notice one of the other men stiffen in alarm. He signals us with a tip of his head. From the street, two Sudanese soldiers dressed in the blue uniforms of the law enforcement unit enter the hotel compound and quickly make their way to one of the rooms in the back.

"Are they looking for someone?" Berhe wonders. "They appeared to be in a hurry."

"Do you think we should leave?" Gebray asks. None of us has yet been registered with the UNHCR as refugees, so we aren't supposed to be anywhere in the country except in a camp.

I don't know what to say or do. I'm not sure if we are in any danger, although the concern in my friends' eyes would suggest that we are. We have already ordered our food. To leave now, before eating, would only raise suspicions.

"Maybe they are just here to eat, too."

Despite the Islamic requirement to fast, it isn't unusual to see a Muslim man or two asking to be served in one of the non-Muslim restaurants. They take their meals in private rooms to avoid being caught breaking the rules.

If these were civilians, we wouldn't give it another thought. But they are soldiers, and we're afraid they will take us away, if for no other reason than because we saw them here. We certainly don't want to be around when they come back out.

The food arrives before we can decide what to do, so we hurriedly eat and slip out before the soldiers reappear.

This is how we live our lives now, always with a low level of fear, sometimes on the edge of panic, and the occasional episode of near terror in those moments when we think we might be arrested and deported. We aren't free to wander about. We avoid gathering in groups of more than three or four. We don't want to attract unwanted attention. I hate that I can't trust most of the people I meet. With the exception of a few regular customers, I'm wary of all strangers. The constant anxiety wears on me. I'm impatient to move on.

Through my discussions with people I trust, I know I have two options for where to go next, but I have simply been hesitant to decide which one of them to take. From Kassala, I can either make the shorter journey to the Shagarab refugee camps outside of the town of Showak, and there begin the process of requesting a pass to travel to Khartoum for a meeting at the US Embassy. Or, for a large sum of money, I can find someone who can take me directly to Khartoum on back roads to avoid the authorities. I decide on the first option, because the alternative is dangerous and offers no guarantee of a safe arrival. Besides, Shagarab is on the way to Khartoum anyway, and so if it doesn't look promising there, I can continue onward.

My first step in this process is to report to a reception center run by the United Nations High Commission on Refugees, where I will formally register my status. Outside of Kassala is one such UNHCR facility. From there I will be transferred to the main camp in Shagarab, so it seems like a good starting point for me.

Omer arranges for a taxi, which takes me most of the way to the reception center. The driver refuses to go any closer for fear of being seen aiding an illegal. After collecting his money, he points me in the direction I need to go. Then he speeds off in a cloud of dust. Carrying nothing but a small bag that holds everything I now own, I walk the last kilometer or so, finally arriving at a large compound surrounded by nothing more than a low stone wall, more a boundary than a barrier.

A lean man in his fifties welcomes me at the entrance. He is wearing a white *jallabiyah*. His body is stooped, as if beaten down by the sun, and he clutches a gnarled stick in one bony hand. The wood is worn down to a high polish by years of handling. I tell him where I came from and why I'm here. He allows me to enter. Together we walk across a large open yard to a house set back away from the gate. The walls are yellow and appear to be freshly painted. He points to a long line, which I join. Most of the men and women waiting there sit or crouch in the shade with their backs against the wall. A few people mill aimlessly about.

There's very little relief from the heat and brightness of the day. More people appear behind me, and soon I am swallowed up in a much larger crowd. Now I am just one more person out of dozens waiting to be received by the UNHCR officials. I find out this happens each and every day. People like me appear at the gate out of nowhere, as if sprung to life by the desert.

We shuffle slowly forward, kicking up dust. It's red, like metal rust. The few bushes inside the walls are the same color as camelhair. They are covered in sharp thorns. The only bright colors come from the clothing worn by some of the people surrounding me, men and women and children of all ages. The rest wear white or gray or tan. Jaundiced bloodshot eyes stare like yellow moons out of dark faces. Most of these people appear gaunt, physically beaten down. Seeing them, I'm transported back in time to the skeletal stranger I once saw in a mirror.

At one point, I'm taken through the house, which consists of four rooms. The smallest is unfurnished and without fixtures. I guess that it might be used as a kitchen. There are two bathrooms, one for each gender. Construction supplies and litter are scattered about, hinting that the structure is fairly new. The UNHCR must be its first tenant. I wonder how many other people have already passed through its doors before me. Hundreds? More likely thousands. If this is happening in hundreds of other places, then unless something changes, soon there will be no one left inside Eritrea for the government to oppress.

On my first morning at the UNHCR reception camp, four brothers show up. They tell me they had been sent altogether to train at Sawa, leaving no one to earn money or take care of their family at home. In desperation, they escaped here. But now they are earning no money at all. Their hope for a better future elsewhere is like the hope I once had for my country, based on little more than a promise. And just as likely to be met with disappointment.

Another four arrive later that same day. This time, they are young boys. Their skin is plastered in dust and streaked from their sweat. Their tattered clothes hang over their shoulders like rags. I learn they are only fifteen and sixteen years old and have been traveling by foot for more than a week from their home town of Keren, over three hundred and fifty kilometers away. The smell of famine clings to them like the dirt. But like so many of the others I talk to, I hear only relief in their voices.

There are many more men and boys here than females. The women tend to keep to themselves, afraid of drawing unwanted attention, especially of the wrong kind. A couple of women arrive with children. They look nervous, frightened, flinching at every sound. I'm told they will have more protection here than out on the road, but I fear for their safety nonetheless. There are so many evil people preying on the weak out there — women and children are especially vulnerable — and the camp doesn't keep all of them out. I hear stories of people disappearing, kidnapped and taken away to be sold for slave labor, for organs and other body parts, and for the sex trade. No one notices when a refugee goes missing. No one cares. No one does anything about it. Why should they? We don't exist.

The next afternoon, three young women in their twenties join us. Their physical appearance tells me they have experienced some significant challenges recently. I later learn that they escaped from the training camp at Sawa while out collecting firewood. They managed to slip away after asking to relieve themselves in the brush. In a rare lapse of attention, the guards failed to notice their absence until they had run off. The women were fortunate to know the area well enough that they could avoid patrols in the thirty or so kilometers between the training camp and the border. They walked mainly at night, slipping from one hiding place to another, using only the light of the moon to guide them. They had no food or water. They slept during the day, and then only in shifts. At last, they came upon a family working their farm, who took pity on them. With enough supplies to last a couple of days and instructions for crossing, they finally reached the border and slipped into Sudan just three days after leaving Sawa. Yet they look like they have been wandering in the desert for a month.

Some of the men here are so bored, so bereft of the usual social constraints, that they don't care if they are caught staring openly at the women. Their intentions are plain to see. It seems both tragic and ironic to me that instead of stripping away the women's femininity, the hardships they endured only seem to have amplified their vulnerability. I pray they stay together until they reach their destination, wherever it may be. Together, they can protect each other. But if they separate, trouble will find them much too quickly.

For shelter, the women occupy one large room of the house, while the men have the remaining two. Bedrolls occupy every inch of space on the floors, including the hallway and kitchen area. At night, the mosquitoes are relentless, driving us mad with their constant whining and unquenchable thirst for warm blood. I try to avoid them, but it's like trying to avoid the sun while walking across the desert in the middle of the day. In the morning, our bodies are covered in itchy welts.

For food, we receive meager portions of bread, which is all the aid workers can offer us. It's hardly enough to call a meal, but it's better than nothing. Once we have been processed, we are forbidden from leaving the compound — for our safety, they say — so we are entirely at the mercy of the aid workers, who arrange to purchase items for us at a nearby shop. We pool our cash to buy soft drinks and milk powder, biscuits, and other items that help make life a little more tolerable while we wait. The workers themselves make a big fuss about having to do this for us, but in the end, it's our money they use to pay for the purchases, including their own.

I am surprised by how few of the refugees have plans beyond registering. I think too many of them simply fled whatever horror they knew without giving their future much thought. How desperate must they have been? Whenever anyone raises the specter of being sent back, terror flashes across their faces. But now that they are here, they will have to decide what to do next. I feel terrible for them. Most will likely end up in one of the permanent refugee camps, where I have heard some stay for years.

The lucky few, like myself, are already in contact with people living abroad, friends or family members who were able to get out legally or escaped after the government began its crack down. Like myself, almost all of us rely on these connections for financial assistance and guidance. They are our bridges to a better life, to escaping this place.

At the moment, only three of us have functioning mobile phones, and everyone wants to use them. We do what we can to accommodate them. Usually, the call is to a number in Eritrea, a friend or family member. They typically hang up before anyone answers, because someone might be listening in on that line. Later, the recipient of the "missed call" will call back on a different line, so I have to run and find the recipient. It's clear that many of these calls are the first chance they have had to reconnect with people back home. It's the first indication they're able to give that they have made it safely across the border. The conversations are often coded or contain no identifying details, so that the government can't easily figure out what they mean. This is how paranoid we are.

Because of the time zone differences in other parts of the world, sometimes the calls come at night. The UNHCR people don't like us to make noise when others are trying to sleep, but it can't be helped. Also, because the signal is usually weak, we have to speak loudly.

Everyone I meet, every story I hear, makes me understand even better the scale of the problem we have in Eritrea and the hopelessness of my fellow countrymen and women. With each new arrival, I see more despair, more desperation. But I also see new hope. The circumstances they are fleeing are so bad that they are willing to risk everything, their lives and livelihoods, willing to leave everything they have and know behind forever. Willing to step into total uncertainty, all for a chance at something better. Not a promise of it, just a chance, and not even a very good one at that.

We are all stunned when a family arrives the next day with a four-month-old baby boy in their arms. What, I wonder, could be so terrible that they would take such a risk? The mother tells us that it isn't her only attempt. She was caught by the border patrol the first time she tried to cross.

We all lean in, eager to hear more of the story. How did she manage to avoid being thrown into prison? How was she able to keep her child?

"I was still pregnant then, only a few weeks and not yet showing," she explains. Her voice is little more than a whisper. "But my husband was away in the ENS and I was starving at home. We had no food, and I had to do something for my unborn child. When the guards found out about the baby, they took pity and agreed to release me. I was lucky. They would have sent me to one of the work camps otherwise."

"You were caught, and yet you tried again, this time with a child?"

"This time, I had my husband with me. We thought we would never have a chance, as he was assigned to a remote area in the south near the Eritrea-Djibouti border. But three months after the baby was born, they finally allowed him to take a leave to visit."

"We knew it was our only chance to escape," the husband said, taking over telling the story. "I knew I would never get another. So we ran. We got some help from a friend, who arranged for a guide to take us safely across the border. This is how we ended up in Kassala."

Once more, the details of their escape are strikingly similar to mine, from the agents they employed to make the arrangements, to the people who risked their lives to guide them each step of the way. Seeing the others nodding in understanding, I realize how common the practice has become.

"We always dreamed of a better life," the mother says. "Our plan is to go to America. Or Canada."

"You're extremely lucky to have made it this far," one person says. "I know many people who tried. I have heard too many sad stories of those who failed."

And again, we all nod. We have all heard the stories. We all knew the risks we took, and how our chances favored failure over success. Yet we all still tried. And we have made it this far. But none of us is fooling ourselves about what lies ahead. Our journeys are far from over. In fact, they have barely just begun.

# Shagarab Refugee Camp, Sudan

ON MY FOURTH DAY AT THE RECEPTION CENTER, several dozen of us are loaded onto open bed trucks for relocation to one of three Shagarab refugee camps. The women and children, including the couple with their infant, are offered seats. The rest of us must stand, making an already difficult transit over heavily rutted dirt roads that much more exhausting.

The fine pale dust thrown up by the tires soon coats our bodies, gets into our eyes, noses, and mouths. Sweat turns it to mud the same color as blood, which streams down our arms. The wind and sun dry it, leaving crusty patches that look like scabs. I'm weak from lack of a proper diet, and my knees buckle with every jolt. But I'm in much better shape than many of the others. My own escape was so much easier than theirs.

There is little chance of conversation as we rattle along. Even if we weren't too emotionally overwhelmed by our situation or too weary to bother, the conditions of the road make talking impossible.

Before we reach the camp, three men slip off the back of the truck and scurry off. A boy standing beside me shouts into my ear that they had already been in the camp previously and left without authorization during a failed attempt to reach Israel. "They're headed over to the nearby millet plantation," he says. "After mixing in with the refugee workers, they'll be able to return to the camp."

I learn that this will allow the men to bypass the registration step that awaits the rest of us upon our arrival. More importantly, they will avoid the Sudanese National Security Service that oversees the process.

As the men disappear into the scrub, I can't help but realize how little freedom I have actually gained by my escape. I have simply traded one form of oppression for another.

We are close to the camp, but it doesn't reveal itself to us right away. When it does, I'm shocked at what I see. I had been expecting something similar to the reception center we just left behind, a relatively quiet and secure place with a wall surrounding it. Instead, what greets us is a city of tents and ramshackle structures, their fabric sides and roofs faded and dusty. Loose flaps whip in the hot breeze. As we draw closer, I see rows upon rows of mud and straw huts called *tukul*. There is no fencing, nothing to keep us in or the animals out.

The moment the trucks stop, hundreds of people appear, eager to meet us. They scan our faces, hoping to find someone familiar to them among our number. It's disconcerting to be the focus of their attention, but even more so when the hope in their eyes gives way to disappointment.

After that, most of the crowd disperses. Today, there are no reunions.

A few curious onlookers remain behind to pelt us with questions. They toss out the names of people and towns we might know, eager for news. Many of us have spent weeks already on the road, so any news we could offer them is outdated, though still fresher than what they might already know. Some in our group have been away from home for so long that they can offer no news at all.

We line up at the National Security Service office to await our turn to be registered and silently recite what we have been coached to say. Among the questions we will be asked are where and when we crossed borders, how long we stayed in each place, whether we are expecting to eventually be joined, and if we hope to locate friends and family already here in Sudan. The NSS officers are brusque. At least the international aid workers and translators appear willing, if not eager, to help ease our concerns. After we finish with the interviews, we are briefed on the camp's operations and our responsibilities as members of the community.

The first-timers among us are given a free meal. The UNHCR is unable to provide food to all of the camp's residents on a daily basis, so this is a onetime occurrence to help ease our transition. We're expected to find our own meals after this. The quality of the food is very poor and the amounts paltry. All it succeeds in doing is slightly dulling the keen edge of our hunger.

It takes me a while to find Alem, the sister-in-law of Meles, the former coworker I met in Kassala. She, in turn, introduces me to Petros and Misgun, who are cousins, and Daniel. Petros married the year before, and his wife has already made her way to Canada, where she is assisting his journey from there. Both Misgun and Daniel left wives and children in Asmara. They are hoping to settle somewhere in Europe, where they will then work to bring their families.

They help get me oriented to the camp. They take me to a place where I'm able to wash up. As with everything else, water is limited, but I'm glad for a chance to wash the dirt and sweat off my face and arms. Afterward, they take me to another part of the camp where we can pay for a halfway decent meal. It seems strange to think that in such a place as this there exist semi-permanent business establishments, but not only are there coffee houses and restaurants, but also shops where I can purchase other goods. Some people own livestock. Some sell wares from two-wheeled carts pulled by donkeys. Others offer services, such as laundry and hair cutting. Even here, in the harshest of environments and under the most restricting of conditions, one can still find the enterprising spirit.

The only permanent structures are the UNHCR and NSS buildings. The rest, shelters and business establishments, are constructed from scrap materials, bits of wood, metal, and fabric. Even mud is used. Tarps are in abundance. Much of the manufactured material is purchased or scrounged from Kassala.

The businesses are located near the center of the camp. Some appear to have been in place for many years. In fact, I'm told that some of the camp residents have been here for decades. I can't imagine that it's by choice, although that may be true for a small number who have learned not just to survive, but to thrive under such conditions. Most people who stay very long are simply stuck here, having nowhere else to go.

It doesn't take long for me to realize that the quality of one's existence here depends on how much one can afford to pay. Besides food and services, money is needed to rent better lodgings than the flimsy, crowded UNHCR-provided tents. For most of the camp's temporary residents, the primary source of income is from friends and family members living elsewhere in the world. Neither the UN agency nor the Sudanese government offers financial assistance.

While in Kassala, I was warned to keep my money hidden, and my newfound friends remind me to be especially careful here. Most of the camp residents are honest, but there are always thieves looking for an opportunity. I secure most of my money in the lining of my waistband and keep just enough in my pocket for spending. Thankfully, most of the people I meet are willing to look after one another. No one is rich, but no one is left to starve, either.

I find one of the most remarkable things to be our access to the Internet. The same establishment where I purchase my first dinner also rents out time on its lone computer for those wishing to send and receive emails. Because it's the only machine here, there's usually a waiting list. I sign up, and when it's my turn, I sit down to compose a message to Wudasie. But then my mind goes blank. I waste several minutes doing nothing but staring at the empty screen. There's too much to tell, and I'm so emotionally worn down I don't know where to start. I end up just telling her where I am and that I am doing fine.

That night my newfound friends invite me to stay with them in their hut. According to custom, they offer me the best they have, one of their *angareb* beds. The legs of the small wooden cots are wound with camelhair or other such material to repel scorpions and other pests. Their generosity overwhelms me, but I politely decline and sleep on the floor instead.

I don't wish to become too comfortable here. I don't plan on staying long.


There are no mosquitoes in the highland city of Asmara. Because of the elevation, they're unable to survive and breed. In the Eritrean lowlands, coastal plains, and along the various rivers and lakes, however, they can be a significant problem, along with the diseases they carry. Here, in the desert of Sudan, there are many different biting insects in addition to mosquitoes, some I have never heard of or seen before. When I wake in the morning, my skin is newly covered in angry, itchy welts.

After consulting with my new friends, I decide to go ahead and rent a nearby hut. I also purchase an *angareb* bed in hopes of avoiding another night like the last. The bed is hand-framed with local wood and lined with old rope and recycled strips of plastic. The shelter is old and dingy, no larger than three meters by three meters, but it offers protection from the sun and wind, and I can improve it to keep out most of the flies and mosquitoes. The roof is made of tree branches and matted grass, which also requires some maintenance. I purchase new mosquito netting so I can pull the bed outside on the hottest nights, where even the faintest whisper of a breeze offers some relief. On such nights, nearly everyone sleeps outside.

Most of my new neighbors in this part of the camp are Eritrean. It's shocking to hear how long some of them have spent in Shagarab. I meet people who emigrated here in the 1980s, while the War for Independence between Eritrea and Ethiopia still raged. They never expected to remain refugees as long as they have. It's evident in their faces that they have forgotten about moving on. This is their home now. Many have cattle, which graze on the stunted and stubborn plants that grow in and around the camp. The animals wake me up at night with the sounds of their shuffling about.

Many of the camp residents were once farmers in their homelands. Others were students or teachers, civil servants or soldiers. I meet many who have a college education like me. Not surprisingly, I even find former coworkers and acquaintances from Asmara.

As I wander about, I notice more and more children, from infants and toddlers to teenagers. There are more boys than girls. Too many of them seem to be unaccompanied, without parents or older siblings. Survival forces them to band together. What hope do they have of a better future, when they have no parent to guide them? How likely are they to fall victim to some wicked person? I thank the Good Lord again and again that my daughters will never have to experience this life.

Within a week, I have settled into the camp's routine. Each day from Saturday through Thursday we check for our names to be posted on the boards outside the front office, which provide instructions for individuals whose status is transitional. The first step in our processing is to be registered as a refugee, whereupon we are provided with two important forms of identification: a Yellow Card, issued by the Sudanese government's Office of the Commission for Refugees, and a White Card, issued by the UNHCR. Both are mandatory forms of ID and proof that a person has been registered as a refugee.

The process for obtaining these cards is long and difficult and can take as long as two months. The interviews can take hours, and only a few are given out each day, and only in the mornings. More people arrive daily from the nearby reception centers, so the line never shortens. Patience can be a hard thing to hold onto, particularly when someone tries to cheat and get ahead in the line. As I am starting to learn, there are illegitimate ways to bypass the system here, as well. They are endorsed by some of the police assigned to the camp, and even some of the aid workers involved in the processing. It isn't hard to find an employee of the Sudanese National Security Service, the Commission for Refugees of Sudan, or the UNHCR who will grant expedited processing and a favorable disposition in exchange for a bribe.

I shouldn't be surprise by this anymore. Whenever there is a chance for someone to make money, they will find a way to exploit it. Still, each time I encounter it, I am appalled. But the monetary bribes aren't even the worst ways we are being taken advantage of. Some of the workers flirt with the females, especially the young and more naive ones. They use their positions to extract sexual favors. When the women refuse, they threaten to make the registration process even longer.

The corruption is widespread. Even those who are victims engage in it. I meet a man who offers to sell me his medical certificate, which is supposed to expedite the registration process. Those with medical conditions, such as diabetes or high blood pressure, are often pushed to the front of the line. I know the sooner I have my identification cards, the sooner I can leave the camp to go to Khartoum, but is this a line I'm willing to cross? What will this man do for himself once he has sold his certificate? He assures me he can get a replacement for 250 Sudanese pounds, roughly 100 US dollars.

"Give me 150 pounds now," he tells me. "You pay the rest after you get the certificate."

Against my better judgment, I take his offer. A week passes, and I start getting that familiar feeling of being taken for a fool. I demand my money back and threaten to tell everyone about him. He denies the deal, but finally agrees to return all but fifty pounds to me.

This is the price I pay for learning my lesson. After this, I force myself to be patient and wait in line like everyone else.


In Sudan, Friday is the Islamic equivalent of the Christian Sabbath, so the office doesn't process any refugees. With little to do to fill the hours when I'm not waiting in line, I wander about the camp. I will usually go and sit in the coffee shops, where it's easy to find a card or board game. Many of these shops have their own diesel-powered generators for electricity, which they sell to others. Electricity is a luxury not found in the huts or tents. For light, we make do with flashlights.

Incredibly, some of the establishments even have small televisions. When they are on, which is most of the time, it's usually a soccer match being shown. Soccer is the one interest we can all share, whether Christian or Muslim, Eritrean or other nationality, young or old. Everyone speaks the language of soccer. Everyone has their favorite team. Generally, they are fans of one of the big three— Arsenal, Chelsea, or Liverpool. The games create an atmosphere of friendly competition and community. They help us forget the wretchedness of our situation and the dire circumstances in our homelands that forced us to flee here. Soccer offers us a glimmer of hope for a better future. Or at least a window into an alternate reality into which we can occasionally escape.

In addition to the coffee and grain shops and small eating establishments, I'm happy to find a thriving business in prepaid cellular phones and services. There are also places for sending and receiving money, a process in Arabic called *tahwil*. What I don't find is very much in the way of reading material. There are no books, magazines, or newspapers available for sale, and very few to borrow among the residents. I can understand why no refugee would want to carry such heavy objects around with them, especially during the rainy season, but it seems incredible to think that so few books have found their way into the possession of at least the long-term residents. Without access to such materials, how will the children ever learn about the world outside the camp? How will they learn to read? I suppose many never will.

Another convenience lacking in our accommodations is toilets. There aren't even any pit toilets here. Any personal business is supposed to be done out in the scrub beyond the boundaries of the camp. Some people are too lazy to bother. It isn't hard to find piles of used toilet paper and human waste in parts of the camp. Because there's no true privacy, I have made it a habit of conducting my affairs in the low light of evening. Sometimes, I walk a half mile before I can be sure of being alone. How anyone gets used to this is beyond my ability to comprehend.

As for bathing, there are a few establishments scattered about the camp where one can pay for a shower. The locals call them *hamams*, the Arabic word for bath. The one closest to my hut has a half dozen stalls. Each has three walls and a door. The floor is cement, but there's no roof. Two boards are laid over the tops of the walls, on which a twenty-liter plastic jerry can is set. The water drains out under gravity. The cost is fifty Sudanese *piasters*, or half a pound, which is the equivalent of about twenty American cents.

The *hamam* also serves as a laundry. Although I prefer to do my own washing, I use the *hamam*'s ironing service to remove the wrinkles. It's one standard I refuse to let go.

The camp administrators distribute water into the living areas by pipes from large storage tanks. The faucets are set close to the ground to discourage us from hoarding it in large containers. We have to use smaller cans or bottles to transfer water to our jerry cans. When the faucets are not running, we purchase water from sellers, who bring it in their carts. In my hut I keep a full jerry can for drinking and washing. I don't prepare food, as I don't have cookware or utensils. On especially hot days, I wet down the floor of my hut to help keep it cool and the dust from rising.

When it rains, we have too much water. The roof leaks. The walkways become treacherous. Mud gets everywhere and disease spreads. I have to be careful, as there is no medical care available here. Instead, if someone is sick enough, they are taken to the hospital, and that comes with its own risks and creates new problems.

Being here is not as safe as I had hoped it would be. Arrests are common. Often they are prompted by little more than someone's baseless accusation. Real crimes do occur, of course. Violence is all too common. Property and money are stolen regularly. Rape is a sad reality for many who don't have someone to protect them. And even when they do, it still happens. There are constant rumors of children being kidnapped. I feel powerless to do anything about it. What is unforgiveable is that the UNHCR and local authorities do so little to prevent it from happening. There are no investigations. So, unless someone is caught in the act, the crime goes unpunished and is quickly forgotten by all but the victim's friends and family.

On top of all this is the constant risk of deportation. There is no rhyme or reason to the detentions. All too often, the police or security forces will come in the middle of the night, when everyone is asleep. People disappear, and we never find out if they left voluntarily, were taken to prison, or were kidnapped.

One day, two of my new friends, Alem and Daniel, tell me they are leaving early the next morning for Khartoum. They have had their White and Yellow ID Cards for more than a week, but they still haven't been able to obtain their travel passes, which is a separate process. The passes grant us freedom of movement throughout the country. Too impatient to wait, they have arranged with smugglers to take them to the capital.

Since leaving the reception center for Kassala, I have been advised by several people not to consider such a dangerous option. My brother Yebio even warned me against doing so. The trips are supposedly run by Rashaida, the same ethnic group as the men who died — or were killed — trying to escape our training camp in Kiloma. They are known for overloading their pickup trucks and driving at reckless speeds through the brush to avoid being caught by the Sudanese police and army. I have heard stories of men being shot at, of trucks crashing, of people being abandoned. When they cross the Atbarah River, a branch of the Nile, the boats are often old and overloaded. Some sink, drowning their passengers.

I know my friends have heard all these stories, too, so I don't waste my time trying to discourage them. I simply wish them good luck and pray they don't become another cautionary tale for those who are considering following behind them.

Other than the permanent residents, the camp population changes quickly. A new friend made one day is gone almost the next. People move in and out of tents and huts around me seemingly every day. In a short time, I hear a dozen different stories of survival and heartache. Then a hundred. We celebrate each success, mourn each loss. One thing, however, remains the same: the endless waiting.

It's so hard to be patient, especially when you know someone is also waiting for you at the other end.

At long last, I receive both my White and Yellow Cards. Now I just need to get my travel pass so I can go to Khartoum. This means submitting yet another application and waiting for the card to be issued. It's difficult for me to wait, but unlike Alem and Daniel, I can't afford not to. My application for an entry visa to join my family in the United States is in the process of being submitted, so there's no need to get to the capital right away. It's not worth the risk of the dangerous smuggler's journey through the heart of Sudan.

Less than two weeks after applying for a travel permit, I receive word that it will be issued. At the same time, Wudasie tells me an appointment for an interview at the consulate is being set up, so now I must make arrangements to pick up the card in Girba and for further travel to Khartoum. All of a sudden, everything seems to be falling exactly into place. Cautiously, I allow myself to imagine a reunion with my family happening soon, not in a matter of months or years, but rather in a few weeks.

# Khartoum, Sudan

TODAY, I AM GOING TO THE REGIONAL OFFICE of the Commission for Refugees at Khashm el-Girba to receive my travel permit. Girba is a small town outside of Kassala, a rather unremarkable place except for the hydroelectric dam they built on the Atbarah River in the 1960s. The reservoir is a source of water for irrigation, as well as electricity for the region. The structure may be small by Western standards, but it's one of the biggest in the country. It's certainly the largest I have ever seen in person.

The reason for going to Girba first is to have my photo taken for the travel permit, which is now required for all adults. With me at the camp gate waiting for a taxi are three women and their eight children. Juveniles don't need a permit, but they must travel in the company of their parents or guardians. We have been told that we will spend the night in Kassala after we are finished in Girba. Tomorrow, I will travel to Khartoum for eventual processing of my entry visa to America. Like me, two of the three women going with me have spouses waiting for them in the United States. The third woman's eventual destination is Europe. I assume they will all be traveling with me to the capital.

Our "taxi" arrives, a small pickup truck with undersized tires and worn springs. The truck sinks low when all twelve of us climb onto the back. There's too little space, so we have to pack ourselves tightly together. "Pay first," the driver demands. The women exchange wary glances. "Pay now or get off!"

The real trouble begins at the Khashm el-Girba checkpoint. One of the guards circles the truck, coolly eying each of us in turn without speaking a word. Finally, he points to the eldest of the children in the women's company, a thirteen-year-old girl, and demands to see her identification. The girl's mother tries to explain that she's too young to have her own, but the guard refuses to believe her. "She is not a child. If she has no identification, she cannot travel. Either she gets off, or everyone stays here."

I try my best to convince the guard that the mother is telling the truth, that the girl is too young. My Arabic is poor, and the guard has trouble understanding my English. He asks if I am the father.

"No."

The guard laughs cynically. "Then how could you possibly know if this woman is telling the truth or not?"

The girl and her mother are now terrified. They don't want to get off the truck, especially after paying for the trip. Nor do they want to leave the safety of the group.

At last, our driver intervenes. He informs us that we have no choice but to offer the guard a bribe, if we wish not to be left behind. Suddenly, it becomes clear that the guard's objective all along was to collect money from us. We reluctantly hand over several Sudanese pounds and hope that it is enough. The guard doesn't look satisfied, but he waves us through the checkpoint and allows us to go on our way.

We ask the driver how much more of this we can expect, but all he offers is a vague "It depends."

"On what?" I ask.

"On how lucky or unlucky you are."

It's impossible to tell what this means. We know he is Sudanese himself and Muslim, but he gives no clue what he thinks of the corruption, or whether he is somehow involved. But we arrive in Girba without further incident.

We have no problems getting our photo ID travel passes. And when we are done, we find a minibus to take us to Kassala. The driver tells us he won't leave until all of the seats are bought and paid for. After waiting a while, we offer to buy the remaining seats. We're anxious to be on our way. None of us wants to arrive in a strange place after dark.

Before entering Kassala, we are stopped and ordered to show our papers once more. After the guard collects everyone's cards and IDs, he takes them inside the checkpoint office, presumably to see if our names are on their watch list. Unlike the first guard, who was dressed in khaki, this one wears the blue of the law enforcement unit. While we wait, dozens of vehicles pass through without any problems. Eventually, our driver gets impatient and offers to go inside to check on our progress. He returns several minutes later with our papers and a scowl on his face. He hands the IDs over to me to redistribute to their owners, then climbs into his seat and starts the engine.

"What was the delay?" I ask.

"The guard was holding onto the passes," he says, and pulls through the checkpoint. "He was waiting for us to offer a bribe."

I don't press the issue, and the driver says nothing more about it. Maybe he's embarrassed by the pervasive corruption. Or he could just feel guilty about taking our money for the unused seats, but he doesn't ask to be reimbursed for what I'm sure he must have paid on our behalf.

By mid-afternoon, we are all situated in a hotel in Kassala.

The next morning, we take a taxi arranged by the receptionist at the hotel, which drops us off at the bus station. The receptionist had also secured our bus tickets to Khartoum— for a commission, of course. At this point, I just have to shake my head. I have never seen so many middlemen in my life. Everyone wants a cut of the money.

Our bus arrives. To our relief, it's large and new, with several modern amenities, including thick cushioned seats and color television screens mounted from the ceiling.

While waiting for the long drive to begin, I try to place a call to Alem and Daniel. I have been told they have since arrived in Khartoum, although not without having encountered a few problems on their way. I'm hoping they can provide me with some assistance once I arrive, starting with a place to stay. The women call their own contacts, as well. Soon after departing, we lose the cell phone signal.

The bus is comfortable, and the road is smooth. For a little while I stare out at the scenery, but there isn't much to see. The landscape is flat, arid, and sparsely populated. Acacia trees rise up from the sands. When the television screens turn on, we draw the shades down to block the glare of the sun. I lose interest in the program and try to sleep, but my mind is filled with too many questions about what comes next.

At last, we reach the final checkpoint just outside of Khartoum. Until now, the ride had been uneventful, and the only interruptions were during brief rest stops. I expect a repeat of our previous experiences — the guards stopping us, boarding, demanding paperwork they know we can't produce so we will be forced to offer a bribe — but nothing of the sort happens. The driver is waved through and begins to weave his way into the increasingly busy traffic. I breathe a sigh of relief.

We arrive at Mina al-Barri, a large and busy bus station around four o'clock in the afternoon. I'm told it was recently constructed to replace the former bus station and market, the chaotic Souq al-Shaebi. A hundred buses of various sizes, makes, ages, and colors, as well as thousands of people of similar diversity, fill the area. Our driver pulls into a line behind a half dozen other vehicles, then shuts off the engine. "Khartoum," he announces, and points to a nearby mosque for those of us who wish to do our afternoon prayers.

The air outside is hot and dry and filled with aromas, both exotic and rancid. Here, spices, diesel exhaust, and dust all mix into a thick, soupy vapor that I will come to know as uniquely Khartoum. We are all tired but happy for our safe arrival.

Following a call from my cell phone, Alem calls back to tell me she is on her way. We arrange to meet at the taxi stand. The other members of the group from the bus have their own friends or family members to greet them, so we bid each other farewell and good luck and go on our separate ways.

When I see Alem, I'm pleasantly surprised to see that an old friend of mine from the National Service, Yohannes, is with her. I knew he came to Sudan many months before, so I had given Alem his phone number in hopes she would be able to connect with him. I hadn't expected them to come together to meet me.

Yohannes is an unusual case, as he didn't come here as a refugee, but rather for medical reasons. While in his third year of conscription, he was assigned to help clear land for a government farm near Keren, and it was there that he began to develop severe back problems from all the hard labor. He suffered incapacitating pain for months while his requests to the government for medical treatment went unanswered. He eventually decided to apply for a medical visa to come to Sudan for surgery.

241

We have a saying, *Akmka hilem*, which advises us to dream only for that which is attainable. This was the advice he had been given, not to bother with asking, because nobody thought his chances of getting treatment elsewhere were very good. He applied anyway, and against seemingly all odds, his request was granted. He said he wanted to try the legal route before attempting the alternative— crossing the border illegally. I can certainly understand his mindset. Besides, how many times have I dreamed for something that seemed unattainable? It seems to be a national pastime of ours.

The visa required getting a medical referral from the doctors at the Ministry of Defense and a strongly supportive letter from his commander. He was granted permission to come here for two months, with limited extensions if necessary. I assume he is still here on one of those extensions, as he has outstayed the original visa, most likely for postoperative follow-up therapy.

When I ask him how the surgery went, he demurs. Before I can press him on the subject, we are on our way.

Alem negotiates with the driver of a three-wheeled taxi the locals call a *rickshaw,* after the notorious bicycle cabs found in Asia, where the style of transport originated. But instead of being human-powered, these vehicles have little gasoline motors. They're small and agile, perfect for navigating the crowded streets of the city.

Alem gives the driver the address to her friend's place, Amar, who has agreed to let me stay with him until I can find a place of my own to rent. I learn I will be living in a two-bedroom flat with seven other people in a house with a number of other flats.

As soon as we arrive at the house, Amar jumps up from his seat on the couch and greets me warmly, as if we are long lost friends. He introduces me to three of his roommates, Seid, Efrem, and Yasir, all Eritrean refugees in their twenties. Yasir speaks Tigre, but the others welcome me in Tigrinya. Amar then offers me some cold water for my dry throat. I think he senses right away that I don't like the smell of the thick cigarette smoke filling the entire room. It filters the sunlight coming in from the one solitary open window in the apartment and turns everything a sickly shade of brown. I'm thankful when he tells me I can have the mattress placed beneath that same window. At the moment, it's being used for a card game. I survey the room and realize I won't be the only one sleeping in it. Besides the couch, there are two beds crammed into the spaces between cupboards and chairs, all occupying an area roughly four meters square. Still, I can't complain. It's far better than having no place to sleep at all, which had been my worry before arriving. I wasn't looking forward to the possibility of having to search for a place to stay in a city I had never been to, filled with people whose language and culture I don't share.

But now that I am here among friends, both old and new, I can relax. The situation is far from ideal, but it's better than I have had in well over a month. It's also not permanent. The first chance I get, I will start looking for a place of my own.

After a much needed shower in the communal bathroom outside the main building, Yohannes offers to take me shopping. I need to purchase new clothes and shoes before my interview at the consulate. The *shidda*-style sandals I have been wearing since Tessenei are no longer suitable. Besides, they remind me too much of my days in Kiloma, and I am determined to put that part of my life behind me once and for all. I also need toiletries and other basic essentials. Amar offers to go with us, but I sense he would prefer not to have to leave his card game.

We walk two blocks down a gravel track to a paved road where we can catch a minibus. Yohannes sticks his hand out to signal for a taxi, but it passes us without stopping. So do the next several. Yohannes seems nonplussed, even though it was clear to me that the buses weren't full. Seeing my confusion, he explains that the signal he's giving with his hand is for the Souq al-Arabi. "See there," he says, when another passes. "The driver is showing us with his own hand signal that he is going to a different market, the Souq Ash Shabi."

"What's the difference between them?" I ask.

"For one, the Souq al-Arabi is bigger and better for clothes. In fact, it's the largest open-air market in the country, so you will have more choices there than anywhere else. You will see. For another, it's in the center of the city, across the River Nile, so it's better for you to get oriented by going there first."

The next minibus to arrive slows when Yohannes signals, and the attendant hops out before it comes to a stop. We climb in and take a seat toward the back. The attendant takes his place behind the driver and whistles for us to pay. Yohannes hands the man sitting ahead of us a five pound note, who passes it up. The change is passed back in a similar fashion. At least this part is familiar to me, as it is exactly how we pay for bus fare in Asmara.

As we drive on, my friend points out places of interest. More rickshaws pass us on both sides. It seems like everyone is in a hurry to get somewhere. "Pay attention," he says. "This road leads to a neighborhood called Jabra. Many Eritreans and Ethiopians live there. You can find plenty of coffee shops and restaurants on this street. It's a good place to go and hang out, especially for people like you and me who don't have jobs."

In other words, it's cheaper to shop there.

We make several more stops along the way, picking up more passengers and dropping some off. Two women get on, and I'm startled to hear them speaking Tigrinya. As is customary in our culture, I greet them with a polite hello, and they reply in similar fashion before resuming their conversation. They aren't surprised at all by my presence here in Khartoum. It seems there are a lot of us here.

I'm learning much in a short period of time simply by watching how people behave. At one point, a young man in a *jallabiyah* gets up from his seat in back and steps quickly to the door. Before the minibus can barely begin to slow, he jumps off and is gone before I can turn to see him walk away. I realize there are no formal stops. People get on and off at their convenience. They know which bus is going to their destination by watching the signals the drivers give. There are no signs on the vehicle saying where the bus is going. I think the route is up to the driver, but most seem to serve the two markets. As these are the two primary destinations for most people, it makes things a little easier for me. Now, I only need to pay attention so I can learn how to get back home again.

"This is called Sahafa," Yohannes tells me. "It's one of the city's main streets."

Ditches run along each side of the road. They are filled with dirt, road rubble, and trash. The buildings are simple in their design and construction. The farther toward the center of town we go, however, the more decorative they become. The streets grow more crowded. People walk in every possible direction, filling walkways and clogging the streets. The driver is forced to slow down.

Finally, we arrive at the *souq*, which also serves as another bus terminal. The place is incredibly crowded, much more than I have seen in even the busiest cities I have visited. Neither Asmara nor Addis Ababa comes close to this. I have never seen so many people and vehicles before. Street vendors are everywhere, in permanent kiosks and in carts, walking about, shouting, hoping to sell everything from sunglasses to brightly colored plastic buckets to music CDs. And these are just the dealers outside the market.

The *souq* is spread out over several square blocks. In the background, the minarets of Mesjid al-Kabir, the Great Mosque, rise above the tarpaulin and sheet metal shades of the established vendors. There's a sense of urgency in the air, a feeling of needing to get from one place to another as quickly as possible, but there's no recognizable pattern to the movement. People are walking in every direction, their hands filled with plastic bags, squawking chickens, and waxed produce boxes.

Yohannes takes me to the section where they sell clothing, and I find that his tastes are completely unlike my own. He points out a seller of sneakers like the ones on his feet, but I would rather have a pair of comfortable loafers. When I tell him this, he takes me to another seller and negotiates a good price on the shoes I like. The whole exchange is conducted in Arabic, which I'm able to follow fairly well. Arabic is one of three official languages in Eritrea, and we are taught in school to at least recognize numbers. The process of negotiating repeats at the other sellers.

On our way back to the house, Yohannes takes me to an internet café so I can email Wudasie and let her know that I have arrived safely in Khartoum. The establishment is owned by an Eritrean man, which explains its name, Wintana, a Tigrinya term meaning "our wants" or "our wishes." Once, we sent *wintana* out through prayer. Today, I send mine out digitally.

With my message sent, Yohannes takes me to one last place, a little coffee shop owned by a woman named Elsa, which she leases from a Sudanese owner. He introduces us and explains that I have just arrived from Kassala. Then we order something to eat.

Since arriving, I had been distracted by the newness of everything, but now that I am among friends, have a safe place to spend the night, and am able to relax a little, suddenly my hunger and exhaustion wrap themselves around me like strong arms. We eat quickly, pausing only slightly to enjoy our tea, then make our way back to Amar's house. The sun is beginning to set, and yet the city is still as busy and noisy as ever.

For the first time since leaving Asmara, I'm certain that I have made the right choice in coming here. I appreciate how much harder it would have been had others coming before me not cleared the way. I have benefitted so much from their experience, from their successes and failures. I can only hope that my own experiences will help others as they make their own long and perilous journeys from oppression to freedom.


Yohannes accompanies me all the way back to Amar's house, then he departs for his own place in the Diem neighborhood, where he shares a room in an apartment with friends he knew in Eritrea. It has been a long, exhausting day for me, and the only thing I want to do right now is lie down, close my eyes, and go to sleep. But the card game is still unfinished, and more of my new roommates have arrived after spending the day in Khartoum. More introductions are made. I silently recite each name so I won't forget them, but in my tired state my mind refuses to hold onto the information.

Amar is sitting with Abraham, a quiet but sincere man whose rheumy eyes and yellowed teeth belie a lifelong habit of heavy smoking. I make a point of committing his name to memory, since it was he who generously offered up his mattress in the living room for my use. For now, he will share a mattress in one of the bedrooms with two other men. Amar then tells everyone that I'm originally from Asmara and have come here for an entry visa to America, where my family awaits. It strikes me as a rather unexceptional story, but everyone perks up and starts to ask questions. Someone mutes the television, and the two men playing *dama* in the corner put down their game and join us. They settle on the floor with their backs against the couch. Amar and Abraham pass along the cigarettes they are smoking. They offer one to me, but I decline. It's a habit I never picked up.

"How did you cross?" they ask. "What was your experience in the refugee camp? Did you have any troubles?"

After we have exchanged border crossing stories, I ask questions about the living situation. Amar explains that he and his friends rent the house from Sudanese owners and sublet it to Eritrean and Ethiopian expatriates for a small amount of profit. He has lived here for a long time by now, learned the language and culture, and makes a modest living this way. "But there's always risk in bringing people I don't know into the house," he continues. "You are friends with people I already know and trust, so that is no problem this time. It isn't always like that. Sometimes, I just have to take a chance. And sometimes it doesn't end so well."

In this city, there is never a scarcity of refugees looking for somewhere to live. The moment one person leaves, another is ready to take their place.

He and two of his friends occupy two of the rooms in the house, including this one, and everyone puts in their share of the rent. Money is also collected for food to be prepared here. There are three additional rooms, all of which open out onto a single, bare courtyard surfaced in plain cement. There are no trees or colorful tiles here. Two of the rooms are subleased to a pair of siblings, while the third is occupied by a woman named Senait, whose boyfriend went ahead of her to Uganda a couple weeks before. They, like the rest of us, save Amar and his two friends, are waiting on entry visas from a specific country. While Amar has settled down here in Sudan, his friends hope for an opportunity to go to America, Canada, or Australia, whichever one can offer assistance first. Knowing their chances are low, they have a backup plan to go to Europe, whether overland through Egypt or over the Mediterranean Sea from Libya. Both of these options are extremely dangerous, so it's understandable that they are not the preferred choices. I offer them a silent prayer that God finds them safely to their destination, wherever that may be.

Eventually, the cigarette smoke proves too irritating for my eyes, so I excuse myself. They are already dry from lack of sleep. The smoke also makes my head ache. Back home, it's customary for smokers to go outside their houses out of respect for those who don't. But here, it seems such norms have been set aside. I am beginning to realize that I should stop expecting things to always be the same. Here, people feel liberated from certain established behaviors. Maybe it's easier for these young people to set their traditions aside. Their ties to their roots are much weaker than mine.

I mention this to Amar when he joins me outside, and he replies that I must be more patient and open minded, or else I will become frustrated at every little thing. "Don't expect it to be easy. Khartoum is a very crowded place. You will see. There are too few places open to rent. Also, don't expect your case to be processed anytime soon. Some of the others inside have been waiting for many months."

I don't want to believe him. My case is already moving through the system. I have a strong advocate in my wife inside the United States, and I have faith that she will be successful in getting me to my family very soon.

But when I return to Wintana the next day, my heart sinks after reading Wudasie's latest email. The US Immigration Office has decided to postpone processing my visa request until after the new year. Amar was right. I need to be patient and not expect anything to happen quickly.


The more I search for another place to live, the more I appreciate how accurate was Amar's description of the situation here in Khartoum. There are too few rooms available and too many people. So while I had originally envisioned renting space from someone with connections to Asmara, I now realize I was being too picky. I did find a few openings, only to be turned away because I can't say how long I will be staying.

Uncertainty infects all our lives. Yohannes, for example, is suddenly forced to leave Khartoum just a couple days after my arrival. When I ask a mutual friend why, he tells me it's because he used up all the extensions on his medical visa, and the Eritrean Embassy refused to grant any more. They demanded that he return.

"How could he go back there now?" I ask, alarmed.

But I find out he hasn't. In fact, he still hasn't gotten the surgery to fix his back. Apparently, the cost is too high, and he can't afford it. A childhood friend of his now living in Europe had offered to assist paying for it, but it still wasn't enough. And because of his legal status in Sudan, his appeals to NGOs for assistance have all been denied on the basis that they can only help refugees. So I am relieved to hear that he went to Shagarab to be processed as a refugee rather than return home. Maybe once that's resolved, he will finally be able to get his surgery. At least he'll have access to legal and financial help he wouldn't have before.

Money is a problem for all of us. I don't have much to spend, so I stop taking my meals in restaurants and coffee shops and start eating at home. I also save money by sharing in the household duties. Amar, Seid, and I do most of the cooking for everyone, while the others clean. Neither set of chores is as easy as I am used to, since we have neither a kitchen nor a laundry. We have to prepare all of the food outside in the courtyard using a small burner set on a little table. And the washing is done by hand.

Growing up, I was always told that it was taboo for Christians to purchase and eat meat prepared in a Muslim butcher shop, since it was slaughtered in the name of Allah. The reverse was also true, for Muslims are forbidden from eating meat prepared in Christ's name. I can remember the day I confessed to my mother how I had strayed from this rule for many years, ever since I was a teenager. I begged her to understand how important it was for me to be able to sit with my Muslim friends at a meal. "We are all thankful for our food before we eat it," I told her. "Why should it matter if we thank Allah or Christ?"

Of course, this was rarely an issue in the National Service, where no distinction was supposed to be made between Christian and Muslim. We all ate what we were given, no matter who prepared it. Here in Khartoum, it's very much like that. We all eat from the same pot, even though some are Christian and others are Muslim. Here, we are a family. We all still give thanks, just in our own personal way.

I wonder what my mother would think now, if she could see me eating this way. Would she disapprove, or would she finally understand that we are all the same? Our circumstances force us to face the fact that we all want the same exact thing: a life of freedom, safe from oppression, and filled with opportunities to pursue.

I wash my laundry in the bathroom sink and hang it out to dry on a line outside, but I learn very quickly that this isn't practical for more than a few small items of clothing. So now I take my trousers and shirts to a Sudanese couple who have better facilities. They charge a reasonable price. It's a small sacrifice I can afford to make.

On cooler days, or during the evenings, the courtyard also serves as our barbershop. We cut each other's hair while chatting and drinking coffee, making it a sort of social event. Efrem has the best touch of us all, so he's usually the one we choose for the job. He makes a big show of complaining, but everyone knows he enjoys the praise. This is just one of the many ways we depend on each other and support each other.

For the nine men and three women sharing the five rooms in the house, there is only the one bathroom. At first, I worry how it will work with so many people, but I learn as the others have that I can make do with far less than I have been used to in the past. We adjust our habits to accommodate each other's needs. Perhaps it's because we know that it's only temporary, which makes it easier to be patient. We are more willing to compromise for everyone's wellbeing. But I think a lot of it has to do with knowing that our lives, as simple and hard as they are now, could be so much worse. We have all seen it by now. Hardship is a good teacher, and its lessons are patience and tolerance.

As the days can be unbearably hot and there is so little to do while we wait for our cases to be processed, we spend much of our time inside watching television, playing games, or reading. I join the British Council Library, which allows me to borrow books and other materials. The library is smaller than the one in Asmara, but it contains a wider variety, simply because there's far less censorship.

As for news, a few papers are printed in English, but most of the local dailies are in Arabic. One of my roommates translates them for us into Tigrinya. It's refreshing to again be able to receive such news, which offer a much broader perspective on events than I had been accustomed to at home. In Eritrea, President Isaias Afewerki abolished the private press years ago, imprisoning many of the independent journalists critical of his policies. Here, I see open criticism of Sudan's president Omar al-Bashir in the media. It occasionally happens that someone is thrown in jail for expressing their opinions, but only rarely, and usually when there is another reason to do so. Those that are imprisoned aren't treated as unjustly as they are in Ethiopia and Eritrea.

Before I know it, I have settled into this new, temporary phase of my life. I miss my family terribly, but it's a huge burden off my shoulders knowing they are safe and working on my case. And despite the ongoing challenges in my own life, I, too, am safe. I no longer have to worry about being sent back to Eritrea. Now, I simply have to wait for my interview to be scheduled.


There are so many people here in Khartoum who are less fortunate than me. I see their suffering and it's in my nature to want to help, just as my newfound friends were compelled to help me. This is how we were brought up, to take care of each other, whether materially or spiritually. It's how my father has lived his life and taught his children to live theirs. When there is need, one does his best to fill it. So we share the chores and the financial burdens. Whenever there are unexpected expenses, we all pitch in to make sure they are met. Christian or Muslim. Ethiopian, Eritrean, South Sudanese. We are all refugees, without a home, seeking peace. If we have learned any lesson from living like this, it's that we can't know for sure what tomorrow will bring. Or if it will even arrive. In this way, total strangers become close friends in a short amount of time. And close friends become family.

One day I wake with a terrible pain in my lower back. I know immediately what is causing it, as I have experienced these same symptoms before. Even when I try to assure my roommates that this isn't the first time, my groans of agony cause them to worry about me. They think I'm about to die.

"It's only temporary," I tell them between pants. "I have had kidney stones before. They will pass." What I don't tell them is that I have previously needed surgery to get relief from them. I pray that my current condition won't require it again. I can't afford a hospital visit, and I don't wish to place such a heavy burden on my friends.

After Titi's heart surgery, Wudasie told me how impressed she was with how advanced medical care is in America. During a particularly painful episode of kidney stones, while I was still unsure about leaving Eritrea, she told me I would never have to suffer like this again after I joined her there. "They will fix you once and for all," she said. I won't say it didn't influence my decision.

But right now, as the pain intensifies by the minute, I'm not so sure I will make it that long.

After hours of suffering, Amar rents a car, and he and Seid rush me to the hospital. I'm too delirious to care by then. After a long wait, the hospital staff tell us they can't treat me. "You must go to a different hospital," the nurse says, and provides directions for getting there. Seid gets angry and starts to argue. "How do you know you can't treat him?" he demands. "You don't even know what is the matter!" But the head doctor comes out and points to the door. He orders us to leave.

I can hear the argument from my seat, and I ask Amar what the problem is.

"*Ma Mushkila*," he says, trying to keep me calm. It's a phrase I will hear a lot before my stay in Khartoum is over. It means there is no problem. He helps me back outside and into the car. The doctors are still shouting at Seid, and Amar goes back to pull him away. I can hear him telling the guards, "*Ma Mushkila. Ma Mushkila.*" The last thing we need is trouble.

We go back to the house. Eventually, the pain goes away on its own, leaving me weak and fearful of its return. Thankfully, it doesn't. Afterward, I remind myself that I must take better care of my body and drink more water so the stones don't form. The last thing I can afford right now is *Mushkila*.

\* \* \*

All too quickly, another half year has passed since my arrival in the city, and there has been almost no progress at all on my case. I'm anxious for change. I'm running out of patience. Even more worrying, I am running out of money.

I should have tried to get a job right away, but I didn't out of faith I would be gone by now. It was only after the weeks turned to months that I began to consider how to support myself. Wudasie sends money when I need it, but I know every time she does it means she and the girls are sacrificing something themselves. I can't keep expecting others to help me.

The types of jobs available to people in my situation are limited. There are the *nadafa* services, which provide janitorial work in shops and offices, and a lot of refugees take these sorts of positions. Others find work serving meals, cooking, washing dishes in restaurants. Still others get paid to do manual labor, mainly at the numerous construction sites scattered about the city. Abraham, for example, works at the site where they are building a new six-story office complex. He tells me that carrying 25-kilo cement bags up the stairs from ground level to the roof is the worst job he has ever had. The bags are heavy, but he's a strong, young man. The worst part is the cement dust that gets in his eyes, nose, and mouth. He's afraid it will make him sick, but he has no other choice. He must earn money to pay for his rent and food.

I try to look for work, but everywhere I turn I'm told no. It doesn't help that I can't speak Arabic as well as others. Most businesses prefer to hire women for anything that doesn't require a lot of strength.

To lift my spirits one particularly frustrating day, Yohannes, who has returned from Shagarab after gaining refugee status, and one of my roommates, Misgun, take me to a favorite Eritrean coffee shop in a neighborhood called Sahafa Zelete. We are enjoying the fine weather and each other's company, when my cell phone rings. I see that it's my younger brother Eyasu, calling me from Eritrea.

"Yikealo?" he says, when I answer. I can tell something is wrong by the way his voice shakes, and my first thought is that he's calling to tell me about Dad. But he's not. "It's about our cousin, Beyene."

"What is it? Is he back in the hospital?"

Beyene had smoked cigarettes ever since high school, and he became a heavy drinker later in life. He recently announced that he has chronic health problems as a result of his bad habits. It hadn't come as much of a surprise. We had watched his health deteriorate for years.

"He passed away."

The news shakes me. I knew he had been admitted to the hospital some time ago, but I thought he was getting better, especially after his release.

I remember how, when we were both teenagers, he had told me how unhappy he was at our ELF and EPLF leaders, at their infighting and how it was sabotaging their ability to defeat Ethiopia. His cynicism had eventually turned out to be all too justified. Even in the weeks and months following independence, when we all believed we were on the verge of victory, Beyene maintained his doubts. I always thought he was being too pessimistic, but time proved his vision of the future was keener than my own. If only he could have seen his own future as clearly and stopped his self-destructive behavior.

It's unfair that anyone should die so young, but his passing seems especially cruel. His father died in a needless accident at a very young age, leaving only him, his mother, and a sister to fend for themselves. The fact that he was so close to me in age hits me hard. While my own medical issues are so much less serious than his, his passing forces me to confront the truth about the time I have left. Every day that passes is another day less I have to spend with my family. I have already lost too many.

I need to fight harder to get myself home.


Yonatan, whom I met at the Shagarab refugee camp, tells me about an opening in a brand new apartment building he's planning to rent with several other people. It will be cheaper than where I am now, but since it's unfurnished, there will also be upfront expenses. "And it won't be any less crowded than your current situation," he warns. "More children, in fact, but less cigarette smoke. You should tell me yes or no today, otherwise you will lose the chance. I'm giving you first choice."

I have always admired Yonatan for his devotion to his Christian faith and his willingness to help others. He is a deeply religious person, which is why I trust him and immediately tell him I'm in. In fact, it was because of his faith that he chose to leave Eritrea, where religious persecution is rapidly on the rise. A few years ago, an American evangelical visited Yonatan's church in Asmara as part of a goodwill mission. Our paranoid government, being suspicious of foreign visitors, and especially of foreign religious evangelicals, took Yonatan into custody when he volunteered to accompany the American on a trip to Massawa. He was charged with assisting a spy. It was only after a close relative and well-regarded *tegadalay* intervened on his behalf that he was released. Yonatan left the country days later, aided by siblings already in Europe and America. The experience may have soured his relationship with his homeland, but it deepened his faith in God and his church.

The three-room flat is in the topmost floor of a newly constructed five-story building. Yonatan and I will share it with four other Eritrean men and a single mother with four children. He tells me he grew up in the same neighborhood as the woman, whose name is Almaz. When I ask about the children's father, he says that the father of her twin fourteen-year-old boys was a *tegadalay* martyr of the Eritrean-Ethiopian border war when they were just three. He doesn't know where the father of the four-year-old girl and one-year-old baby boy is. "Their mother's aunt is sponsoring them from Europe," he adds.

Of the four men, three have confirmed destinations and sponsors in Dubai, Angola, and America, respectively. The fourth escaped Eritrea without a plan after being brutally disciplined at the Sawa training camp. He was lucky enough to find a job here working for an ice-making company, which allows him to partially support himself. Yonatan also helps him out. He tells me he's committed to getting the young man out of Sudan, but first he has to get himself to Europe or the US.

To furnish the apartment, Yonatan and I go to the Souq al-Shaebi, where he purchases two bed frames and mattresses, one for Almaz and her young children, and one for himself. We also get three extra mattresses, two for the twins and one for me. On a second trip, we buy a small dinner table, a gas stove and propane tank, and cooking utensils.

The rest of the expenses, including food and rent, are divided among us, as are the household chores. Almaz prepares the meals, while the men shop for groceries, wash dishes, and manage any other tasks that need to be done. The twin boys are polite and helpful. I find them to be surprisingly good company and kindhearted, despite all they have been forced to endure in their short lives.

In the following weeks, Yonatan helps Almaz lease a small coffee shop nearby so she can earn money to help pay for some of her expenses. He also assists her in the daily running of the business, as well as with tutoring and disciplining the kids. He says it's his Christian duty, but I think a lot of his dedication to her is because they have known each other since childhood. I don't know for sure, but I also suspect he has grown quite fond of her.

For a little while, life seems about as normal as it can get.

One Sunday, Almaz doesn't open her shop. Instead, Yonatan asks us all to stay home. He has a big announcement to make, but he's waiting to tell us what it is. Almaz is cooking outside, and from the delicious smell coming in, I can tell it's not our regular modest fare, but something special. "Today," Yonatan announces over lunch, "our roommate Elias has accepted Jesus Christ as his savior." His gaze sweeps the table and settles on me. "Today, we celebrate his conversion from Orthodox to Protestant."

I realize why he's looking at me. I am now the sole Orthodox Christian in the group, despite Yonatan's past attempts to get me to convert. But he can try all he wants. I'm perfectly satisfied with how I practice my faith. I just hope he doesn't take it personally, and things become awkward between us.

Living on the topmost floor of the building means we have to hand carry water from the ground level whenever there isn't enough pressure to deliver it to our faucets, which happens much more frequently than it should, given how new the building is. We take turns filling buckets and jugs and wrestling them up the stairs. We do this early in the morning or wait until evening on the hottest days. Thankfully, the twin boys are always willing to help.

On especially warm nights, we pull our mattresses out into the uncovered hallway. If we're lucky, we get a breeze.

We are located right next to a busy bus station, or *Minelberi*, and it can be noisy, even at night. Crowds of travelers, drivers, workers, sellers, and other people fill the plaza at all hours. During the day, the buses are constantly idling, filling the air with their fumes. The vendors shout at every passerby to buy their bottled water and soda, packaged fruits, candies, biscuits, and cigarettes.

We are in a neighborhood where unfinished buildings are a common sight. Khartoum is filled with them, since so many projects hit roadblocks before they are completed. Some builders run out of money. Others run afoul of local officials. The unfinished structures fill up with homeless people. Many of them are Christian refugees from South Sudan, who are distinguishable from locals by their darker skin. Hundreds of thousands have made the difficult journey north to escape poverty, drought, and political instability. In 2005, following years of civil war, Sudanese president Omar al-Bashir agreed to grant the region independence from the north pending a referendum to be held at some future date. In the five years since that promise was made, no referendum has been held, and resentment between the north and south has grown. The situation in South Sudan must be terrible indeed to drive them to come here, where they know they are unwelcome. It's easy to draw parallels with the migration of Eritreans to Ethiopia in the years we were at war with each other.

On nights that I am unable to sleep, I take my chair to the balcony overlooking the street. I can see the homeless people down below. Their bare legs stick out of makeshift tents constructed of plastic sheets, scraps of fabric, and cardboard. The shelters offer no privacy and only a small amount of relief from the sun. Even worse, they are easy targets for the police. What the security forces don't tear down during their raids, the hot, dry winds known as *khamsīn* sometimes do. I wish I could help these people, but there are so many of them, and the police are more ruthless with them than they are with us. Helping them would only invite more trouble instead of relieve it.

We are just a few weeks away from presidential elections, and Omar al-Bashir has finally committed to holding a vote of referendum of independence— *if* he wins reelection. But the general election itself has been marked by violence and accusations of corruption, forcing its postponement multiple times. As the day draws nearer, tensions rise. The police raid the encampments more often. They arrive without warning in their big trucks. Kicking and shouting, they knock down the shelters and smash what few possessions the people have. They claim they are looking for alcohol and drugs, both forbidden in Muslim religion and culture, but even if they don't find them, they still gather everybody up and take them away to prison.

A man I met in the Shagarab camp does janitorial work for one of the courthouses in Khartoum. He tells me the refugees taken into custody are whipped with a stick on their backs until they bleed. "I have witnessed this myself," he says. "It's terrible."

"How can they treat their own people like that?" I say, before remembering the Sudanese aren't the only ones guilty of such inhumane treatment against their own.

"Not just their own," he says. "Don't think your refugee papers or your nationality protect you."

"What do you mean?"

"They are Christian, those coming here from South Sudan, and it is true that some of them bring alcohol and try to drink it. That makes them targets. Sudan is an Islamic country ruled by Sharia law. This is how they punish those who don't abide by their rules."

I know this isn't strictly true. At least, it doesn't have to be. "Those people are homeless," I say. "They had no choice but to come here to escape death."

"What does that matter? There are people here who are happy to punish you for anything. For having a different god. For being homeless or hungry. For drinking alcohol. For being from someplace other than Sudan. For not observing their customs. For sleeping on the street, dressing differently, or speaking differently. Not everyone is like this, but enough people in the right positions are to make life difficult everyone. And lately it has been getting worse."

"I hope it stops when the president is reelected."

"*If* he is. If he isn't, we should be prepared for even more violence."

The longer I stay here, the more I understand his worry. I wonder how it is that people everywhere can't figure out how to be kinder to each other. Why do we have to suffer so much, especially when we are at our most vulnerable?

In the predominantly Eritrean and Ethiopian neighborhoods where we live or visit, the police aren't welcome in the coffee shops and restaurants. When they do come in, it always creates a tense situation. They treat everyone as if they are criminals rather than people simply trying to survive, who want to escape oppression and reunite with their families. They typically show up without warning and shout at everyone. They demand to see our papers. But having the necessary documents is no guarantee they will stop harassing you. Sometimes, they take everyone to their station for no reason. It's a way for them to extract bribes. Because of this, the shop owners don't like the police. And in turn the police harass and accuse them of attracting the refugees in the first place. All the business owners want to do is help us and make a living for themselves.

It doesn't take long for me to become a victim of such a raid myself. It happens completely without warning one day when I am out with friends. One moment I'm sipping coffee, the next police are barging in from off the street. We have very little time to react before they are screaming for our photo identification cards. *"Bitaka! Bitaka! Show us passport!"*

We pull out our documents to prove that we are allowed to be here, which they snatch out of our hands. Just when we think they are going to leave, they order six of us to climb onto the back of their truck. "Stay put!" they scream. "Don't move!" We have no choice but to obey, since they still have our papers. Five more people are pulled out of a nearby internet café and added to our number.

We're taken to a police station in the al-Sahafa district "to be processed." What this means is that we each have to call someone to come and vouch for us— more coded words meaning "bring bribe money." I finally get a hold of my friend Amar, from my first house here in Khartoum. When he arrives, he's required to provide the name of the Sudanese owner of the house he rents. To make things simpler, he claims I still reside there. Once I fill out some paperwork and pay a small sum of money — all that I have in my possession at the time — they take my photograph and release me without further difficulty.

Once we are outside again, Amar asks if we need to go back to the coffee shop. He has been through this routine before and understands what has happened. I nod, even though the shop is the last place I want to go right now. But I need to recover the money I stashed in a secret place when the police ran in.

We learn very early on that whenever there is a raid, it's better to hide as much money as possible to keep the police from taking everything. I'm lucky this time, since the Sudanese pounds I stuffed into a basket inside the shop are still there when we return. Some of my friends aren't as fortunate. They lose everything they have. This is why I never carry too much of my money with me when I go out, even though I know it's a risk to leave it anywhere else, even at home.

"Someday," I tell myself, "I won't have to worry about such things."

After seven months, Yohannes and I have become like brothers, checking up on each other every day. His back still bothers him, but he has learned to manage the pain. We usually arrange to meet at one of the local coffee shops or internet cafés, even if it's only for a quick hello and to share news of home. Our conversations are often about people we know who made it out of Eritrea. Thankfully, those stories are more common than those about friends and family members who were caught. We try to keep track of anyone who has arrived here in Khartoum, and especially those who are close to reaching their final destination. Without this tight network of contacts, life here would be much poorer, and moving onward would seem next to impossible.

Another frequent subject of our conversations is the local police raids. In fact, the memory of my own recent capture is still very fresh in my memory the day Yohannes calls and tells me to stay home. Although he doesn't say he has bad news, it's clear to me that this is what he intends to deliver, and when he arrives with Misgun, Daniel, and Muna, the Ethiopian woman who runs a coffee shop we like to visit, I know it isn't just bad, but serious.

My people almost never deliver news of a family member's passing over the phone. It goes against our culture. While I'm not shocked to hear of my father's death, it still devastates me. Aboy was very sick when I left Asmara, and I have been dreading such news as this every day since.

My housemates, Almaz and Yonatan, immediately set about serving tea and our ceremonial sweet bread, *himbasha*, which she has freshly baked. This tells me that they were forewarned so they could prepare to have me receive visitors wishing to pay their respects. It's also customary for visitors to stay with you in your house for at least three days while you mourn, but I don't want to sit here and mope about. As much as I feel like my friends are my family, it's hard for me to think of this apartment as my home. It only makes me feel more guilty for leaving my father behind in his time of need. To sit here and receive visitors would be to accept that my current circumstances are normal, and they aren't.

My friends don't question me when I break from custom. They take me to a local coffee shop, and this is how we celebrate my father's memory. They ask me to tell stories about him and I oblige, until my tears of anguish are diluted with tears of love and happiness.

One memory stands out. It was during the celebration of Christ's birth, *Lidete Kristos*, several years after the stroke that left my father bedridden. Natsanet's grandmother had just returned from church, and the family was getting ready for an afternoon gathering. We were outside in the shade beneath a trellis covered in grape vines, except for my sister Ellen, who was looking after my dad inside the house. My mother was in and out, buzzing with more energy than I can remember her having in a long time. The sight of her grandchildren having such fun brought her so much joy. My brother and neighbor slaughtered a bull and were preparing it for the families. My two sisters-in-law were busy cooking sauces and baking *injera*.

When the food was ready, we sat in two big circles, adults on one side and children on the other. A prayer was said. The neighbor remarked that the *zigni*, a spicy meat sauce, was especially delicious. His eyes were watering, and he was waving a hand in front of his mouth, which made us all laugh. A homebrewed beer called *suwa* was served, the perfect accompaniment to the spiciness. The traditional way to eat is to use the *injera* and our fingers. My father was the only one to use a spoon, which he could manage with assistance from my mom and sister. Everyone was laughing and enjoying themselves, even Dad. Yet, when I looked over at him, I could sense a deep sadness in his uneven smile. I wondered what could keep him from being completely happy.

Then it was time for the coffee ceremony, which is one of our most cherished traditions. Very little can come close to the comforting aroma of freshly roasted and brewed coffee beans, and nothing brings family and friends together quite like the promise of a hot cup. As we sat and enjoyed it, I took the opportunity to glance about the table once more. I was especially thrilled to see Ellen there. As a medic stationed far away in the National Service, she had missed too many of our family celebrations, including my own wedding, several graduations, and a few funerals. It made me realize how truly special the day was.

But there were empty seats, as well: my own wife and eldest daughter; my older sister, Saba, who lived in Europe; and others, some unable to get permission from their units to come. This was the reason for my father's sadness. Our family had been splintered. He knew it would never get put fully back together again.

"He's in a better place now," my friends say, to comfort me.

I want to believe this, and yet I'm too consumed with guilt. I hate that so much of my father's family was absent at that special holiday celebration. I hate that even fewer of us will be there to attend his funeral.

"You did what you could, Yikealo. You spent as much time with him as you could. You waited until the very last possible moment to leave Asmara, so you could be there for him during his last days. He knows you had no choice but to go when you did. At least he got the chance to see you escape. Now, you have your family waiting for you in America. They have already been waiting too long."

This is what my friends tell me, but it doesn't ease my pain. I know how much my father suffered because of how broken his family had become. That pain could never be eased by seeing us leave.

"He prayed every day for the Lord to take him home," I say at last. "After his youngest brother and sister died so close to each other recently, I know he was ready. Now he's there himself."

I pray the Lord hears my father's wish and receives his soul exactly as he wanted, once more in the company of lost loved ones.

In early April, on the eve of the Sudanese election, Wudasie emails to tell me that my petition for immigration has been completed and is being forwarded to the American Embassy in Cairo, Egypt. I have been granted an interview for the second of June, just eight weeks away.

How am I going to travel to Egypt? We knew it was the general policy to assign immigrant visa applications by Eritrean citizens to the American Consulate in Cairo, whereas the consulate in Khartoum processed non-immigrant visas. But we were also told that each office has the freedom to handle any type, choosing which ones to consider on a case-by-case basis. Wudasie and I have been pushing for my request to be processed here, since this is where I am living. When asked why it won't be, we are given no explanation. I suspect it is because of tensions between the American and Sudanese governments. This is becoming a familiar refrain, and it makes me wonder about American foreign relations policies in general.

Still, it is progress. An interview is an interview, so I try to stay hopeful. I just have to apply for another entry visa, except this time to go to Egypt.

The Egyptian Embassy in Khartoum requests that I hand over all of my official paperwork. This is a hard thing for me to do, as I have become wary of relinquishing control. But I have no other choice. Days pass while I wait for the consulate and the Department of Foreign Affairs here in Cairo to communicate with each other. Each time I return to the embassy, they tell me to go home and wait several more days before checking in again. After several weeks, they finally admit that they have yet to receive any sort of response from Cairo. They can't even tell me whether they have begun processing my paperwork at all. It's just as I had been warned about when I was still in Eritrea. In Cairo, nothing happens quickly. With the date of my interview drawing nearer, I grow more and more desperate.

Finally, a friend tells me nothing is happening because I am *habesha*. "They won't allow you to enter Egypt because they do not like *habesha*."

This is the name we call ourselves, the highlanders of Eritrea and northern Ethiopia. Here, it not only distinguishes us from other groups within our countries, it identifies us as Christian. But why would this matter to Egypt, which has tolerated Christianity for many years?

"Egypt suspects *habesha* are using their country as a gateway into Israel," my friend explains. "You know those two countries have a long history of hatred and distrust between them."

"But I am not going to Israel!"

Outside the consulate, I'm approached by one of the so-called "facilitators," who tells me there might be a way to expedite the process. To do so, I must hand over my passport and some money to an independent party, a middleman, who knows someone on the staff who can personally manage the visa request. By now, I'm used to such arrangements. I have been forced to take such deals at nearly every step along the way, and I have reluctantly come to see them as just as essential as the official processes. And just as risky. But I have also developed a sixth sense about which ones to trust and which not to. And this one strikes me as suspicious.

When I tell Wudasie, she shares my concern. "There's a good chance you will lose our money," she says, something I already have far too much experience with. "But money can be replaced. That isn't the issue. What if you lose your passport? Without it, everything will become a hundred times harder."

We decide not to do it, so I miss my chance to interview in Cairo for the entry visa. After ten months in Sudan, I'm still no closer to getting to America than the day I fled Asmara.

\* \* \*

One day, Wudasie calls. "I think we should try for Kenya," she says. "The American Consular Office in Nairobi can handle immigrant visas. Traveling there will be easier than traveling to Egypt, and they don't care about *habesha*. You need to ask for your file to be transferred to Nairobi."

I would, except my papers are still in Cairo. And when I request for them to be transferred to Nairobi, they tell me I must first ask to have the Kenyan office grant my petition for consideration. If they accept, only then will Cairo permit the transfer. It all seems unnecessarily complicated, but I do as I am told.

It takes several attempts, but finally the American Consular Office in Nairobi agrees to take my case. Now I can turn my attention to getting an exit visa from Sudan and an entry visa into Kenya.

Once again, it isn't straightforward. The first obstacle is an all too familiar one, a requirement to pay off certain people to ensure that certain things happen within a reasonable timeframe. This time, I don't have the luxury of saying no. It's becoming clearer to me every day that there is a *de facto* system for making headway in such bureaucracy, and it involves paying extra for such services. The problem is that it's often hard to distinguish the real dealmakers with those who just want to take your money and disappear.

For 250 Sudanese pounds, roughly $95, I am connected with a retired police officer, a Sudanese Muslim, who manages the transaction and delivers my exit papers. It takes just one day and happens so quickly I can't help but feel cheated, as if I had just waited a little longer, I would have gotten through the official process without paying extra. But Wudasie waves it off, and I realize she's right. I shouldn't obsess over such minor details. This is just how business is conducted in Sudan. At least with this step done, I can focus on the next hurdle.

Now I need to apply for an entry visa into Kenya and arrange my travel to get there. I go to the Kenyan Embassy in Khartoum for the stamp, but they tell me I don't need one. At first, I'm pleasantly surprised, until they explain why.

It turns out that Eritrea is one of the signatory nations within Africa's Inter-Governmental Authority on Development, along with Djibouti,

Ethiopia, Kenya, Somalia, Sudan/South Sudan, and Uganda. As an Eritrean citizen, I am theoretically allowed to enter other IGAD countries from my home country visa-free.

And that is where the problem lies. I would still need to show that I have an exit visa from my home country, and in order for me to get it, I would need to return to Eritrea.

When I tell Yohannes this, he tells me I can still purchase a plane ticket and fly to Nairobi without any problem. "It's only when you arrive at Jomo Kenyatta Airport that you *might* be denied entry by the Immigration and Customs officials."

"Might?"

"It really depends on the Immigration agent at the airport. But there are ways to push things in your favor." He knows this because our mutual friend from our days in the Zonal Command, Asmeret, is now in Nairobi waiting for her chance to move to Canada. Once again, it seems we have to operate outside of official channels, utilizing people who know how to get around bureaucratic obstacles.

We call Asmeret, and she agrees to put me in contact with a man in Nairobi who deals with these types of situations. This time, the cost will be $200, but for that amount of money he will personally receive me at the airport and facilitate my entry. I still have my doubts, so I call another friend, Zemu, who is also living in Nairobi. He confirms that this isn't unusual. Even Wudasie, who has a better sense for such things than I do, tells me to go ahead.

Amar helps me purchase a ticket to Nairobi and coaches me on what to expect while checking in. The airport employees will stop me if I give them a reason to have any concerns, so I need to act like I take this trip all the time. "Whatever you do, don't draw any unusual attention to yourself." Next, he introduces me to Abdallah, an Eritrean taxi driver whose specialty is facilitating this exact type of situation from here. For one hundred and fifty Sudanese pounds, he will accompany me from my apartment to the airport and hand me over to a Sudanese friend of his who will stay with me until I have cleared the security checkpoint.

I have only a day before my flight to Kenya, so I quickly tell everyone who had a hand in my stay here in Khartoum for the past year thank you and goodbye. That night, I can't fall asleep. Many different feelings fill me — sadness, dread, excitement — but none is as urgent as my need to keep moving forward. I'm ready to take another step away from my homeland and another closer to my new home.

As promised, Abdallah arrives on time and takes me to his Sudanese friend at the airport, who helps me get my ticket and gate assignment. He's not allowed to enter the security screening area, so I thank him and say goodbye. As expected, the immigration officer takes a moment to inspect my exit visa and ticket. He speaks in broken English, then hands the documents back. But instead of letting me pass, he demands cash. I call Abdallah, who speaks with the officer for a moment. When they are finished talking, the man waves me through. I don't know what arrangement they have made, but I'm sure it includes a promise of some form of payment to be paid later on my behalf.

Within the hour, I'm on the plane, a small Russian-made commuter jet. Then, within minutes of everyone settling down in their seats, we are speeding down the runway and rising up into the air. Now I am past the point of no return. If I'm unable to pay my way into Kenya, then I could very likely be stuck with nowhere to go but back to Eritrea.

I spend the first half of the flight praying that the person waiting for me at the other end is there, and that he will be able to deliver me safely through the immigration checkpoint as promised. For the second half, I will have something new and far worse to worry about.

# Nairobi, Kenya

THE PLANE IS ONLY HALF FULL, maybe four or five dozen passengers. Eight of us are Eritrean, five women and two other men beside myself. One of them, a younger man named Kibrom, sits next to me in the middle of the plane. He tells me his plan is to get to Europe and work to bring his family later. I ask him how long he has been in Khartoum, and he tells me two years. He says he misses his three daughters terribly, but when I ask about his wife, his face pinches. I don't know the reason for his reaction, but it's rude to pry, so I don't. Either he will tell me eventually or he won't. When he hears how long it has been since I last saw my wife and firstborn, he expresses his deepest sympathies.

Our first stop will be Juba, the capital of autonomous Southern Sudan, where we expect a several-hour wait to take on more passengers. About halfway there, an old acquaintance chooses to pay me an unexpected, and most unwelcome, visit.

The ache in my lower back had been a dull throb all morning, easily ignored. I had been hoping it was just stress. Or, at worse, mild dehydration — flying always seems to do this to me — so I had made sure to drink lots of water prior to boarding. Now, as the pain intensifies, I wish I hadn't had so much to drink. My kidneys are working overtime to rid my body of it, but I'm unable to urinate. The agony leaves me writhing and moaning in my seat. Kibrom grows alarmed. I try to explain to him that it's just an old affliction and that it will pass. He doesn't look convinced. He asks if there's anything he can do to help. He wants to know if he should tell the flight attendant. Afraid of the consequences, I shake my head and try moving instead. Walking has worked in the past to ease the pain. But now we are beginning to make our descent into Juba, and the flight crew orders me to sit back down. I'm doing exactly what I was advised to avoid: drawing attention to myself.

Once on the ground again, I am supposed to remain seated on the plane while the passengers board for the next leg, but the flight attendant permits me to get off with the departing travelers so I can use the restroom. She is probably worried that I will upset the new arrivals. I hurry off, nauseous from the pain, and I barely make it to the bathroom without being sick. But I get little relief before I have to return. Once back in my seat, it takes forever for the plane to leave Juba. Meanwhile, I'm certain I will die of agony before I even make it to Kenya.

Throughout the flight, the pain comes and goes and comes back again several times. At last we are on the ground at Jomo Kenyatta Airport. Once more, I'm barely able to walk without being sick. Out of fear of being deported for harboring some kind of communicable disease, I try my best to hide my discomfort when the Immigrations official demands my papers. My hands shake when he takes my fingerprints. He looks at me strangely, but doesn't ask why I'm sweating so badly. Finally, someone comes and pulls me aside. I see him signal to a man in the waiting area and the official tells me I'm free to go.

My contact's name is Michael, another Eritrean transplant. I explain what's happening to my body, and he patiently allows me to stop at several of the restrooms before we leave the airport. Each failure to find relief makes me more anxious. If the stones don't pass on their own, I will have to have surgery.

Michael helps me into his car. I have only one bag, which he places in the trunk. Then we drive into the city. On the way, the pain abruptly fades. I pray it means the episode is over, and not the prelude to something worse. The experience leaves me utterly drained, but for the first time since arriving, I can give thanks to God for seeing me safely here. I send a separate prayer to my friends and fellow refugees for their selflessness in assisting me.

Asmeret, who was my initial contact here in Nairobi, has already told Michael my story, so he's familiar with my history in the Eritrean National Services and my long separation from my family. He asks me about my time in the refugee camp at Shagarab and about living in Khartoum. I sense that his interest isn't mere curiosity or paid courtesy. He seems genuinely concerned about my plight and that of our fellow

Eritreans who fled to Sudan. When I ask why, he explains that this is
what he is meant to do, help others. This is why he spends a lot of time
driving people around, helping to settle them in, connecting the
newcomers with people who can rent them apartments. I feel an
immediate bond with him.

He tells me that he escaped to Kenya from Ethiopia in 1998, in order
to avoid being swept up by the successor to the Dehninet Security Forces
after the border skirmish in Badme erupted into all-out war. "Because of
the first war, there were thousands of Eritrean refugees already in Kenya
by then," he tells me. "But it seemed like no one in the international
community had even heard about the problem back then. It was only
after the second war started, when the flow of refugees spiked that they
began to take notice. It has only gotten worse since then, so they can't
ignore it anymore."

I nod thoughtfully. It has been a long, hard struggle for us. Our
people just can't seem to find peace.

The traffic in the city grows heavier, forcing Michael to stop many
times while we wait for it to clear. During the lulls, he talks casually with
random people outside the car. He speaks Swahili with ease. I ask him
how difficult it was to learn. "I had no choice," he replies, shrugging. "I
had nowhere else to go when I left, no family anywhere who could help
me relocate. So, from the beginning, I knew I would be staying here.
Learning a new language became necessary for survival."

"You speak English?"

"Yes, of course. Kenya was once occupied by Great Britain, so many
people speak it, but not everyone. Here, the common language is Swahili.
Anyone who plans to stay here long eventually learns it, or else they never
really fit in." The ease of his smile tells me he's happy calling Nairobi his
home. And I'm glad for him, rather than sad that he cannot go back to
Eritrea. I hope that when I finally reach America and have settled down
with my family, I will be just as comfortable with it being my home as he
is with Kenya being his. I wonder if he ever thinks about going back to
Eritrea, before realizing it's a stupid question. Of course he does. We all
do. Nothing can erase that, not acceptance of, or comfort with, one's new
situation, and certainly not the passage of time. Someday, God willing,

when there are enough positive changes to the status quo and we can truly live as free as we deserve to be, we will return.

Michael takes me to a place called the Asmara Bar & Restaurant. I suspect he has chosen this place specifically to welcome me to his city and to make me feel at home. But I can't help feeling a little homesick. At least until I see my old friend Asmeret waiting for us inside. Then I forget my sadness.

She, too, seems so much happier than I remember her in Khartoum, just a few months ago. And even that was an improvement over our time in Asmara. She gives me a big hug and a kiss on the cheek. Her smile lights up the room, and when she laughs I remember the girl whose irrepressible humor always helped lighten the mood back in our command.

"How is your case going?" I ask.

She tells me she's still awaiting the arrival of her entry paperwork into Canada. But rather than a sense of resignation, I get that she's expecting to hear good news any day.

I mention Zemu, a fellow service member from Asmara, who I have come to learn is living nearby. "Yes!" she exclaims, and immediately pulls out her phone. "Let me call and see if he can join us!"

Ten minutes later, our happy threesome has grown to four.

The reunion becomes even more jubilant with the arrival of our food. To top it off, I order a beer. Impossible to get in Khartoum, where alcohol is forbidden, it's the first I have had since leaving Eritrea, and I relish the sharp, clean taste and the way it satisfies the thirst like nothing else can, much as good company quenches loneliness. I feel the tension I had been holding inside all day draining away. At one point, someone says something funny, and it makes me laugh. I almost stop, because it's such a strange sound to my ears. I had almost forgotten how good real happiness could feel.

Zemu takes me to the house he's renting, a single story home with six rooms arranged in two parallel rows looking out on a central courtyard. The owner is Kenyan, who leases it to an Eritrean, who in turn sublets the rooms to other needy Eritreans and Ethiopians awaiting processing for entry into other countries. Five of the rooms, including Zemu's, are occupied by families. The last is leased by a single man. At the moment, all of us are Eritrean.

Zemu's three sons range in age from four to ten. Their mother is already living in America and has been working for the past three years to bring them there. Like me, this is their final stage. The boys take my bag and stow it in the corner of the room near one of the two beds. They are eager to hear my story, but Zemu knows how anxious I am to let Wudasie know of my safe arrival in Kenya, so he tells them to wait and he takes me to an internet café, where I can email her. The place is buzzing with activity. All fifteen computers are being used, and there is a line of people waiting their turn. I can tell from their speech that most are Eritrean or Ethiopian, undoubtedly refugees like me. After waiting about a quarter hour, it's finally my turn. I write a quick email and send it. Then we head back to the house.

Zemu explains to his sons that our friendship stretches back many years, from the time when we were coworkers, then fellow members in the same command in the National Service. "Please treat Yikealo like he is an uncle to you," he says. It doesn't take long for the youngest boy to warm up to me. He has no clear memory of his mother, other than what he sees in pictures and in letters. She escaped the country when he was barely a year old. I kneel down and tell him he will be with her soon. Then I tell him about my daughter Titi, whom I haven't seen in seven years, and Natsanet, who left to be with her mother over three years ago. When I stand up, he grabs me tight and won't let me go.

Holding to custom, Zemu invites me to stay with them until I can find a place of my own. Back in Eritrea, we like to say we open our homes to anyone who needs shelter. I have witnessed this myself many times in my years there, as well as in Ethiopia, but I have never seen it put to such practice as here in the refugee community.

"I can't," I tell my friend. "There's too little room here." They own almost nothing, just a pair of beds and a single small table for eating. The kitchen holds barely anything at all.

But Zemu insists. "The boys and I will share the big bed. You can have the other."

There's nothing to be gained by refusing his hospitality. I tell him I'm deeply touched by his family's kindness and generosity, which goes far beyond what is customary. I promise not to impose on them for very long and will repay them all for their sacrifice.

With that settled, the boys compete with each other to be the first to tell me about their lives and experiences in Nairobi. I learn that Zemu stays home with them most of the time, since he doesn't have a job. He teaches them what he can, so they won't fall too far behind in their studies. He plans to enroll them in school as soon as they arrive in America. They make do with the money his wife sends from the States.

"And where are you in your plans?" he asks me.

After I tell him, he nods thoughtfully and tells me I shouldn't expect things to be done anymore quickly than I have experienced elsewhere. The fact that he is going through the exact same process as I am gives me an idea of how long I should expect to be here. He and the boys have been in Kenya for months without any new developments.

While this dampens my spirits, I can't allow myself to become depressed. I have already been through so much and have come so far. I'm confident the worst of it is finally behind me.

After the heat and dryness of Sudan, I'm not used to the cooler, wetter weather here. It hasn't rained since I arrived, but the ground was wet when we left the airport, and the skies have been broody and threatening rain all day. I shiver and rub my arms, and Zemu retrieves a blanket and throws it over my shoulders. Suddenly, I'm exhausted. The sun hasn't yet set, but he hands me a torch anyway. "You will need it if you have to go to the bathroom during the night."

I know I probably will be up several times. Even though the pain in my lower back is mostly gone by now, I'm still having some difficulty, which tells me the issue hasn't completely resolved. A dull ache has taken up residence in my side, but I can't tell if it's a remnant of the kidney stone passing through and will fade away, or another stone waiting to follow. I hope it isn't the latter.

Zemu and the boys say goodnight. And so ends a very long day, one that started in Sudan and ended in Kenya. Now I wish for dreams filled with nothing but thoughts of joining my family in America.

After a breakfast of fried eggs and fresh baked bread Zemu purchased that morning from the local mini-mart, I look forward to filling my day with learning how to live in yet another new country. Zemu introduces me to the Kenyan woman who cleans the compound and its two shared bathrooms. She also does the laundry for a small fee. The clothes are dried on a line, which can sometimes take days when the weather is cloudy or rainy, as it is now. She speaks English, so we are able to communicate effectively. She tells me about a Kenyan tailor nearby who can iron my clothes, should I prefer.

Our first trip from the house is to a local marketplace, where I can purchase a new SIM card so I can use my mobile phone again. I'm eager to speak with my family instead of emailing, but I still have to wait a while after installing the card and making sure it works, since the time difference between here and Illinois means everyone there is asleep. I don't want to cause them any panic with an unexpected call in the middle of the night.

From the market, we head out on a *matatu* — minibus — to a place the locals call Isli, which Zemu says is a corruption of the original British name of East Leigh. "It's a much larger shopping area with many, many different businesses," he says. "I go there often and collect my remittances from my wife." The bank he uses is Somalia-based Dehabs-hill. He recommends I set up an account with them, too.

Before we arrive at the market, the bus comes to an abrupt stop to wait for a crowd of people to clear out of the way. Hundreds are gathered in some sort of rally. The man they are giving their attention to wears a *jallabiyah* and is speaking into a microphone. I have no idea what he is saying, but Zemu says he's preaching Islam. I might have guessed this, as most of the women listening wear *burqas*.

We decide to get off the minibus there and walk to the clothing stores. I need to purchase a sweater and jacket, since what I already own won't do for the weather. Zemu had earlier prepared me by saying that Isli is the largest and most crowded market in Nairobi, but I'm still astonished by the crowds. There must be thousands of people, all rushing from one place to another. We're jostled repeatedly, cut off, pushed. When we try to cross the street, drivers speed past us in loud, rumbling trucks and the smaller *matatus*, honking their horns and shouting. I don't know if it's physical or emotional exhaustion, but I'm overwhelmed by it all. I realize that this is the last place I want to be right now. I just want to get what I need and go back to the house.

Zemu, in contrast, seems to become more energized by the crowds. He explains that this is the common market for the local people, which is the reason for the mass of humanity. "There is another, much more upscale shopping center," he says. "There, you will see British architecture and high-rise buildings. It's in a part of the city called European Nairobi." By the description, I have a feeling it's a lot like the pricier Italian district in Asmara. I notice he doesn't offer to take me there. Neither of us has money to spare.

Heading back to the house, we happen to run into Kibrom, the man who sat next to me on the airplane from Khartoum. Remarkably, he's living on the same street as Zemu. He asks if we want to join him for coffee at a small shop in the lobby of the building where he lives. I agree to go, but Zemu politely declines. "I have to check on my sons," he says. I sense there's more to it than that, but I don't push.

Over the next few days, I begin to understand Zemu's situation more clearly. He's very thrifty out of dire necessity. He shops carefully for food and prepares all of their meals himself. Learning this, I'm torn by his generosity. I don't want to impose on him or make him feel like he must spend his money on me. I offer to help pay, but he's too proud to accept it.

So that Zemu doesn't feel obligated to feed me or take my charity, I take my meals with Kibrom instead. The Asmara Restaurant where I enjoyed my first meal here in Kenya is too expensive to eat at for every meal, so we seek out the smaller and cheaper Ethiopian cafés and restaurants sprinkled throughout the neighborhood. Without the distraction of kidney stones, I'm much more comfortable again. We sit for hours and tell each other stories. I learn that Kibrom was conscripted in one of the first *giffas* soon after the ENS was established, so he served much longer than I did before he escaped. "I had no choice but to leave," he tells me. "There was no money, no end in sight. I couldn't help my family." His wife and children are still in Eritrea, waiting for him to send for them once he reunites with his mother and an older brother in Europe.

It has been two years since he's seen his family, yet he remains surprisingly optimistic. "After everything else I have had to go through," he says, "this part is easy. They are the ones who are suffering, back there inside Eritrea. After I get to Europe, I hope the rest will be very smooth. I'm sure my family will follow very quickly." His eyes sparkle with hope and excitement when he talks about his children, and especially for the education he hopes they will receive in Europe. But then a sadness comes over him. "I had this same dream for them after the War for Independence. Back then, we hoped our future children would grow and learn in our own free country. We still have this dream, but now it's set in a completely different country."

Zemu's house is on Chai Road, which is one of the busiest in Nairobi. It can be noisy, but it's also conveniently located. Nearly all of the basic necessities for daily life — pharmacy, books, internet, barber services, food — can be found within a two-block radius. The businesses are often run by Eritrean expatriates. The rent is cheap. But there is also a fair amount of crime, drawn by the high population density, especially of unsuspecting foreigners who won't report being victims to the police. Many of the shops have iron bars installed on the doors and windows to thwart thieves, and my friends are constantly reminding me to always be aware of my surroundings.

A lot of cultural and political trouble in the city, like the sort the area is well known for, started during the administration of Daniel Arap Moi and remained prevalent ever since Mwai Kibaki took power in 2002. The large population of Eritrean and Ethiopian expatriates in this part of the city reminds me of the Sahafa Zelet neighborhood in Khartoum. Zemu tells me there are numerous such neighborhoods in Nairobi, pockets of refugees from any number of different African countries. The city is home to immigrants from all over, but it is less like a melting pot than a mosaic.

Many of the residents aren't legally employed, since they can't get the paperwork permitting them to get a job and earn money. Like me, they are dependent on remittances from family and friends around the world. But high unemployment plagues nationals, as well. It's common to see adolescents and teenagers wandering aimlessly about the city dressed in shabby clothing. They frequently get into mischief. Many are addicted to drugs, whether from chewing *chat* leaves, a legal stimulant, or from sniffing glue, petroleum, or other chemicals. Every city has the same problems. Even in Asmara you can find kids sniffing glue at the Mercato, right in front of the city hall. The numbers there are rarely large, however, as they are frequently rounded up and taken to Sawa for military training. If there is one positive thing about the *giffa*, it is that it offers these youth a chance to clean up in the ENS. But it gives them no more certainty or optimism for their future.

Over time, Kibrom opens up to me about the true situation with his family still remaining in Eritrea, which is apparently not good. I had first sensed that something was wrong on the plane from Khartoum, but hadn't wanted to pry. It seems that his long and frequent absences from home while serving in the ENS had put too heavy of a strain on their relationship. Their family was falling apart. This is what prompted him to escape. Once free, he hoped that they could start mending the marriage. Instead, he learned that his wife was having an affair with another man. She refused to talk to him about it, although she permitted him to stay in touch with his two daughters. It was through them that he learned his wife was pregnant.

"I have no choice anymore but to divorce her," he tells me.

"But aren't you trying to take them out of Eritrea?"

"I have to. It's what is best for my girls."

"And your wife?"

He gives me a cheerless look. "She is the mother of my children. With another child from a different man, it will be more complicated. Neither my mother nor my brother wants to help me bring her or the other baby, but it's the only way I can help my daughters."

"Do you forgive her?" I ask.

"Who am I to judge?" he replies, evading the question.

"She was unfaithful."

"She isn't the only one who has done wrong in their life. I have made mistakes, too. The only difference is, I bore no children from my infidelities."

I want to ask him what he means by that, but I'm afraid to know. What sorts of mistakes did he make? What were his infidelities? He may not have brought any new life into this world from his mistakes, but did he take any? He won't tell me what he did during his time in the army.

"Should my children suffer for the sins of their parents?" he wonders aloud. "No, I would rather put the past behind us and move on for their sake."

It seems a common theme for us all who have children. We make such immense sacrifices for them, so they won't have to pay for our sins.

"Anyway," he adds, "they deserve a better life than the one that awaits them in Eritrea."

Zemu's story, unlike Kibrom's, isn't spun with dark secrets, yet his dedication to his children is just as great. His dream is very simple— for his boys to go to university some day. "I never had the chance to go myself," he tells me. "So now I do what I must to give them the opportunity." He purchases used textbooks and home schools them in mathematics and English. The eldest son tutors the youngest on the alphabet and numbers, while Zemu helps the middle child. But their education isn't limited to academics. "I try to keep them busy so they don't get into trouble. I take them to church. We go to the Eritrean Orthodox Church down the road. I don't want them to become like those kids we see on the street."

His dedication inspires me to help out with the tutoring. It feels good to have a purpose again, but it makes me miss my own daughters all the more.

\* \* \*

A few weeks after coming to Nairobi, I hear from Araya, a former coworker of mine newly arrived from Sudan. He tells me about a vacant room available in a house on the outskirts of the city and asks if I'm interested in renting it with him.

Araya is one of the lucky few lottery recipients of a Diversity Visa to the US and has come here to Kenya to wait while the consulate processes it. Wudasie's younger sister, Aster, won her DV many years before, when they were far easier to get. Like me and so many others, Araya crossed into Sudan illegally. After gaining refugee status, he went on to Kenya, using his connections to find the place to rent after his arrival here in Nairobi. He tells me we will be sharing the room with Semhar, the new wife of his first cousin, who has already gone ahead to Europe. "But it won't be for long," he adds. "Her case is already far into the process."

Araya takes me to see the house, a two-story affair in a neighborhood known as Kariokor, a corruption of Carrier Corps, a British military unit that had been stationed in the area during the First World War. The room we will rent out together is on the upper story. It's small and contains a single bed, but it comes pre-furnished with a spare mattress, television, and some cooking utensils. "It will be cramped for the three of us," he says, and gives me a wry grin. "Do you remember the tiny space we had to share when we worked in the same office back home?"

I nod. Neither of us could have known all those years ago that the experience of working together in such cramped quarters would prepare us for living together in them in another country.

The house is run by an Ethiopian couple with one child. They occupy the entire first floor, which has a living room, bedroom, and kitchen. The second floor has two bedrooms, but the other one is occupied by a pair of Ethiopian brothers. Araya and I share the bed and give the smaller mattress to Semhar.

There is a convenient open-air market nearby with many small shops and restaurants serving traditional foods, but with access to a full kitchen and a three-burner gas stove now, I stop eating in restaurants again to save money. Semhar insists on doing the cooking, which is customary in our culture. This leaves the other household chores to me and Araya, including the grocery shopping and cleaning. We purchase freshly baked bread from a nearby Eritrean family who are also in the process of moving to America. I don't know how long they have been waiting. I have stopped asking whenever I meet new people like this. I don't want to get depressed or raise my hope with unrealistic expectations.

As expected, Semhar's last day in Kenya quickly arrives. To celebrate, she prepares *tsebhi derho*, a spicy chicken dish marinated in lemon juice and cooked with chili, onion, and garlic. It's usually reserved for special occasions, and this certainly qualifies as such. Whenever one of us reaches the end of our long journey, we all share in the joy that our friend is about to reach their destination. Semhar buzzes excitedly about the kitchen as she readies the meal. Her happiness infects us all.

We barely have time to finish our meal before we have to say goodbye to her. This time, instead of sadness, the departure leaves us euphoric. It gives us hope that our own journeys will soon end.

As if delivered by this wave of optimism, I receive word within days that my interview at the US Embassy has finally been scheduled.

To prepare for my upcoming interview, I pay another visit to the market at Isli. At the very least, I will need a decent pair of shoes to go with the modest slacks and shirt I own. Araya asks to come with me, as he has yet to see it. As before, the streets and walkways are crammed full with *matatus*, trucks, motorcycles, and pedestrians, but by now I am an old pro at navigating through them to the market. Partway through our own *matatu* ride, an ambulance siren cuts through the noise of the crowds. Traffic comes to a standstill. For many long minutes, the siren wails somewhere nearby. We crane our necks to see what's happening. At last we see its flashing lights. The ambulance speeds by us, traveling on the wrong side of the road. Countless other vehicles chase after it, taking advantage of the opening. The locals just shrug at the blatant lawbreaking and go about their business.

At the market, I find a pair of shoes in a style I like. The shop is run by two Somali men, an older gentleman and his teenaged son. Both are dressed nicely, in clean slacks and stylish shirts. Up close, I realize the boy is much younger than I had originally estimated, but just how young he is becomes clear when he speaks. While his father tries to help us, the boy keeps interrupting, trying to get us to consider more expensive shoes from the other display cases. When I tell him I already know what I want, he gets angry and demands to know if we are *habesha*. Highland Eritreans and northern Ethiopians have proudly used the term for many generations to distinguish ourselves from other groups in the Horn of Africa. Eager not to be confused as coming from Ethiopia, a country that shares a thousand-mile border and a history of direct conflict with Somalia, we are both quick to say that we are Eritrean. But he seems determined to be offended either way. "Because of your country," he says, accusingly, "we can't have peace in mine!"

The charge stuns us. How do we respond to such a claim?

"I don't understand," I say.

"Your government interferes in Somali politics," the boy says. "Don't deny it!"

We have heard these charges before, so we can't claim ignorance. Nor can we say that they are absolutely false. Some Somalis blame us for their own political troubles, in part because their former president, the deeply despised Mohamed Siad Barre, backed the Eritrean freedom fighters toward the end of our armed struggle for independence. Soon after the war ended, Barre was ousted from office and exiled. This led to the rise of brutal warlords and years of civil unrest and political instability. Then, starting in 2006, years after Eritrea and Ethiopia agreed to the ceasefire, our countries fought a proxy war in Somalia, which killed or displaced nearly two million of their people.

Araya tries to tell the boy that we, personally, had nothing to do with any of that. "We are refugees, too, same as you."

But the answer does little to placate the boy. His eyes flash with rage. Araya pulls me away, saying we should leave. At this point, the father finally intervenes. He snaps at his son, ordering him to be quiet. Then he turns to us and apologizes profusely. "The boy is only repeating what he hears from his friends." The explanation seems only partially sincere. It isn't hard to see that the elder Somali feels the same way about us. Like his son, he blames us for Somalia's woes. But he apologizes now because he's at risk of losing a sale.

We leave without buying anything.

The incident shakes us both to the core. Many of the Isli shop owners are Somali, as are many of the shoppers around us, but this is our first intimate encounter with such open animosity directed toward us. It sours our appetite for shopping, so we depart as soon as we can.

We end up stopping at a small Ethiopian-owned boutique instead. It's in a part of town that, despite its old, fancy storefronts, restaurants, and hotels, now shows signs of neglect and decay. Open ditches line the sides of the road, some filled with litter. It reminds me of parts of Khartoum, and for a moment I miss my hometown of Asmara. As difficult as life has become there, as poor as most of its residents may be, the streets of Eritrea's capital city have always been kept immaculate.

Most of the stores here are run by Kenyan nationals, although a significant number of them are rented out to *habesha* immigrants, who operate them. The prices are far higher than in Isli and the selection is smaller. I'm still discouraged by the incident at the market, but Araya tries to cheer me up. He points out a pair of shoes he thinks I will like and says, "Picture them on your feet as you greet your family in the airport in America. Or walking down an American street, free at last."

I know what he's trying to do. He wants me to put the past behind me and only focus on the future, because that's all that matters right now. But the past is who we are. We wear it like a shirt that others can see and easily judge. A shirt that has the stains of our history embedded within its threads.

If we shed it, then we choose to shed our entire identity.

I have been in Kenya for barely a month, and the differences between this country and Sudan are already very striking. Both have a representative republic for their government, but Kenya doesn't use Sharia law. Instead, there is civil law here based on the British system. This makes life a lot easier for Christians. In fact, most people here are Christian.

282

Communication is also easier for me. In Sudan, the main language is Arabic. Swahili is widely spoken here, but English is common because of the former British occupation.

Another example of the British influence is the flow of traffic. I'm used to cars driving on the right side of the street, but here it's the opposite. Sometimes when I cross the street, I forget to look in the appropriate direction and find myself nearly run over. It's especially dangerous on the main roads, where cars can speed by very quickly. The *matatu* drivers make things much worse with their loose interpretation of the rules and their even looser adherence to them. There are so many of the minibuses, and they are all very competitive. It is a cutthroat business. I frequently see drivers blatantly flouting the law, if they think there is a passenger to steal away from another.

I thought the *Mowasalat* minibuses in Khartoum were noisy and the drivers reckless, but they are nothing compared with the ones here in Nairobi. The *matatu* drivers blast their music as loud as they can to alert potential riders of their presence. They honk and shout at people standing or walking on the side of the road in their constant search for paying customers. The outsides of the vehicles are plastered with all kinds of advertisements, magazine pages, and photographs of famous people. The minibuses in Khartoum and Asmara are typically uniform in color, usually white. Sometimes, boring is preferable.

I try to ignore them. To save money, we walk most places anyway.

One day while sitting at a crowded café with Araya, I see a policeman running past with a pistol in his hand. He's chasing after a man at the other end of the street, who disappears around the corner. I'm surprised when no one steps in to stop the thief, and when I ask the man sitting at the next table why, he replies, "Why should we? It's too dangerous to get involved with the police."

"You don't trust them?"

Being a refugee immigrant, I have grown used to distrusting the police, but I have also been told that we have far less to fear from them here in Nairobi, at least in terms of harassment and unwarranted detentions. Still, I have been advised that it's best to avoid contact with them under any circumstance. The problems aren't because they hate refugees or Christians, as I have seen elsewhere, but because we are easy targets for corrupt officers. If one happens to know you are a refugee, they will put you in handcuffs and threaten to take you to jail. Meanwhile, knowing you have no recourse, they search through your pockets for valuables and money to steal. Sometimes, it's simply impossible to avoid them, since not all of the police wear uniforms. As I had already learned to do in Khartoum, I typically carry around the bare minimum amount of cash I might need whenever I go out.

Wudasie assures me that in America the police don't act this way. I hope she's right, but I have a hard time believing it. It seems like it's always the same, no matter which country I go to. People in positions of authority are always tempted to abuse their powers.

Kibrom says the Kenyan government knows about the problems of corruption in their police force. They claim to be fixing it, and those who have lived here for several years say they have seen improvement. But it still happens often enough that we are naturally distrustful.

Rather than answering my question about the police, the man at the other table says, "Maybe the thief has a knife or a gun. Would you want to be injured or killed? No, it's better to just let the police do their job and stay out of it."

The sound of a gunshot shatters the quiet a moment later. We all jump and turn to look. The man I am talking with nods, as if he expected this, then returns to his coffee. After a little while, the police officer reappears. He has the thief in restraints. Thankfully, neither of them appears to be hurt.


The longer I stay in Nairobi, the more people I meet from back home, both strangers and old friends. One day, I'm invited to a house occupied by two families from my old neighborhood in Asmara. One of them has been living here for well over a year because of delays processing her paperwork. The other family won a visa lottery and is supposed to leave in a matter of weeks.

On another day, I happen to run into a different neighbor from back home, a youngster in his mid-twenties who came here recently to process his Diversity Visa. He tells me he's on his way to Kampala, Uganda, to visit his sister first, and he invites me to go with him. It's a fourteen-hour drive by bus one way, but while I would very much like to go, I have to decline. I'm too nervous about missing an opportunity or doing anything that could jeopardize my case. It's a terrible feeling, this sense of helplessness and paranoia. I feel trapped, too afraid to move very far outside this narrow path I am on. Every story of success I hear should raise my hopes, but they also raise my anxiety.

Asmeret tells me about another old friend of mine here in Nairobi, Mesfin, a former colleague from the same Zonal Command as us and Zemu. After he vanished without a trace more than three years before, I had assumed he was dead, so I'm delighted to hear that he's still alive and doing well.

In the days before Mesfin went missing, I had been in the middle of trying to get Natsanet's exit visa. Knowing my frustrations, he had confided in me that he was also trying to leave the country. "I have arranged for my family to be smuggled across the border in a Land Cruiser," he'd said. "It's very safe, Yikealo, minimal risk. There's even room for you and your daughter, if you choose to come with us."

I had wondered many times after that if I made the wrong decision by declining the offer. Would we have ended up in America together far sooner than it has actually taken? But after not hearing anything from him for so long, I decided I had made the wiser choice. I was convinced he and his family had been caught. Now, knowing he's alive and safe here, I can't help but wonder once again. Would I already be with my wife and family had I accepted his offer? Was I not brave enough? Had I not wanted my freedom enough? If I had known four years ago how difficult a time I would have, would I have chosen any differently? My highest priority then was making sure nothing bad happened to my daughter. I still hadn't exhausted every legal option, and the risk was simply too great to take the gamble. There are never any guarantees in the future. The only certainty we can have in life is in knowing how the past has unraveled.

My reunion with Mesfin and his family is one of my best days since arriving in Nairobi. I can't believe how happy it makes me to see him again. It's even better to see how beautifully they have settled in. His wife greets me as if I am an old and dear friend, then she treats us to the traditional coffee ceremony. I immediately feel right at home. Even though I miss my own wife and daughters, watching Mesfin's girls, now eight and ten, make me feel like they are here with me.

Mesfin tells me he has a job in construction in Juba, the capital of South Sudan, where he splits his time. It's a thousand kilometer drive, but only an hour and a half by plane. The arrangement is similar to Kibrom's, who commutes between the very same two cities on a regular basis. "Of course it's hard being separated from my family," Mesfin says, but the work allows them to be self-sufficient, especially as there are so few jobs here in Kenya's capital. "In fact," he adds, "we are even able to pay for our girls to go to an international school for their education. They are doing very well."

Their hope is to one day leave Kenya for Canada or the US. They think it's close to happening.

It's so easy to see how well he has done for himself and his family in the past three years. The house he rents is modest, but well-constructed and in a safe neighborhood. The living room where we take our lunch is nicely furnished. The girls have new clothes. *This is how we should all be living*, I think to myself. It's how we would be living in Eritrea, if everything had gone the way it was supposed to go.

Mesfin insists on taking us to a section in the heart of the city called European Nairobi, which Zemu had first described to me the day I arrived. Araya and I accept the invitation, since neither of us has yet been to the area. We take a *matatu*, but the experience this time goes well beyond what I am used to. The closer we get to our destination, the higher the buildings tower over us and the shinier they get. The streets are more tidy and less crowded, the roads better maintained. Everywhere, people walk around wearing elegant suits and dresses. I see people of all colors and ethnicities. Uniformed police stroll casually up and down the sidewalks. They don't stare at you, as if they are trying to figure out if you are trouble. Or worth trying to rob. There is none of the chaos, the reckless driving and noise, the shouting. European Nairobi is nothing like Isli at all. It's like an entirely different city in another country altogether.

"Here," Mesfin tells us, "the streets are very safe. You don't have to worry about anyone harassing you."

I think back to the day we were assaulted by the Somali boy in the shoe shop. It would be nice to live in a place where nothing like that ever happened, where you weren't judged by your appearance, or by the place you came from. You simply . . . were.

Araya and I can't get over how clean and tidy the coffee shop is where we visit. Or the bathrooms, with their shiny facilities. I'm suddenly painfully aware of how underdressed we are for the location. Even the friendly servers are better dressed. So are the fancy tables with their cloth covers. And we pay dearly for the privilege of sipping a tiny cup of coffee in such a sterile, safe setting, coffee that is produced and delivered by a machine into a paper cup, which is tended by someone who has probably never seen a coffee pouring ceremony in their life. It costs so much more than I would ever pay on my own, yet the experience is so much less satisfying. After quickly draining our cups, we decline Mesfin's offer to sightsee and instead head back to the sanctuary of our familiar neighborhood of Kariokor.

While it's always a joy to reunite with so many old friends and acquaintances from back home, every one of them I meet reminds me of how Eritrea has betrayed its citizens. How many of her children will never know their homeland because of President Afewerki's repressive policies? How many will forget how valiantly their parents and grandparents fought to win the freedom that was then denied them, or stolen piecemeal away? Eritrea has so much to offer, from its abundant natural resources, to its cultural and architectural treasures. From its people's beauty to their generosity. In general, the country isn't vulnerable to the same kinds of natural disasters many others experience. We don't have earthquakes or tsunamis or tornadoes. We have a rich and diverse past. We have endured so much, gained so much, and yet lost so much. We have defeated stronger militaries, evicted the cruelest of enemies.

But how do we defeat an enemy when it is ourselves?

\* \* \*

287

One of the first things I had done upon arriving in Nairobi was to visit the American Embassy to inquire about the status of my case. The equivalent office in Cairo was supposed to have forwarded my file here, but at the time of my inquiry it hadn't yet arrived. For several weeks after that, I checked back nearly every other day, but I always received the same answer: "Not yet."

After a month, I decide to email the American Embassy in Cairo, hoping to hasten the transfer. Their response? The file had been sent in mid-June, more than two months before.

Fearing my paperwork has been lost, I call Wudasie, who in turn calls the US Immigrations Office and the State Department. They assure her that the diplomatic pouch containing my case file is actually still en route and not lost. The reason it takes so long is that it first has to go to Washington, DC. "That process could require up to eight weeks," they tell her. If this is true, then it should show up any day now.

It actually takes another month— a month of anxious waiting, sleepless nights, constantly living on the verge of panic.

After so much waiting and so many delays, I expect the process to resume its slow plod through the system. Instead, everything seems to happen all at once, at a pace that leaves me dizzy. I'm quickly scheduled for a required medical examination, which will be conducted at the Migration Health Assessment Centre near the United Nations building in downtown Nairobi. MHAC is part of the International Organization for Migration, an intergovernmental organization headquartered in Switzerland. The center is responsible for administering medical physicals for those immigrating to the British Commonwealth nations and the US.

On the day of my exam, the female doctor, an American woman approaching sixty, asks about my medical history. I'm hesitant about sharing everything with her for fear they will use it to deny my visa. She encourages me to be honest, so I tell her about my recent kidney issues. She asks a few questions about this, but otherwise doesn't seem troubled at all. I'm sent to have x-rays done. A nurse draws my blood and takes a urine sample so they can screen for tuberculosis and other communicable diseases, including the sexually transmitted kind. Another doctor assesses my mental and emotional states. They ask if I am addicted to any drugs, if I smoke, drink. *No*, I reply. *No*, and *Occasionally*. When I'm finished, they schedule the interview.

This close to the end, it's hard for me to wait. With each day, my anxiety grows tenfold. I start to doubt my ability to convince the interviewer that I'm worthy of being allowed into the United States. What if they ask me a question I can't answer? Will they look for reasons to not let me in? Rationally, I know I'm being too critical. There is no reason to turn me away. Even Wudasie tells me to just be honest in my answers and to stop worrying needlessly. But with every day that passes, the more convinced I become that I will fail.

By now I have talked to dozens of others who have had their interviews before me, so I know it's natural to have such doubts. I also know I shouldn't worry. Most of them had come out of their meetings feeling immensely relieved and satisfied. Still, not everyone succeeds. One man was forced to return to Eritrea to retrieve documents to clear up some kind of discrepancy. I don't know if he ever made it back out again. He would have had to sneak in and then escape a second time, multiplying his risk of capture several fold.

I have done everything I can to make sure my papers are in order. My record is as clean as can be. Yet I still worry. What if something comes up and I'm asked to go back to Eritrea? I don't think I would risk it, even if it meant never going to America and seeing my family again. Besides, what possible documents could there be at this point to make my chances any better?

The day before my interview, another man tells me that he has been ordered to provide a DNA sample to prove that the woman petitioning for his visa is his biological mother. This brings me all sorts of new anxiety, just because it's something I hadn't previously considered. The request seems so arbitrary. Yet the young man doesn't act concerned in the least.

"What possible reason would they have to require such a strange thing of you?" I ask.

He pulls a recently taken photograph out of his pocket by way of explanation. The woman in it looks far too young to be his mother. I would have guessed she was his sister.

"That's what the interviewer thought, too," he says. "They want to make sure I'm not lying."

That night I check all of my papers one final time. I make sure all of the pictures of myself, my wife, and my family tell the story I need them to tell. The photo of me is the same man I see in the mirror now, except with a bit more hair on his head than I have left. Even this tiny discrepancy causes me to lose sleep.

In the morning, I rise early and put on my best clothes. I make sure they're freshly laundered and ironed. I appraise myself in the mirror—striped black and white shirt, gray V-neck sweater, black pants and socks, black windbreaker. For a moment, I'm struck by a memory of that far-off morning, when I had dressed in the dark in fairer clothes before setting out for what I had hoped would be a wonderful new opportunity for my family. That day had ended in tragedy, and the days since have all been a struggle.

Lastly, I slip on the too-expensive Italian leather shoes I bought in the Ethiopian boutique up the street. If I were home in Asmara, I would add a necktie to the outfit. I feel incomplete without one, but I'm told it's unnecessary. Anyway, it won't hide my nervousness.

As I lace up my shoes, another memory comes to mind— the *shidda* I wore so many years ago. I feel both guilt and nervous excitement, guilt for betraying my culture and all the things our martyrs fought and died for during our war for liberation, and excitement knowing that this truly is the final step in my long journey. "I am still Eritrean," I remind myself. "I will always be Eritrean."

It's my government that forgot who they are and betrayed the sacrifice of our fallen *tegadelti*.

Arriving at the American Embassy, I'm trembling with excitement and nerves. I try to calm myself, but it doesn't help. The words I have been reciting for days now suddenly get jumbled up in my mind. I have all the documents I might need in my hands. It's a thick packet, yet it feels inadequate. It holds my life in it, and my fate.

In my first visit here a couple weeks before, when I came to deliver my papers to IOM, I was advised to hire someone to assist me in the process, even take my place at certain critical junctures, rather than trying to do it all myself. I remember being put off by the suggestion that I might need someone who can communicate in English better than I. Now I wonder if it might have been the wiser choice to heed the advice. It's too late to worry about now. I just hope I don't end up regretting it.

A young lady greets me through the glass window separating us. She's young, maybe in her late thirties, white. She smiles warmly. As if by magic, I feel the iron band around my chest begin to loosen. "Please sit," she says, encouragingly, and gestures at the chair. I sense she's trying to put me at ease.

To her, this is just another day of work and I am just another case, one of possibly thousands this office processes each year. How many others like me have passed through her door and sat in this very same chair? Where did they come from? What were their stories? Does she understand that every single one of us is unique? Does she also see that we are all the same? The details may differ, but for all of us, this moment is life-changing.

She opens my file and scans a few pages. She asks me a couple questions regarding my level of education, my wife's profession, her academic background. She asks me if I know my daughters' birthdays and what grade they are in at school. She wants me to recite the address of my family in Illinois. Then she takes the photos of my family I offer and studies them. She makes a quiet comment about my hair. I can see the edge of a smile on her lips, and my heart races. Before I realize it, the interview is over.

"That's it?" I ask.

She nods and stands. This time, she extends her hand through the iron bars in the window so I can shake it. "That's it. Congratulations."

I stand up, but I'm unable to speak at first. I can't believe it was so easy. I take in a big breath and let it slowly out. All the remaining tension in my body leaks away.

"Oh, but there is one last thing," she says, almost as an afterthought, although by the shape of her brow it doesn't seem like such a trivial thing.

"Based on these numbers, your wife's income doesn't meet the minimum requirement to sponsor you."

Once more, I can't breathe, except this time I feel like I'm drowning rather than soaring in rarified air. My face goes numb. "What does that mean?" I slowly ask. I don't want to hear the answer. "Does that mean I can't go?"

"Oh no. It just means we need some additional verification so we can be sure you'll be properly supported after your arrival. Don't worry."

I leave the embassy with mixed feelings. On one hand, a huge burden has been lifted from my shoulders. At the same time, it's like that burden is being held just over my head, waiting to be dropped on me at a moment's notice. I don't know how we are going to fulfill the income requirement. I don't even know how much is considered enough. How will Wudasie possibly find more money to sponsor me?

I don't know how she does it, but she finds a way. The consulate accepts the revised documents, which now include a statement from her sister's family as co-sponsors.

And just like that, it's done. The papers are signed. The visa is being processed. It's finally official: I'm going to see my family at last. I still can't believe it, not even when I have my plane ticket in hand. I clutch it tight against my chest and imagine it disintegrating into dust. But it doesn't. It's real. The last wall before me has come down.

I remember this feeling I once had when I was a younger man and the thirty-year war for liberation of my beloved Eritrea had just been won. I remember the exhilaration of knowing that the terrible weight of oppression had been lifted from our shoulders. I feel the same way now. It has been a long and often painful journey, one filled with loneliness and despair and punctuated by moments of utter hopelessness, anger, and betrayal. I can't count how many times I was sure I would never see my family again. The moments of pure joy are far fewer than anyone deserves in a lifetime, yet they shine so bright in my mind that they blank everything else out. This is one of those moments.

Yet at the same time, I'm also sad. I am Eritrean, and Eritrea will always have my heart. I know that will never change, no matter where I go and how long I stay there. Someday, my people will truly be free. I will never give up that hope, or the hope of someday returning to the soil from which I sprang. I don't know when that will be, but I do know this:

From this day forward, I will not grow downward.

# Editor's Note

What is the price of freedom? Not just the tens of thousands of dollars it takes to escape an oppressive regime, navigate a refugee system, and make one's way to freedom. And not the cost in lives and livelihood of a war to gain one's freedom. What is the cost to a people who have already won it and risk losing it again?

In a speech before the Massachusetts Anti-Slavery Society in 1853, the American abolitionist Wendell Phillips argued: *"Eternal vigilance is the price of liberty,"* because *"power is ever stealing from the many to the few."*

A century and a half later, these sentiments are certain to resonate with the estimated five million people of the small African nation of Eritrea. In the decades since they won their independence from Ethiopia, the country's powerful few have stolen nearly everything they can from the vast impoverished majority of its citizens. The crimes continue to be perpetrated to this day, concealed behind a veil of secrecy so opaque that few outside the isolated country are aware of what is happening there— *if* they are even aware of the tiny nation's existence at all. There is good reason why Eritrea is known as the "North Korea of Africa."

When Isaias Afewerki led his freedom fighters to military victory in 1991, he was lionized as a hero of the common man for finally ending a bloody thirty-year conflict that claimed many tens of thousands of lives.

As their soon-to-be democratically elected leader, he promised to guide the newly independent nation along a progressive and pragmatic path toward modernization. For a populace eager to shrug off the mantle of foreign occupation and take its long-sought place on the world stage, these were welcome words indeed. Instead, the so-called "Abraham Lincoln of Africa" delivered the exact opposite: forced militarization of the populace, the consolidation of nearly all private enterprise under the watchful eye of the Party, widespread corruption, severe poverty, global isolation, lies, and oppression.

None of this happened overnight, but rather in the insidious manner most often employed by aspiring dictators. Eritrean citizens were like the proverbial frog in the stewpot, oblivious to their fate, either too complacent, too forgiving, or too hopeful of positive change, that they failed to notice the gentle touch of progress stiffening into the regressive claw of totalitarianism until it was far too late to alter their course. More than a quarter century after he helped liberate his people from an oppressive foreign regime, President Isaias — Eritreans are known by their first names — revisits the very same tyrannical horrors perpetrated upon the Eritrean people by their former foreign oppressors. He has never allowed a political referendum on his leadership, despite his many promises to hold democratic elections for his position. Instead, he appears to be grooming his eldest son, Abraham, as his heir apparent.

Many Eritrean youth, both male and female, are forced into compulsory military service before they finish high school. There, separated from their families, they train under the most inhumane of conditions, then continue to toil for the state for untold years. Their pay cannot support a single individual, let alone an entire family. This effectively perpetuates a cycle of poverty and dependence from one generation to the next. Eritrea's disproportionate military force is deployed to the borders to prevent people from leaving. It is used in the cities to quash dissent, to spy on others, to detain and force even more people into compulsory servitude, and to inflict torture on those taken to their many prisons.

President Isaias is the sole decision maker in his government, and his edicts are frequently erratic and abusive. He imposes his "reign of fear through systematic and extreme abuses of the population," which the United Nations characterizes as crimes against humanity.[1] These abuses include the imprisonment of more than ten thousand political prisoners, many of whom are never charged or formally tried in a court and are instead subjected to torture for reasons of punishment, interrogation, and coercion.[2] Many of these prisoners eventually die while incarcerated. In 2016, a UN Commission of Inquiry found that the government's totalitarian practices and disrespect for the rule of law manifested "wholesale disregard for the liberty" of Eritrea's citizens.[3] Yet despite international pressure to change, human rights violations continue unabated.[4]

The effects of such despotic rule on the citizenry are entirely predictable. Those desperate enough and capable enough to escape the country do so by any means possible. And they do it knowing full well the terrible risks they will encounter, both natural and manmade. They do it with full understanding that they will very likely fail. This is how driven they are to escape. So pervasive is the abuse that even the president's younger son, Berhane, tried to flee the country in 2015, but he was caught illegally crossing over the border in Tessenei, the same border town where the author made his own crossing into Sudan in 2009. Many of those caught while attempting to escape are shot on sight. Some who make it out end up becoming victims of sexual abuse in the hundreds of refugee camps scattered throughout the region. Some are caught up in human trafficking. Too few make it to Europe, far fewer to the Americas. And of those who do find a place outside of the camps, too many are marginalized, criminalized, and forcibly repatriated to a country that will punish them as traitors. Sadly, the fates of too many remain a mystery.

No one becomes a refugee by choice, whether out of convenience or laziness or a shortage of patriotism. No one leaves home if their basic human needs are already being met. No one risks the often treacherous journey to a foreign land, where they know they will almost certainly face racism and other forms of persecution. Where they will spend the rest of their days as second-class citizens. Or worse.

One of the best descriptions I know of for the utter desperation that must be felt by refugees is encapsulated within the poem "Home," by the Kenyan-born British-Somali writer, Warsan Shire:

> *i want to go home, but home is the mouth of a shark*
> *home is the barrel of the gun*
> *and no one would leave home*
> *unless home chased you to the shore*
> *unless home tells you to*
> *leave what you could not behind,*
> *even if it was human.*
> *no one leaves home until home*
> *is a damp voice in your ear saying*
> *leave, run now, i don't know what*
> *i've become.*

It is true that Eritrea doesn't know what it has become, other than the mouth of a shark. It is why so many of its nationals have fled.

The numbers are simply staggering. While no reliable census data is available, the United Nations High Commissioner for Refugees reported that by the end of 2015, nearly half a million Eritreans have ended up as global refugees and asylum seekers— roughly twelve percent of the country's "official" population estimate.[5] *That's one in every eight Eritreans.* But even that number is almost certainly underestimated by a considerable amount, since so many more Eritreans end up displaced from their homes and separated from their families for reasons of poverty, drought, violence, religious persecution, and disease. It is likely that as many as one in three Eritreans have been uprooted. How can a country survive — how can it grow, advance, and prosper — when so many of its citizens remain unsettled?

The truth of what is happening to these people remains largely hidden from the wider world. Within Eritrea, free speech is aggressively suppressed. There is no independent media inside the country to ensure objective reporting; it has been completely abolished since 2001, when President Isaias expelled or imprisoned dozens of journalists. Eritrea's state-owned news agency censors local and global events, keeping its citizens — and the rest of the world — largely uninformed or intentionally misinformed. In fact, since Reporters Without Borders first began publishing its annual *Press Freedom Index* in 2005, Eritrea has consistently ranked at or near the very bottom of the list; only North Korea has ranked worst, edging Eritrea out for the bottom spot in the past two years.[6] The only independent and politically non-partisan source of freely reported news and information focused on Eritrea is Paris-based Radio Erena, which is run by exiled journalists. The signal is often electronically jammed inside Eritrea.

Outside its borders, anyone who succeeds in escaping is typically reluctant to speak out about their experiences for fear the government will retaliate against family members and friends they left behind.

For these reasons and more, the scale and scope of Eritrea's plight remain largely underappreciated and badly misunderstood. But word is slowly and steadily getting out. People are starting to take notice, to heed the struggle of the Eritrean people and diaspora, almost solely as a result of the few brave expatriates who managed to escape the government's tyranny and are putting their safety on the line to speak out about it. They want the world to know what is happening behind the iron veil surrounding this isolated nation— the nation for which they still hold a deep and unshakable love. They refuse to give up hope that conditions will one day improve enough for them to return home— that is, when home is no longer the barrel of a gun. It helps that international pressure is increasingly being exerted on the country's leaders to change, even as pressures continue to mount from within. But will President Isaias heed these signals?

There may be, at long last, the faintest glimmer of hope. Just in the few weeks leading up to the publication of this book, tensions between Eritrea and their largest foe in the region, Ethiopia, have eased. This has been brought about entirely by peace gestures from Ethiopia's newly elected prime minister, Abiy Ahmed Ali. Just days ago, in fact, the two nations signed a fresh peace accord in Jeddah, Saudi Arabia.[7] But will this finally end the perpetual state of war between them? More importantly, will President Isaias Afewerki, now in his mid-seventies and suffering from health problems, or his descendant, take the opportunity to loosen the government's chokehold on a people who simply want to breathe free?

Time will certainly tell. But Eritreans aren't collectively holding their breath. In the month since the border between the two countries was reopened, nearly ten thousand fled over it into Ethiopia, and they say they won't return until there are clear signs of reform. The skepticism is well-founded. When the president's own son is in attendance during the secretive peace treaty negotiation, what hope do the people have for regime change? And so far, Afewerki still hasn't released anyone from their National Service commitments or freed any of his political foes from prison. This is what he has cost his people: the loss of their national pride and trust. It will take more than signatures and empty promises to recover them.

~K.J.H.
October 22, 2018

[1] Nick Cumming-Bruce, "Torture and Other Rights Abuses Are Widespread in Eritrea, U.N. Panel Says," The New York Times (8 Jun 2015) https://www.nytimes.com/2015/06/09/world/africa/eritrea-human-rights-abuses-afwerki-un-probe-crimes-against-humanity-committed.html?_r=0

[2] Amnesty International, "Eritrea: Rampant Repression 20 years After Independence," (9 May 2013) https://www.amnesty.org/en/latest/news/2013/05/eritrea-rampant-repression-years-after-independence/

[3] Human Rights Watch, "World Report - 2017," (20 Jan 2017) https://www.ecoi.net/en/document/1173976.html

[4] Human Rights Watch, " Eritrea: Rights Abuses Continue Unabated," (12 Mar 2018) https://www.hrw.org/news/2018/03/12/eritrea-rights-abuses-continue-unabated

[5] Human Rights Watch, "World Report - 2017," (20 Jan 2017) https://www.hrw.org/world-report/2017/country-chapters/eritrea

[6] Reporters Without Borders, "RSF Index 2018: Hatred of journalism threatens democracies," (2018) https://rsf.org/en/ranking/2018

[7] Aaron Brooks, "Eritrea and Ethiopia sign fresh peace accord in Saudi Arabia," The East Africa Monitor (20 Sep 2018) https://eastafricamonitor.com/eritrea-and-ethiopia-sign-fresh-peace-accord-in-saudi-arabia/

# Acknowledgments

First and foremost, I would like to thank my wife and my two wonderful daughters for being the light of my life. No words can ever express my love for the three of you.

My wife deserves particular recognition for urging me to write this book in the first place. And then reading, re-reading, and editing the endless drafts. I could have not done it otherwise without her.

I also thank Mr. Kenneth James Howe, my publisher and co-author, for his professional input, and for the detailed research he conducted on Eritrean history. He made an invaluable contribution to this book.

Many people have been involved in my refugee journey from Asmara to Sudan and Kenya, many of whom are described in the story, although renamed to protect their identities. In particular, I thank those who helped me cross the border into Sudan, those whom I befriended in Shagarab Refugee Camp, and the dozens who opened their arms and homes in both Khartoum and Nairobi. Without your encouragement, aid, and support, I could never have reached my destination and reunited with my family. For this, I say thanks again.

Last, but not least, I would like to thank my parents, my siblings, my mother-in-law, and my brothers- and sisters-in-law. Be it known that you will always have a wonderful place in my heart.

~Y.N.

# Glossary and Acronyms

**NOTE**: Regarding spelling and pronunciation of words and names from the Tigrinya and Amharic languages, there is no direct conversion from the Ge'ez alphabet to the Roman alphabet. Rather, these terms are spelled phonetically, often in multiple ways that reflect local variants. The reader should be aware that they may encounter different spellings in other published materials.

**Abo/Aboy** Father.

**Ades** A thin lentil soup served to soldiers and conscripts during training.

**Afagn Guad** An especially vicious arm of the Dehninet known as the Strangulation Squad, whose function was to protect the Mengistu regime. They preferred murdering their victims by garrote, then leaving the brutalized bodies in a public place as a message.

**Agar hakim** Eritrean Army medic.

**Agar Serawit** Eritrean Army Ground Forces.

**Agefa** Palm fronds used as cover for temporary shelters.

**Angareb bed** A low, four-legged bed, typically framed in wood with a woven rope or fabric surface. Oftentimes, the legs are covered in a rough, bristly material to prevent ground pests from climbing to the sleeping surface. (also commonly known as a Swahili bed)

**Ascari** A native Eritrean who fought as part of the Italian colonial army.

**Bagayit** A dish of cooked spiced meat.

**Burqa** An outer garment worn by women in some Islamic traditions to cover their body, and sometimes their face, in public.

**Dahlak Kebir** The largest island of the Dhalak Archipelago, situated in the Red Sea off the Eritrean coast. Home to as many as 800 prisoners in the notoriously brutal Dahlak Kebir Penitentiary.

**Dama** A variant of the board game checkers played in Africa.

**Dehninet** The Ethiopian paramilitary squads that rounded up known and suspected rebels and supporters of the Eritrean resistance during the time of the Derg. (aka: Dahnanet Security Forces, Hezbi Dehaninet, or Hizb Dehninet, roughly translated to People's Protectors" or "Public Security organization")

**Derg** The short name of the Coordinating Committee of the Armed Forces, Police, and Territorial Army that ruled Ethiopia under President Mengistu Haile Mariam from 1974 to 1987. Although replaced by a civilian government, many of its leaders remained in

301

power until Mengistu's exile in 1991. (aka: Common Derg, Dergue; from the Ge'ez meaning "committee" or "council")

**Dimtsi Hafash** Radio of the Masses, an EPLF radio station transmitting news about the resistance during the Eritrean War for Independence.

**ELF** The main independence movement in Eritrea seeking independence from Ethiopia during the 1960s and 1970s.

**EPDM** The Ethiopian People's Democratic Movement was a political party formed in 1982 in Wollo Province as an armed resistance movement against the Derg. It is now called the Amhara Democratic Party.

**EPLF** The Eritrean People's Liberation Front was an armed resistance movement fighting for Eritrean independence that emerged in 1970 as a left-wing group from the Eritrean Liberation Front (ELF). The left-wing nationalist and Marxist–Leninist group was renamed the People's Front for Democracy and Justice (PFDJ) after independence, it now serves as the country's sole legal political organization. (aka: Shaebia)

**EPRDF** The Ethiopian People's Revolutionary Democratic Front is a leftist political coalition formed by the merging of four political parties, including the Ethiopian People's Democratic Movement and the Tigray People's Liberation Front.

**EPRP** The Ethiopian People's Revolutionary Party was established in 1972 to overthrow the monarchy of Emperor Haile Selassie.

**Eritrean Liberation Front** see ELF.

**Eritrean People's Liberation Front** see EPLF.

**Ethiopian People's Democratic Movement** see EPDM.

**Ethiopian People's Revolutionary Democratic Front** see EPRDF.

**Ethiopian People's Revolutionary Party** see EPRP.

**Gedli** Eritrea's armed struggle for liberation from Ethiopia.

**Giffa** Roundups by Ethiopian and Eritrean government officials for conscription into the armed or national services.

**Gotera** A district in Addis Ababa named for a type of container used to store grain.

**Habesha** A term used to refer to certain populations inhabiting the highlands of Ethiopia and Eritrea and consisting of culturally, linguistically, and ancestrally related groups.

**Hafash widib** Civilians who secretly supported the tegadelti in Ethiopia and Eritrea. They acted as informants and organizers of underground cells. During the war, the Ethiopian government rounded up, imprisoned, tortured, and killed thousands of the hafash widib.

**Halewa Maasker** The Zone 3 Core Guard Unit headquartered in Asmara.

**Hamam** Bath (Arabic).

**Himbasha** A slightly sweet Ethiopian and Eritrean celebration bread that is often served on special occasions.

**Injera** A traditional flatbread used in place of utensils in daily Eritrean and Ethiopian cuisine.

# GLOSSARY AND ACRONYMS

**Jallabiyah**  A general term for a traditional Arab garment worn by both males and females. It is typically worn over other clothing.

**Jebha**  Militant arm of the Eritrean Liberation Front (ELF).

**Junta**  A general term for a military or political group that rules a country after taking power by force. In reference to the Ethiopian junta, otherwise known as the Derg, it refers to the TPLF military group that wrested control from Emperor Haile Selassie in 1974, when it assumed control over the Ethiopian federation (including the province of Eritrea). Mengistu Haile Mariam was its leader until 1987, when, under pressure, he abolished the Derg and replaced it with civilian rule, although many of the Derg leaders remained in power in the government.

**NSS**  Sudanese National Security Service.

**Kiflitat**  Non-combat departments of the Eritrean National Service.

**Kitcha**  A thin, unleavened wheat bread.

**Maetot**  An Eritrean national program established by President Isaias Afewerki in which youth in grades nine through eleven engaged in public works projects in agriculture, environmental protection, or hygiene during their summer holidays. Although the stated purpose of the program is to instill a proper work ethic and exposure to other ethnic backgrounds, the work is essentially slave labor.

**Matatu**  A privately-owned minibus (or other vehicle) used for conveying passengers throughout Kenya and surrounding countries.

**Medeb**  Raised sleeping platforms, usually made of dried mud or concrete.

**Meshemae**  Plastic grain sack, sometimes reused as a barrier between a medeb and sleep roll.

**Nakfa**  The main currency denomination of Eritrea.

**People's Front for Democracy and Justice**  see PFDJ.

**PFDJ**  The People's Front for Democracy and Justice is the founding and ruling political party of the State of Eritrea. Formerly, known as the Eritrean People's Liberation Front (EPLF) under the leadership of Isaias Afewerki, the PFDJ (EPLF) rose to political power in Eritrea after the defeat of Ethiopia's President Mengistu Haile Mariam in May 1991.

**Piaster**  Sudanese unit of currency equivalent to 1/100 Sudanese pound.

**Revolutionary Ethiopia Youth Association**  see REYA.

**REYA**  The youth wing of the Workers Party of Ethiopia (WPE), which began as a volunteer movement of the Mengistu regime to clean up neighborhoods, rehabilitate communities, and construct new ones. The organization compelled Ethiopian and Eritrean youth 18 and over to join out of fear of being considered anti-government. Members were mobilized to carry out the group's revolutionary activities. Following the overthrow of Mengistu's government in 1991, REYA was banned, and its former members were persecuted as Mengistu sympathizers.

**Shaebia**  Arabic term for the Eritrean People's Liberation Front (EPLF).

# GLOSSARY AND ACRONYMS

**Shidda** Plastic sandals worn by the freedom fighters during the War for Independence (1961 - 1991). Cheap to manufacture and easily repaired using spare scraps of rubber, often from used tires, the sandals have become a symbol of the resistance and the freedom fighters who sacrificed their lives for Eritrea's liberation from Ethiopia.

**Shifta** A general term in the Horn of Africa for thugs or bandits. Applied by Ethiopia to describe the Eritrean freedom fighters, who adopted the term as a badge of pride.

**Souq** Arabic term for open air market.

**Suwa** A fermented drink made from barley malt and buckthorn flour. Each brewer has their own unique recipe, giving it a highly localized character.

**Tahwil** Arabic term referring to the process of sending and receiving money and the shops that provide such services.

**Tegadalay** Male Eritrean freedom fighter active during the 30-year War for Independence (1961-1991).

**Tegadalit** Female Eritrean freedom fighter active during the 30-year War for Independence (1961-1991).

**Tegadelti** Plural form of tegadalay and tegadalit.

**Tekoratsi sidrabet** Eritrean government's money transfer service for making payments to service members and families.

**Tewedeb** A style of music and dancing associated with the Eritrean Liberation Front (ELF).

**Tigray People's Liberation Front** see TPLF

**Tihni** A processed barley meal.

**Tor Serawit** Ethiopian army during the time of the Derg.

**TPLF** The Tigray People's Liberation Front was established in 1975 in western Tigray and grew to be the most powerful of the armed liberation movements in Ethiopia. In collaboration with the EPLF, the TPLF inflicted a total military defeat on the Derg regime of President Mengistu Haile Mariam on 28 May 1991.

**Tsebhi derho** A spicy Eritrean dish of chicken marinated in lemon juice and cooked with chili, onion, and garlic.

**Tukul** Simple hut made of mud and straw.

**UNHCR** United Nations High Commissioner for Refugees.

**Wetehader** General term for a soldier in any branch of the Eritrean Defense Force (Army, Air Force, Navy).

**Weyane** Ethiopian rebel soldier of the TPLF. (aka: woyane)

Make sure to look for the companion title to
*I WILL NOT GROW DOWNWARD*

# RELENT
# LESS

an **immigrant** story

# wudasie nayzgi

with Kenneth James Howe

Made in the USA
Monee, IL
16 June 2021